MICHAEL NOVAK

The Tiber Was Silver

with a
New Foreword by Ralph McInerny
New Introduction by Hadley Arkes
and
New Afterword from Michael Novak

Sapientia Press
of Ave Maria University

Sapientia Press
of Ave Maria University
24 Frank Lloyd Wright Drive
Ann Arbor, MI 48106
888-343-8607

Printed in the United States of America.

Library of Congress Control Number: 2004095307

ISBN 1-932589-13-9

For my Mother and Father

Table of Contents

Author's Note of 1960 vii

Foreword by Ralph McInerny ix

Introduction by Hadley Arkes xiii

PART I: *Autumn* 1

PART II: *Early Winter* 59

PART III: *Christmas* 111

PART IV: *Late Winter* 201

PART V: *Spring* 267

Afterword 2004 303

Author's Note of 1960

GOD, THE ARTIST, is not clearly revealed in the universe He made—only imaged. There are traces of Him, and everything in the world leaps from the crucible of His love. Nevertheless, it is a grave mistake to identify Him too readily with what occurs on earth.

I am not Herbert, nor Richard, nor Padre Benedetto, nor Padre Bracciano, nor Paolo, nor George, nor any of the others who people my creation. I do not agree with all the ideas of any of them, though I am, in a way, responsible for all the ideas (even the contradictory ones) of all of them. One of the joys of the novelist is to pretend he is God for a while and see things, through the eyes of many rational creatures, in many different ways at once—none of which may be wholly right or even adequate. God is not scandalized at inchoate, groping, and even wrong ideas; neither is the novelist.

This work is fictional; its characters and situations were dictated by the needs of expressing as briefly and fully as possible what it was like for an American to study for the priesthood in Rome, in the second half of the twentieth century. Its people and incidents are imaginary. For fictional purposes, two historic events, the Hungarian Revolution, and the launching of Sputnik, have been compressed into one winter.

M. N.

Foreword

BY RALPH MCINERNEY

I LIKED THIS NOVEL when it first appeared and I enjoyed it even more coming back to it now, and this for two reasons.

First, it is a fascinating story, told with an authority rare in a first novel. A young man, preparing for the priesthood in Rome, studying theology at the Gregorianum, resident in the house of his small religious community, is in the crucial year that will end in his ordination to the subdiaconate. Crucial, because irrevocable. He will not only become a vowed celibate but will take on the obligation of reading the daily office. Soon after he will become a deacon and a year later, priest.

Novak puts before the reader the drama of this decision by means of long discussions—with his spiritual director, his fellow students, his superior—and lengthy internal monologues which enable us to participate in the momentous decision. The time of the novel is a single year, but the narrative reaches back in time and projects into the future. The novel is saved from being overly cerebral by a series of events that underscore the stakes of the decision that Richard McKay is in the process of making. Will he or won't he? The reader wise enough to skip a foreword will already know the answer to that question. The unwise reader must find out for himself. I can assure him that there lies before him a suspenseful, meaty story with the issue in doubt until the very end.

Second, is the setting. A novel, as the term suggests, has an aspect of newsiness. But the news of the day becomes history and a novel returned to after an interval of 45 years can invoke a lost time and place. Novak's Rome is vividly presented. His protagonist is an artist—one of the elements of the drama is the compatibility of his art and the priesthood—and Novak establishes the credibility of this conflict by presenting the Rome and environs that are the setting of the story through the painter's eye. The silver of the title is a recurrent value, as painters say, and some doctoral student could devise a dissertation on the role of silver in Novak's novel. The buildings, the streets, the immemorial places of Rome, are evoked with an authority that could make the novel serve as only a slightly dated guide book to the eternal city.

The time is the late 1950s, just before the Council, Pius XII is on the throne of Peter. The garb and discipline of seminarians are of that time, the vehicles that infest the streets are too, but Novak enables us to see classical and Renaissance Rome as the permanent stage on which later generations strut and fret their hour. But it is the evocation of the pre-conciliar Church that is perhaps the most fascinating aspect of this novel.

Any reader wishing to sample the thinking and discontents of that time will find in *The Tiber Was Silver* a precious historical document. The contrast between one lecturer—Bernard Lonergan?—and the rest of the Jesuit professors enables Novak to portray student discontent with a scarcely understood Scholasticism. Questions arise as to the relevance of the Church in a world where the Cold War threatens. The age-old tension between the active and contemplative is made concrete. Those interested in the archaeological layers of the Novak personality will find here strata that partly contrast with and partly foreshadow his later viewpoints.

This is a first novel, and I could not help wondering why Novak never settled into this genre. One finds some of the flaws of a first novel, of course, but I am struck by the high degree of technical and dramatic skills the author possessed. It will be said that everyone has one novel in him and this was Michael Novak's. Perhaps. But few novelists have more than one story at their disposal, they all spend capital acquired early on, and Novak could have worked the vein of this novel in any number of later ones, if he had chosen to. I wish he had.

When I first read the novel, I was of course struck by the character bearing the name McInerny. Michael and I did not know one another at this time, so it is pure coincidence. Cornelius McInerny emerges as a likeable character after a shaky debut. My one complaint on this score is that on p. 218, Novak seems to think McInerny is a Scotsman! Only if Novak is a Pole. Nonetheless, I would award the novel a silver medal.

June 2004

Introduction

BY HADLEY ARKES

ON THE DUST JACKET of *The Tiber Was Silver*, in its first edition, was a picture of the young writer in his late 20s, a former seminarian, now publishing his first book. He would be on his way back, from Rome to Harvard, to begin his graduate education. His fellow Harvardians, still forming themselves, would be looking ahead to the time when they might have their own works in print. But he had already established the touch of a serious writer, and in the manner that counted: a publisher, not devoted to the stylish losing of money, thought there was a market for this young man, and the portraits he was able to convey with words.

1956: Year of the Hungarian Revolution. In our minds' eyes, many of us can readily bring back scenes, vivid and precise, from the late 1950s and the early 60s, and so that time, when Eisenhower gave way to Kennedy, does not so seem so far out of reach, or so far away. 1956 was just before the time when John XXIII would take the place of Pius XII, but there was already so palpably at work in the Church the stirrings that would bring forth Vatican II.

The point is brought home then: 1956 is, after all, a long while back, longer than we had realized, as the years swept past. And then again, that picture: that lithe young man. Is he really the same as that accomplished writer on theology and politics we have come to know in the fullness of his years? With the filling out of his experience, and the seasoning of his judgment, has come—to put delicately—a certain filling out of his frame as well. He does not have the same spring on the basketball court, and his hook shot is creakier. But the same passion and joyousness has remained, and the striking thing is that this book, published in 1961, wears so well. There is, in it, nothing out of date, and it wears well, I think, because there is in fact such a clear connection between the accomplished writer, on politics and theology, in later years and the writing struck off by this young man in Rome in the vigor and exuberance of his 20s.

Exuberance? Consider this knock-off of Gilbert and Sullivan in a college skit written and produced by the novel's hero, ensconced in an Italian seminary in 1956:

> *Three old apologetes are we,*
> *Pride of the university,*
> *Full of the air of certainty—*
> *Three old apologetes.*
>
> *We can explain every mystery;*
> *We can refute every heresy*
> *(Up to the nineteenth century)—*
> *We three apologetes.*
>
> *Three fundamental theologians*
> *Free from all nasty modern notions.*
> *We may not move but we go through the motions—*
> *We three apologetes!*
>
> *Up pops an error fresh or stale.*
> *What on earth shall we raise for a wail?*
> *Cite the decrees that never fail—*
> *Us three apologetes!*
>
> *Do you know the inquisition tricks?*
> *Well, down in the basement just for kicks,*
> *Fridays we burn three heretics.*
> *We three apologetes.*
> *Three old apo-lo-getes!*

And yet, for a work done in early years, with this kind of spiritedness, *The Tiber Was Silver* shows an uncommon tautness and restraint.

There is no overwriting; the writing is spare, with energy and verve coming through all the more forcefully with the economy of the narrative. At the same time there is a sensitivity to so many things in the setting of Rome—in the sky and the churches, and the conventions that color in the moral landscape: A custodian lifts an eyebrow when he sees a young priest speaking, in a familiar way, with a young, attractive girl, and that moment, gently noticed, marks a world now distant from our own.

The protagonist in the novel is a young seminarian, Richard McKay, and it comes as no surprise that he sounds at times like that former seminarian many of us happen to know. He struggles with the question of whether he is truly fitted for the priestly life. The question that cannot be stilled is whether he really needs to immerse himself in the world—in the action, the argument, the abrasions, the sweet savoring of victory and honors, or the taste of defeat. The writer says of Richard McKay that he sought to sink his destiny deeper and deeper into the issue of immortality. He would see people on the bus in Rome, and he had the impulse to shout, to the man or woman across from him, "You will live forever!" The narrator says:

> The sight of people wounded him. He would have liked to have journeyed all around the world, and lived for all time, and heard all the woes and all the loves of every man that lived. Each tale would be so beautiful. Each would be painful.

A short while later he is responding to the doubts registered by his superior, Padre Bracciano, and he admits that

> He *was* worldly. He did love art, love the cities, love people: everything captivated him! Governments, reforms, proposals, everything about the earthly city. To build up everything that was truthful and was good, to conserve it . . . these were what he wanted on earth.

In these passages, of course, are disclosed everything, and they confirm just why the man we have come to know did in fact immerse himself in the world, even while his protagonist finally held fast in resisting the lure of the world. The young seminarian in the novel meets an attractive young woman, an artist, and he is evidently drawn. The challenge facing the writer was to convey just how much Richard, the seminarian, was indeed drawn, attracted, and yet how plausible was his decision not to go over the wall—not to turn away from the priesthood to the world of marriage. Some see a certain prophecy here: Back in America the writer, settled in at Harvard, would meet an attractive young woman who was a serious artist, and they would marry, just two years after the publication of this novel. To stretch the prophecy a bit, the writer also had in the book a character named McInerny, long before he would meet, and enter into the most productive collaboration with, Ralph McInerny, the renowned philosopher and writer at Notre Dame. The McInerny in the novel was named Cornelius, Connie for short; and Ralph McInerny's late wife was Connie.

But we can readily put aside even these mild hints of prophecy, for the happy thing is that the main prophecy was not fulfilled: The novel strayed decisively from what became the truth of the matter for Michael Novak, for he did choose the world and marriage, but in that straying was a boon for the rest of us. G. K. Chesterton remarked that, in all of life, there is a "silent swerving from accuracy by an inch." Yet that swerving was the "uncanny element in everything . . . a sort of secret treason in the universe," that made the most notable difference.

Michael Novak, swerving, chose the world and marriage, and yet, in swerving, he found another way of pursuing a kind of religious vocation in the fullness of his work and life. His writings have brought him an international standing, as a theologian and political sage, and the family he has shaped with the artistry of his wife, Karen, may run even deeper than his books. But he remains, through it all, the same fellow, radiating promise, pictured on the dust jacket back in 1961. And in the most truthful way, Richard McKay, in the novel, turns out to have been the forerunner.

June 2004

PART I
Autumn

1

"I'D LIKE TO COME here every day forever," Richard said.

Paolo was silent. Together they leaned on the balustrade at the top of the stairs of Santa Trinità del Monte and looked over the city of Rome, golden in the painter's hour of the afternoon.

"Would you like to paint this?" asked the young Italian.

"I'd love to," Richard said without looking at him. They lapsed into silence to enjoy the view. The October breeze was fresh and scented. It whipped over the balustrade and pulled at their cassocks. It struck the towers of the golden church behind them and swept careening up into the high blue sky. It's five o'clock, Richard thought.

Below, on the long Spanish stairs, tourists in whites and reds and yellows climbed up towards Santa Trinità. Their heads were back; they pointed; delight radiated from their faces. The flower stalls of the stairway were bright with flaming-red chrysanthemums, a little purpled now in shadow. A twelve-year-old Italian girl behind one of the stalls scolded a barefoot, grimy boy of five and pointed to the dark stucco flat beside the steps; the boy stamped his foot; the girl shouted, but the sound was lost.

Cars jammed the street. Dark-green buses roared up to the fountain and spun in a wide turn down the narrow cavern away from the ancient stairs. Tourists at the mouth of the shadowed buildings looked through their cameras, stepped forward and back, and tried to achieve fountain, steps, and tall twin golden spires of Santa Trinità in one frame. Richard smiled. Shadows already darkened the fountain in the square and the lower steps and even many of the flower booths.

3

The photographers might not notice the line of shadow now, but in their living rooms later in the winter, when they flashed the slide on the bright screen before their families and friends, there it would be, with only the mellow tan-gold of the spires and brilliant blue of the sky to hint how beautiful the autumn day had been. They would sit helplessly by the projector and explain with exuberance how bright the flowers actually had been and how stirring the noise and silver falling of the fountain and the excitement of the street. "Pictures can't capture it," they would say. "Keats' room is off to the right, just out of the picture, the corner room he loved. Keats, the English poet. And the English tearoom is off the picture to the left."

Richard leaned back from the rail. He slapped Paolo's shoulder. " 'niamo?"

His companion leaned back and smiled, shrugging off the slapping, to which he was unaccustomed. "You love Rome, Richard? You should have been born in Rome. It's in your blood."

Richard smiled and tipped back his *romano*, the clerical shovel hat, and they walked away to the right. The tan-orange stucco of the church and convent was quiet in the sun. The breeze blew in from the faraway sea and the Vatican hills across the town. "I would have liked that," he said in Italian. "I would have liked that. However, I'm an American. And I'm pretty glad about that, too."

"Imperium Americanum?" suggested the Italian slyly.

"Civis Americanus," nodded Richard. "It is lovely here. Feel that breeze from the sea. Look at the leaves turn. You know, I love this walk along the Pincio. I remember Henry James writing of it."

"Remember who?"

"Henry James. Remember, I gave you that short thing to read."

"Ahh, mi ricordo." They walked along under the trees for a while. "The *giovinetta* sitting in the *Colosseo* under the summer moon. In the days when fever blighted Rome—before Mussolini," he ventured, looking at his American friend warily.

But Richard didn't wish to argue that afternoon. "It's too lovely, Paolo." He swung his arms widely, breathed deep, slowed his stride. "Smell the air."

"Romantico!" sighed the other seminarian. The two of them in their long clerical ankle-length coats and shovel hats walked down the tree-lined asphalt street. They looked and thought but did not talk. The grilled entrance of the French Embassy, tiny parks, here a monument to the hero of one of Rome's countless civil wars, there parked Fiats; idling tourists, lovers, and other clerics; French sailors in blue jerkins and berets with red pompons on top like huge cherries; a white-faced German lady in faded print dress painting at an easel—sight after sight from Rome's *turista* streets registered faintly in their memories, to be recalled vividly in later times. *Haec olim meminisse juvabit. . . .* It was Richard's third year in Rome; the first two had sped by like a dream. He was almost twenty-five, a year and a half from ordination to the priesthood. Paolo was twenty-three, but would be ordained at the same time. It was Paolo's fifth year of studying in Rome.

Paolo's home was in Milan. His father was a journalist, a Christian Democrat of the party's left, an ardent admirer of De Gaspari and now Fanfani, and not a little anti-clerical. "He still sticks every time he sees me in my *sottana*," chuckled Paolo. "But he is glad—so long as I am different from the rest." Paolo's dark-brown eyes would sparkle merrily. His hair was light brown and cut short, a little longer than a crew cut. He knew more about painting and architecture, in an informal way, than Richard could ever hope to know. His father had seen to his political education, and he was realistic in a way Richard had found that seminarians scarcely ever were. His father had seen, too, to Paolo's reading in world literature—not merely the Latin and Greek, which Italian schools had urged until recently, with the resultant pseudo wisdom of resignation and "nothing new under the sun," but also the Russian novelists, English writers, Confucius, and Gandhi and the modern Americans. Paolo had read Hemingway and Faulkner and Lewis; in their very first conversation he had replied to Richard, *Sí*, he had read Dostoievsky, Shakespeare, Byron, Shelley, Graham Greene; *no*, none of Dickens, Waugh, Eliot, Turgenev. He had read nearly everything in French, classical and modern—far more than had Richard.

Most Italian clerics seem to have entered the seminary at twelve or thirteen, and now even at nine or ten. Paolo had entered at sixteen. He spoke little of the Italian minor seminary, and that little with distaste. "I was always ready to leave the whole first year," he once told Richard as they walked together through the Vatican museum. "Only my director kept me. He was a wise old man. He kept saying: 'Wait. And think. Do not act quickly. Do what you really want to do, not what you feel like doing now.' I am glad I had him."

Richard had felt lost in his first days at the Gregorian University at Rome. Paolo was a member of his same religious community, but they had not met to talk yet. Then one day at class Paolo saw him standing all alone and came to speak to him.

"Do you speak English?" Richard asked as Paolo came up to him.

"*Un po'*," blushed Paolo. "Not like your—how you say?—countrymen." He pointed to a knot of seminarians from the North American College with their maroon sashes and flowing shoulder cords. The light in the Aula Magna was dismal, and the air coming in through the great front doors and the skylight high above was damp. Richard looked over the swarming crowd of seminarians of all countries and colors and types. The chatter was deafening.

"*Io,*" formed Richard carefully, "*io non parlo bene Italiano. Voglio studiare.*"

"And I wish to learn English," replied Paolo, bowing slightly. Paolo Veronese," he added, extending his hand. "*Un Suo confratello.*"

"I recognize you," said Richard. "But I did not know your name." He formed the English carefully for Paolo. Paolo smiled. "Richard McKay. Padre Riccardo."

"*Lo so,*" smiled Paolo. He had wanted to talk to Richard. He had heard he was a painter. He wanted to get to know Americans.

From then on they had begun to sit together in the semicircular, steeply pitched classrooms of the Greg. Richard offered Paolo part of the bun and cheese he had brought with him to stave off his hunger through the long mornings; Paolo was at first surprised, then accepted graciously, bowing slightly. They chewed the doughy bread and cheese. From then on for a week or two the midmorning snack had become a ritual between them, until Richard got used to the Roman meal schedule and no longer needed it. In blundering Italian and blundering English they had slowly encouraged one another's progress in the languages. Their enthusiasm for one another's ideas and reticent dreams made the pain of learning a language easily forgotten. Italian was easier; Richard learned it quickly. He proved to have a quick ear, except for the Midwestern drawl of his O's and A's. Paolo tried to imitate him by talking through his nose. Paolo's own English was splendid; his vocabulary, if anything, was too literate. His pronunciation, of course, was slow and faulty, and his natural modesty prevented him from speaking as boldly and as well as he might have. In two years both had become rather fluent, and their conversations flowed from one tongue to the other.

"Excuse me," Paolo had said once in the break between their classes. "I wish to go to the water closet."

"The what?" Richard had asked. "Oh," he said, laughing.

"Don't you call it that?" Paolo had asked, his face fallen a little.

"Sure. Sure. The water closet." And he explained the usages. He himself never learned new words from a grammar comfortably again.

Richard McKay was taller than Paolo and built athletically. He had been born and had lived all his life in Gary, Indiana. He had played football and basketball in high school. He had belonged to the Radio Club and the Photography Club; in his senior year he was the photographer for the school paper and the yearbook. He was a good dancer, and he dated Jean McKinley very often. But he had decided on following out a perduring dream of the priesthood. He had worked almost a year after high school. Then he had entered the postulate near Chicago. Quiet, talented, he had made a good seminarian. After his years of college work and novitiate, he had been sent to Rome, a privilege that he deeply cherished—in great part because of his love of art.

The community to which Paolo and Richard belonged was of Italian origin. A Milanese priest had founded it in 1876. Its special mark was devotion to Our Lady, under the title of the Annunciation. Yet, really, nothing except for its attentive piety toward her especially marked it as Our Lady's. Like those of a hundred other communities, its actual spirit and work were determined more by decade-to-decade needs than by written constitutions, though these were in turn wide enough to embrace plausibly nearly any new work that came along. In America the work of the Fathers had been mostly among the almost illiterate immigrants from South Italy and Sicily—immigrants creating by their religious ignorance so great a problem that the American bishops hardly dared inform the Holy See how poorly instructed Italy had let them depart. The community now had a dozen parishes scattered through New York City, Chicago, Buffalo; they were in Germany, too, and in the Lowlands, and now in Canada and Australia—wherever the Italian immigrants had gone. And, inevitably, especially in America, the Fathers were being drawn into education. A bishop in New England was insisting that they take a small college. Four bishops begged their provincial to take a high school. The ending of the immigrant problems and the dearth of vocations from the parishes was forcing the provincial to concur. He began to see that education was a vital arm of the apostolate. He had only three priests with degrees, and two of these were in theology; but one of them was in economics—a man who had come late into the priesthood. And six or seven men were fluent in French or Spanish or Italian and, of course, Latin, and could, with some concentrated reading, teach courses of literature in those languages. Some of the younger men might be sent for degrees. In a year or two it might be done!

Richard's family consisted of a brother two years older than himself and his parents, the Michael McKays of Chestnut Street in Gary. The McKays had lived in one house all their married lives, a wooden frame house, now quite old, in the worker's part of Gary. Michael McKay was a railroad switch operator. His father and his father's father had been with the railroads in the Middle West since after the Civil War, with the railroad gangs of Irish laborers. Many were the stories old Mike McKay could still tell, with a drink or two in him to warm him up—of the campfires his father had told him about as a boy, and the cold cars to sleep under, and the cold, brittle stars of the plains, and the glorious fights. The Irish were always fighting. One night it would be because there was no drink, another because there was. A shovel over the head had ended not a few evenings for some of these rough foreigners who built the West, had ended not a few lives.

"Real days," Mike McKay used to say. "When men was men."

"Oh, Michael!" would say Maureen McKay. Pert, thin, still somewhat pretty in the dainty-rough Irish way, Maureen O'Boyle McKay was forever blushing and shushing at her husband. Irish affection is a wonderful thing to observe, and she and her husband were masters of the range of it: blustering, teasing, and compassionate all in a swoop. "You've got two of the most civilized boys the McKays ever seen, and here you are encouragin' them to be like their fathers."

"Civilized, yes, but a damn sight less men, I'll tell ye!" said Michael McKay in answer. A red-faced, small, wiry man himself, his hair was still sandy or reddish blond, although its predominating shade was brown. His eyes were blue, with that mammoth Irish innocence and cleanness. Twenty-eight years now he had worked at the yards; he was supervisor of the switch controls and track clearance. He drew good pay, and his boys were growing up straight. Kevin had gone through college and come safely through Korea; he had a good job now with an insurance company. Richard was going for priest. A ripe, good Irish family. Maureen was as good and loyal as ever. He patted her far arm as he embraced her and bore her in to himself. "Aren't you now, Maurie?" He pinched her arm.

"Now Michael McKay! When will you remember I'm no longer sixteen! Aren't I now *what*?"

Richard looked up at the old branches over his head and the dark-green, silvered antiquity of their leaves. Autumn in Rome was never so bright and fire-hued as in America; leaves in Rome merely tarnished from their dull summer silver-green to a vague brown, and fell. Many of the trees remained green all the winter. "And here I am in Rome." It seemed a miracle still.

"Che dice? Diventa pazzo?" smiled Paolo.

"Yes, foolish. Over Rome. It is good to be here, isn't it?"

"Um, more or less," shrugged the Italian.

"Doesn't anything ever get you excited?"

"I'm not a cold Irishman, if that's what you mean."

"You're the first one who ever called the Irish cold!"

"Chesterton did. 'The Irish are as cold as the cliffs of Dover.' You showed me yourself."

"I suppose you'll say Italians are cold, too."

"The Italians—have sentiment. English, Germans, they try to hide it. Their affection goes for flower gardens, puppies, the army, or the queen. Their literature—very sentimental. Sentiment will out! Americans, now . . ." Paolo said slyly. "They aren't so cold as the English or the Germans. They're more like us. They've got something—warm about them."

"Thanks."

They turned left. "Piazza del Popolo," Paolo nodded. They stood at the top of the steps. Below lay the great stone piazza, reddish in the sunset, ovaline, significant. Four churches marked its four sides, but they did not belong so much to the images that rushed to Richard's mind as did Communist May Day crowds or Garibaldi's black shirts. An Egyptian spire rose in the center of the piazza, symbol of other empires, other times. Concrete bastions with heavy iron chains fended traffic from the obelisk; little Fiats darted past like desert ants and exited from the piazza through the narrow city arch beside Santa Maria del Popolo. Streetcars clanged outside the city walls. Off to the right and to the rear, up behind the trees, lay the Borghese gardens—where Goethe wrote part of *Faust*. A cheap English bookstore lay over there among the little shops, across the expanse of cobblestones. Billboards for newspapers and chocolates and movies lined the opposite wall of the piazza as if it were a stadium. The trees above the opposite wall flashed the brilliance of the western sun and the reddening clouds.

Slowly Paolo and Richard descended the stairs, hiking their cassocks to give room to passersby. The noise of traffic did not take away the sense of quiet and emptiness, or the memory of political harangues and shouting and the birth of revolutions. A cripple sat, legless, holding out a cup, athwart one of the landings of the stairs. Almost everyone who passed stopped, fished for a coin, dropped it in his cup. A young fellow, held there by his girl, fumbled for his wallet. Richard felt the shame of passing without giving.

"*Padre, padre . . .*"

"*Niente . . .*" he replied, smiling a compassion that could offer nothing else. "*Studente. Non ho niente . . .*"

He wondered if the beggars understood, really. Could they really believe he had not a lira, that he was allowed no pocket money, not at all, when they saw the well-built religious houses, the seminarists with cameras, the wrist watches, the new shoes, the neatly lettered buses all through the city?

He and Paolo descended to the piazza and crossed it, against the swerving, considerate traffic. A strange sorrow pulled at his heart, a now familiar distant sorrow. "Lord," he said, "I love you. Thank you for the lovely walk."

The piazza was somehow hotter, and purplish in the shadow. They crossed over to the wall opposite and climbed the steps. Maybe it was only his fatigue. He shook it off and tried to recover his habitual joy. He began to laugh and talk.

On the far side of the piazza, and in the maze of side streets of the medieval city, he suddenly stopped his companion and asked him: "Paolo, are you thirsty?"

"*Sì.*"

"Would you like a peach?"

"*Sì.* But we haven't any money."

Richard pointed down a side street. A tray of fresh peaches and other fruit projected out from a tiny store. Bushel baskets of fruit and vegetables stood around it. No one was in sight.

"Riccardo, that would be stealing!" Paolo warned.

"No, it won't. Not if we use our heads. Come on."

Paolo pulled his cassock about him and followed Richard down the side street. Like most Italian clerics, he wore no trousers under his cassock, and his black socks flashed with every step.

Richard took off his *romano* as he drew near the front of the store. The smell of fruit was heavy and sweet in the afternoon air. Flies buzzed on the fuzz of the peaches and around the shiny pears. Richard peered inside. He pushed through the colored plastic bands that served as a screen door. The inner part of the store was dark and hot. The storekeeper was pouring turnips from a sack into a basket. He was fat and sweating, with his shirt sleeves rolled up. His apron was very dirty. His portly wife held her hands at the edge of the basket to catch escaping turnips.

"Che cosa?" growled the fat man as the clerics darkened the door.

"We're thirsty," Richard smiled. "May we take a peach?"

The fat man lifted his hand and swore threateningly. "Parasites! Thieves! No-goods!" He pointed his thick arm up the street. *"Via!* Get a move on! Pumpkin heads!"

Used to Italian oratory, Richard stood there with a meek smile. "But we're very thirsty."

The fat man took a step towards them in anger. The turnip bag began to slip away from him and two turnips bounced across the dirty stone floor.

"Mario!" the old wife shouted from the little box on which she was sitting. "Don't be so stupid! Are you an idiot? The boys only want a single peach. We are not so poor we can't afford it. Take one," she said to the boys sternly. She commanded her husband: "Pour that bag right!"

The man gesticulated with his hands.

"Pour!" said the formidable voice of his wife.

"Grazie; buon giorno!" Richard said in a glad, almost singing voice.

"Buon giorno," said the wife with kindness and sternness. "Faster," she said to her husband.

He mumbled.

Richard selected a large peach for Paolo and another for himself. He handed the first to Paolo with a grin. "Never say die."

"You've set church-state relations back another decade," Paolo said.

"I hope they don't start proceedings for divorce on account of me."

"He's used to it," Paolo said.

"All the worse. I didn't expect an argument. People usually like to give. I'd give anything to them." He felt guilty now that the husband was angry.

They washed the peaches in an old bronze fountain, running them under the cold clear water and shaking them to dry. Then they set off on their way, trying not to drip the succulent juice on their cassocks.

"I feel a hundred times better," Richard said. "Someday I'll have to come back and pay them something."

"You better bring a bodyguard. He won't want to see you again."

"He doesn't really mind," Richard said. "They like to shout and fuss, but they're awfully goodhearted underneath."

"He was probably a Communist."

"All the more reason for stopping then," Richard laughed. "If we're going to fight, might as well be in local skirmishes. Over peaches on a hot afternoon. Think of it, he may even get into heaven for his kindness."

"We'll probably go to hell for our imposition."

"Ah, Paolo, don't ruin the taste of a perfectly good peach."

"In paradise it only took an apple."

Richard swung his hand at him. Paolo ducked and had to catch his hat.

2

RICHARD ENTERED the silent library. He turned the porcelain switch and four bare bulbs in green shades became illumined. Shelves lined the walls in the silence; only a little of the morning's light filtered through the high, narrow windows. Richard straightened chairs that were awry. He sat slowly at the librarian's desk and pulled three new books from the large bottom drawer. He opened the cracking cover and flipped the new pages of the one-volume digest of Toynbee's *A Study of History*. He fingered the soft covers of an essay on Paul Claudel in French and Moeller's *La Littérature du Vingtième Siècle* and flipped their pages thoughtfully.

Four years before he had been reading Graham Greene and Mauriac, Camus, and Péguy. He missed that reading now. He set Moeller's tome on the desk. *Vingtième siècle.* The dried, disciplined image of American Catholicism seemed hateful to him when so much was happening in France and England. *Vingtième siècle!* He longed to appreciate his time; he gave way before images of grandeur and achievement. He wished to create a burning image in his painting, a piercing penetration into anguish and despair, a moment of what it was like to live in the twentieth century. He wished to capture something, to pull back the edges of the veil, even for a little. But all he could do was grope. Inside himself he felt strong feelings, but he could never find them to express them. They were there, but what were they? He fingered his lips and cupped his elbow in his hand. The morning sun fell on the dusty volumes on the shelves; out in the hall somewhere a broom fell to the floor.

Adolf Hitler and the diving stukas, damp newspapers, and leaves blowing in a December street. He remembered a Sunday dinner at his grandmother's. "We interrupt this program to bring you an important announcement: the Japanese have bombed Pearl Harbor." An eight-year-old's incomprehension and fear as he looked about the room at the faces of his elders. War. War. The headlines and the newscasts as he went through grammar school. Germany's capitulation on a day in May. Pictures of the atomic bomb on Hiroshima, and a faint sense of sickness. Confetti and auto horns and dangling tin cans in the streets in August. *Vingtième siècle.*

"Has it not become colder? Is not night and more night coming on all the while? Must not lanterns be lit in the morning? . . . God is dead. God remains dead." The tradition of the West had been destroyed. Richard lifted up *A Study of History.* Centuries flipped before his eyes. After a while he set the heavy book upon the blotter. The waters of an ocean tossed restlessly, trees spun round and round, a crow cawed over a lonely field, a huge fire blazed up and obscured everything. He felt desire stirring in him and his fingers itched. If only he could bring it to the surface, reduce it to form. If only he could . . .

Footsteps sounded at the door. The double doors rattled as one side was opened. A short, stocky man stood at the door and looked for Richard.

"*Buon giorno,* padre," Richard said quietly, rising to his feet. Unaccountably, he found himself blushing, and made a mental note to examine himself about it later.

"Sit down, sit down," motioned the superior in a direct, quick way. He was balding, nearly fifty; his sparse hair was black and curly. His eyes were friendly but serious and accusing.

Richard sat down, but on the edge of his chair.

Padre Bracciano showed him the invoices in his hand. "Did you order these books?"

Richard looked at the slips. He colored. "*Si,* padre."

"Did you get permission?"

"I did, padre." Richard found his throat sticking. "From you."

"From me? When? I remember no permission."

"*Si,* padre, in the spring. Before we went to the villa."

Padre Bracciano's brown eyes stared intently at him. The eyes were troubled, not believing, not disbelieving. "I do not remember."

"But I did, padre. I gave you a whole list. I brought it into your office."

"I . . . remember a list vaguely. Yes, I remember a list—but not for all these."

"There were fourteen titles, padre. I think there were fourteen. I explained it all to you; you seemed willing. We had no novels, almost no new books at all."

"We have many books," expostulated the superior, spreading his arm toward the shelves all around the room. "You could not read all these books in four years. The classics are here—Suárez, Bellarmine, Cajetan, Bossuet, Bremond. You could not read even these in four years. In my day we were *forbidden* to read novels. The students should not have the time. I want no more novels!" he convinced himself as he spoke. "I want those on the list brought to my room for approval."

"*Si,* padre."

Padre Bracciano picked up a pencil sketch lying on the desk. It was of the column of Trajan. He asked after a moment: "This is yours?"

The superior scrutinized it for a time. Then he set it down. "You have a great deal of talent. But this is a house of theology. We do not have time for everything, for novels and for drawing."

Richard was silent. The superior hesitated whether to say more. "Write out a list of the books you wish to buy," he said. "I always wish to have a list. I want a list of all the books you have bought since you have been librarian."

"But I have given you a list, padre. Each time."

"I want them all on one list." Padre Bracciano's eyes searched Richard's face. "I must speak to you sometime about your drawing. Your obedience is to study. Drawing is all right for a hobby."

"*Si,* padre."

"You'll bring the list to my office."

"*Sì,* padre."

The superior nodded. He looked around at the shelves for a moment. Then he turned and left.

Richard looked after him for a time. Slowly he opened the side drawer of the desk and rooted out the records of his acquisitions. He pulled out the old Underwood typewriter from the lower compartment of the desk and inserted a sheet of white paper. He began to type out a list of the twenty or thirty books he had bought since becoming librarian the previous winter. He had asked Umberto, Herbert, Paolo, and a number of others for suggestions in his purchases. He had conferred with Padre Carlo, the assistant superior, and with Padre Eugenio and Padre Giovanni, two priest students in the house. He had studied book reviews and conferred with professors. The slow renovating of the library had become his joy and personal concern.

The resentment he felt towards Padre Bracciano indicated how far he had begun to take the task as a proprietor. He felt that Padre Bracciano had been rude, suspicious, and unfair. But he could see that his own pride was involved and was the source of his resentment. His reactions were habitually so ambivalent that he found it hard to judge a situation truthfully. Surely his resentment was real. Was it justified? Was it a mature reaction? Was it merely thwarted selfishness? He pounded the typewriter keys and knew that he was pouting. He slammed the carriage to the left. That kind of thing burns me up, he thought. But he is my superior. My task is to obey, not to pout.

As he got halfway through his list, the doors rattled open again. Herbert Klein looked in for him. "The boss gone?" he grinned.

"Yes," Richard nodded.

"Good." Herbert carried a push broom with him and drew it into the room. He shut the door. He was short, strongly built, blond, blue-eyed. He spoke Oxfordian English, with only the faintest sense of German harshness. When Richard talked to him, he often felt that Herbert still heard bombs falling and mortar dust sliding down from the walls; he often felt that Herbert remembered terror and pain. The past summer, he and Herbert had spoken often about the war, a fantastic war, an unbelievable war. Blitzkrieg and tanks and bombs, propaganda, excitement, swastikas, droning chants. Herbert had been a member of the junior Hitler youth. He had worn a uniform and, with solemn face, had marched, resolutely kicking his skinny legs. After the war, he began to grow ashamed of those early days; but he was never apologetic. He would defend the attitude and atmosphere of Germany if anyone attacked them. But he was ashamed nonetheless.

"Germany," he had said to Richard that summer on the Adriatic coast, "still has a role to play in history. The West will fight the East—in Germany." He rubbed his hand across his jaw and blushed. They sat on a barren, sandy hill overlooking the blue sea. The breeze blew through their shirts and through their hair. "Nazism was a mistake. Paganism is outmoded. Paganism can never rule the minds of men again. Christianity has opened up men's minds to the value of the person once for all. The world can never be happy in Greece or Assyria again. There cannot be another Caesar."

"What about the Communists?"

"Communism is a scourge, a blight, a punishment! Communism is the end of the person, the end of—everything!" Herbert spat out bitterly with a gesture of his hand. "Communism is a nightmare!" His older sister had been raped by Russian soldiers; his father was missing at Stalingrad; his two brothers died in the Ukraine.

Richard was silent. After a time, Herbert's bitterness passed, and he began again. "Germany is the field where Christianity and Communism are going to tangle. They will leap at each other's throats. They are incompatible. Politics is the messianic battleground."

"Christianity is not politics."

"Unless we settle what to do about the bombs, and world domination, and poverty, civilization is impossible."

"Why don't you become a politician, not a priest?"

"Because the ultimate struggle is Christianity's. The kind of government, the proximate concerns—these are important, but only to put Christianity in action. If Christianity is lost . . . the moral sense of the West is gone. Liberalism has no moral sense, not even that of the Greeks, no morality at all, except what it has not destroyed of Christianity. Kant spoke of an imperative, which Freud says is a compulsion, which Nietzsche says is an illusion. 'Live alone!'—'live dangerously!'—these are all the West has outside of Christianity."

"So you will be a political priest."

"A priest who understands what the issue is. Save the political world so that men can save themselves. Nature, for grace to build on."

"So that is why you wish to be a priest . . ." Richard threw a pebble at a lizard lying in the dry sand three or four yards away. Alarmed, the creature sped noiselessly through the tough growths of grass. The Adriatic shone in the sun. "So that is what we are about . . ."

Now Herbert had a push broom in his hand. "Did he give you a talking down?"

Richard nodded.

Herbert made the sign for stupidity. "*Questi Italiani!* What about? The new books?"

Richard nodded, not able to restrain a smile.

"I told you! He doesn't want any changes. The Eternal City—it never moves. Even the Spanish are going fast compared to them."

"You don't like Italians because they deserted you in the war."

"Deserted us? That was a break! We had to rescue them in Greece, rescue them in Albania, rescue them in Libya. After 1943, the Allies rescued them!"

"Meanwhile, Germany kept the lands she had to rescue."

Herbert shrugged. "In war, nearly everything is fair. What I came to ask you—will you help us make the beds for the new men?"

Richard hesitated. He wanted to use his free time for tacking some canvases on frames. It would be the last chance before classes began. "All right," he said grudgingly. "For a half hour or so. Can't you find enough help?"

"I knew you would, Ricky," said the German, patting him mockingly on the shoulder, as he had seen Americans do. "Americans are very generous. To a fault."

"Only for a half hour!" Richard warned. Herbert left with a wave. Richard didn't feel very generous at all. He felt he should have said yes immediately, with no strings attached—as he should have obeyed his superior. In a moment of anger he wished that such love were inhuman, too much to ask. He turned back to his typing. He squirmed to think of his pettiness.

3

THE NEXT DAY Richard and Herbert were returning from a trip into town. As they rang the bell and then opened the front door with the buzzing of the lock, Herbert hurried right on through the vestibule and into the house. Richard looked at his watch and then stopped at the porter's window.

"*Buon giorno, Rosetta, come sta?*"

"Ah! Padre Riccardo! *Buona sera!*"

"Why is it that every time I say *buon giorno*, you say *buona sera*? When is morning and when is afternoon?"

"*Eh beh!* Just to be different, padre. There's no rule." The old woman smiled. "You look very tanned. You look good."

"I put on a little weight."

"A good thing! Last spring you looked so thin." Rosetta pinched her cheeks together with her fingers from behind the small porter's window.

"Yes, I feel fine this year! Ready for another year!"

"*Bravo,* padre. . . . Today has come back Padre Carlo."

"Yes, I know. I'm supposed to see him." Richard looked at his watch.

Of all the students, the Americans were the most responsive to Rosetta and her family. She was over fifty now, heavy, tired already, tired long ago. Her hands had washed clothing in the icy streams of the Abruzzi before she had come to Rome, after the war. Giacomo had been in the Italian army from 1936 until 1943, away all that time in Ethiopia, in Libya, in Southern Italy. The *bambino* had grown, God knows how, with no father, almost no food, through all these years of war. Rosetta passed her hard, rough hand through her straggly gray hair. The lot of Italian women was bitterness. Riccardo was a little what she wished her son were like: considerate, mild, serious. Yet all the child had known was hardship, hunger, fear. Fear, always, of the Germans. Fear of bombs. Fear for his father. Fear because of his mother's long sorrow and tired back and sleepless eyes.

"How's Antonio?" Richard asked.

"What am I going to do, padre? That boy will drive me to my death." She set down her sewing. "The more I want him to be good," she gestured from her chin, "the more he is bad. Lazy! Spendthrift! Who knows what he is doing when he is out so late? He won't talk to me. *Vitellone!* Good-for-nothing!"

"He's young, Rosetta."

"No, padre, today I have a headache." Rosetta put her hand to her forehead. "I am tired, and when he comes in so late I do not sleep. So today I have a headache. Everything is ugly."

"Would you like an aspirin?"

Rosetta hesitated.

"Sure you would." He looked at his watch. "I'll get you one."

"But *padre superiore . . .*"

"He won't mind. I'll be right back."

"No, no, padre. It's not worth the trouble . . ."

"It'll only take a minute." Richard pushed through the inner door and hurried up the hallway to the stairwell. He climbed quickly to the infirmary. The door was locked, but he remembered he had aspirins in his room. He had doubts about what Padre Bracciano would say if he saw him giving aspirin to Rosetta. The rule forbade fraternizing. He had only meant to say hello. Surely it was only charity to give her the aspirin. He found the bottle, shook out two, and started down the stairs. Charity or obedience: the dilemma always seemed to leap in front of him. He thought it right to solve it this way.

"Here you are!" he said to Rosetta. The door swung closed behind him.

She set the aspirins beside her for a moment. "But it wasn't necessary. I don't want you to get in trouble, padre."

"I won't!" he said. "It's the least I can do for you. You work hard for us."

"You are very good, padre."

"I have to go now, Rosetta. See you later."

He hurried again upstairs and washed his face and hands. Then he descended a flight to Father Milton's room. He walked slowly as he approached the battered green door in the wall of the ancient corridor. The worn indicator outside the door read *occupato*. Richard hesitated, hand uplifted. He knocked. No answer. He knocked again.

"Avanti!"

Richard pushed open the door.

Father Charles Milton, "Padre Carlo" in Italy, sat at his desk rummaging in the bottom drawer. "Rich, how are you? Come on in. Be with you in a minute. Come in, come in."

"Good to see you again, father. Welcome back."

"Good to be back." Father Milton smiled broadly. "Good to see all the old faces. Find a seat."

Richard looked for a chair, but neither of the two high wooden chairs was empty. He lifted a box from one and set it on the floor, then sat down. The priest continued fussing and offering small talk about his trip and whom he had seen on returning and whom not. He was a very tall man and very thin. His hair was curly black; he had high cheekbones. He wore yellowish plastic-rimmed glasses, had a large nose and large lips, which he was always rubbing with his hand.

Father Milton was a native of Cincinnati and for years had taught economics in a small college in Ohio; then he had decided to become a priest. At forty-two he was highly thought of in the congregation. He had a keen business sense and administrative talents; above all, he was mild, good-natured, and not at all ambitious. For the American seminarians at the *collegio*, his presence was a great blessing. He understood their problems in adjusting to a European regime and smoothed their conflicts with the European version of religious ideals. Richard watched him as he rooted through the drawers of his desk. He wished he could feel as close to him as Frank Perrone did.

"Well, Richard," the priest said at last. "Can't find it. It will wait. So how are you? How did the summer go?"

"Fine, father. Very fine."

"You liked Villa Maria better than last year, then?"

Richard blushed. "The Adriatic was beautiful the whole summer. We got to Ravenna and Venice, and to Florence on the way home."

"Firenze! You saw Firenze then! Ah, lovely, lovely Florence." Father Milton rubbed his lips with avid pleasure.

"It was my second trip. The finest city in the world!"

"Ah, what about Venice? And Rome? And you haven't even seen Paris, have you? Or even San Francisco? You're rash, Richard, rash!"

"And stubborn," Richard answered. "The others would have to be heaven. But I loved Venice, too. It's hard to decide: Venice, Florence, Rome."

"Rome has got the history—and the Church."

"Venice has St. Mark's, the canals, the music—but, above all, the piazza. Though, in another way, I like St. Peter's, too. . . . Father, why do you always get me into these impossible comparisons?"

"You're an artist, Richard. I like to hear you talk." Father Milton laughed and flashed his teeth in the friendliest manner he could manage. "But, Rich . . ." He changed his tone. "I've got a message for you."

Richard knew he was coming directly to the point. He waited.

"Father Provincial is worried about you, Richard."

Richard had his chin in his hands. He felt his palms growing wet. "Worried about me?"

"Well, he wrote to me. In fact, I saw him while I was in New York." Father Milton spoke slowly.

"What's supposed to be wrong with me?"

'Well, you've been losing weight."

"I gained some of it back! I'm one-seventy again."

"What were you when you came?"

"One eighty-three. But I lost almost twenty pounds right away."

Father Milton shrugged. "Well, you're going up again. Hmm, what he was asking about. Well. . . ." The priest rubbed his lips. He focused his green eyes on the desk in front of him. "Well. . . ." He looked at Richard and blurted it out quietly, with a sense of helplessness: "Do you really want to be a priest?"

Richard sat there in a cold silence. "What?" he asked, disbelieving.

"I . . . I see I said that too directly. But . . . that is what he basically wants to know." Father Milton flashed his friendly smile again, but stiffly.

"What . . . kind of question is that, father?" he asked quietly. "Aren't I here? Didn't I take my final vows?"

"But this is another sort of thing, Richard." Father Milton sat up, rubbing his lips more rapidly. A serious expression came into his eyes again. "Vows can be rescinded. But ordination . . ."

"I can't look at vows that way, father."

"I'm sure you can't. You shouldn't. But . . ."

"But the fact is Padre Colletto thinks I do not *want* to be a priest."

"No, no, not that."

"That I *should* not be a priest."

"No, Richard. See here." Father Milton shifted his legs on the rung of the chair and gestured with his thin, bony hands. "He only wants to be sure that you are happy."

"But what gives him reason to suspect that I am not?"

"Well, perhaps word gets back to him . . ."

"What word? And how?"

"Now easy, Ricky. You know the council has to send back a yearly report."

"Yes."

"Well, perhaps Padre Bracciano saw fit to add a note."

"Concerning my unfitness."

"Concerning things he doesn't understand."

"Doesn't understand! He doesn't understand much about me at all! He could write a book."

"I know it hurts, Ricky. Now look, he's not an American. It's hard for him to understand our ways. And you happen to be outspoken."

"That's what exasperates me! I *am* outspoken. He should know my attitude."

"But neither he nor Padre Colletto are Americans, Ricky. They're classmates. They think alike. Your frankness looks like insubordination. Perhaps"—the priest formed the words slowly—"sometimes it is insubordination. But all of us are guilty of that. Obedience is hard for all of us."

"Obedience! That isn't my problem," Richard replied. "I do everything I'm told. I don't break any rules. Padre Bracciano—he's a fine superior and all that, but he simply is—suspicious. I don't try to pull anything over on him. I'm just myself. I obey. Ask him." His conscience twinged concerning the aspirins for Rosetta. But that was charity, he reasoned. Charity takes precedence.

"What about the visit to North American College, Richard?" Father asked quietly.

"I *had* permission for that. He admitted it afterwards. He gave the permission, but he forgot about it. He knows that."

"You missed vespers that afternoon," the priest said resolutely.

"But that's what I had the permission for—to miss vespers."

"Well," shrugged Father Milton, "I'm just repeating what the provincial told me. That was one of the things Padre Bracciano must have mentioned."

"I went in to Padre Bracciano right after he brought the matter up. He remembered then that he'd given the permission. Why would he have written about it? That's the third time he's done something like that!"

"Like what, Richard?"

"Accused me of something we had already straightened out. He gave me permission to keep three dollars to buy a set of post cards for an aunt of mine. Then he called me in because someone had told him I was spending money. He did the same thing in the library."

"Easy, Rich, easy. I know it's hard. These things sometimes happen, and they get me down, too. I can only tell you to be careful. Look. Try hard not to say anything or stand out in anything that will antagonize Padre Bracciano. Just be prudent. We can't always do the good things we'd like to do, you know—prudence sometimes demands—"

"Prudence! Prudence! Prudence! Father, there's one word that's beginning to drive me mad. *Prudence.* You can use it to halt anything or to cover anything. Sometimes I think it holds our life together, like putty, and there's nothing else of substance there!"

"There's a false prudence, of course, and a true prudence."

"Of course! But what everybody means by prudence is 'take the safest course possible.' Try that anywhere you hear the word prudence and you'll have a perfectly adequate translation."

"Richard, Richard," laughed Father Milton, stroking his lips. "Just don't say these things to Padre Bracciano and you've grasped my point. Or anywhere they might get back to him."

"But where is that, Father? Everywhere?"

Father Milton smiled and nodded. "Isn't it worth it to play it safe for now, Richard? You've got years ahead of you. Keep your thoughts under your hat. You've got good ideas. Pray over them. The Lord will make much use of you. But, for now, silence. And pax."

"Peace . . . well, I'll try. I'm really not as upset as I sound. You're the only one here I have to talk to, and so I talk pretty frankly. Tell Father Provincial not to worry. I'll be a good boy." He smiled wryly. "That was what I decided this summer anyway. I promise to keep my nose clean."

"I'm glad, Richard. I told Father Provincial you'd say that. I spoke very highly of you. And I don't mind your speaking up with me. As a matter of fact, I usually agree with you· You've got a lot of good will."

There was a silence.

"What should I do, father, about the library books?"

"The library books?"

"I still want to build up what we have. We need so many things. The Dead Sea Scrolls, *Sources Chrétiennes* . . . we've bought very little over the last twenty years. No novels. Nothing but theology. Old stuff at that."

"Hm. I agree with you. Let me talk to Padre Bracciano about that. Maybe we can set aside a larger fund." He reached over and made a note. "I'm going to be gone in a month, so I'll have to see him soon."

"Where to, father?" Richard colored. "If I may ask."

"Surely, Ricky. To England. Father General gave me some business there that may keep me away all year. I won't be much use here as a councilor."

"We'll miss you."

"Thank you, Ricky. I hate to leave. Hmm, well, I'll mention to him about the books in the first meeting of the council. Meanwhile, you just obey. You've time enough to make decisions. Now is the time to obey."

Richard nodded. He could think of nothing more to say, and his throat was tight. He sat there for a moment.

"May I—have your blessing, father?"

"Sure!" Both men arose. Richard knelt *"Benedictio Del omnipotentis . . . descendat super te et maneat semper.* Amen." The priest slapped his outstretched hands down upon Richard's head with affection.

Richard lifted his cassock from his heels and stood. "Thank you, father."

"Glad you look so well, Ricky, and enjoyed your vacation. Plunge in now and have a good year. It's your third, isn't it?"

The green eyes were studying him with affection. "Yes, third," Richard said, anxious now to leave and to turn away.

"You'll have, let's see . . . Lampada, Schuman?"

"Some young German prof is taking Schuman's place."

"No! He was old when I went through. They said he was teaching in the temple when the boy Christ appeared." He flashed his big grin, his head tilted to one side, his skinny hand holding on to Richard's. "Well, be good, Ricky."

"Thanks, father," Richard said evenly. He pressed his jaws together and stepped out into the corridor. He hurried off for the chapel and knelt in prayer.

He knelt there a long time. It had come to that then. Behave or get out. He had wanted so badly to be a priest. For six years

now he had given everything in preparation; he loved the life, and
his ardor hadn't diminished even by a little. Now he had been
given, no matter how sweetly, an ultimatum. But what did they
ask? How was he to change? He had done nothing wrong; his
heart reproached him on nothing definite. Yet there was, somewhere, a movement of inner dread. There was something that he
didn't see. It frightened him to think that he was unknown to himself, and he refused to believe it. He called to his mind the images
that had always consoled him, the images on which he built the
walls of his vocation. People milled in the streets, hundreds of people; he looked at their tan, concerned faces; his heart was moved.
They walked in a hurry down the streets, away from a pursuer.
Time was always faster. Time sifted through their lives like the
granules of an hourglass. The days dropped away and left them
emptier and emptier. Did they know? Did they know where they
were hurrying?

Rome had heightened his perception of fragility. The people in
the streets of Rome were but one generation out of hundreds who
had seen the same streets, a living film of activity and joy, to be shed
and replaced by another while the streets and the buildings and the
hills remained. Griefs and loves passed away. People with new
desires and a new sense of self-importance came to replace the present. In 1856, in 1914, in 1932, there had been other people who
had been the living. Richard's heart sometimes ached with the
thought. The loves of human beings were the one value of the
world. He could not believe that they evaporated. He could not
believe that suffering and anguish were meaningless.

He had struggled for six years now to sink his destiny deeper
and deeper into the issue of immortality. It was this his life signified,
or it was nothing. Men live forever: that is what his life called out.
Men live forever: that is what his cassock signified. "You live forever!" That is what he sometimes wished to shout, on an impulse, to
a man or woman sitting across from him impassively in the bus.
The sight of people wounded him. He would have liked to have
journeyed all around the world, and lived for all time, and heard all

the woes and all the loves of every man that lived. Each tale would
be so beautiful. Each would be painful.

And now himself? What was to become of himself? If he could
not be a priest, what would he be? A priest was one who labored
fulltime for immortality, totally for men. A priest was concerned
with being and nothingness, with love, with grief, with responsibility, with destiny. A priest's whole life was lived with the ultimates.
What, then, if not a priest? Was anything worthwhile for him in
comparison? His fingers clenched and unclenched on the dark pew.
He opened his eyes and looked down at them. Painter's hands. He
had his art. But was that the same as the priesthood? Is that what
the Lord had made him to do? *No!* his heart said. He wished to be a
priest. Priest and painter both. As Fra Angelico had been. Fra
Angelico. . . . Why so much opposition? Why did his acts meet with
such resistance from superiors? Was he unworthy of the priesthood?

A new coldness overcame him. Perhaps that was it. He was
deluding himself that he wished to be a priest. Secretly he longed to
be a painter and to live—an ordinary life, in the world, among people, in love with things. He wished for children, a family, the solace
of a wife. He longed for human comfort, for a heart with whom he
could speak. No, no, he thought. He pressed his fingers to his eyes.
Beyond that . . . beyond that was a taste he had begun to relish, a
delicate taste, a fragile taste but strong: the love of the Unseen. An
ultimate love, beyond sensuality and emotions, eternal, cold, unaf-
fected by the hourglass, victor over death. It was sure and deep and
immensely fortifying. Ever beyond, never seen . . . alluring, promising, intoxicating. He searched to grasp but could not. His heart
reeled with desire for his Beloved, for a sight ever promised but
withheld, for a revelation that would never come until the snapping
of the cords. The Lord would come as terrible light, with overflood-
ing love. Come, Lord Jesus! he often prayed. Come! . . . I have
nothing else.

He tried to make himself empty. But he was a hypocrite. He
knew in fact that he was not empty. He liked praise and attention.
He liked every mark of human love and consideration. It pained him

to feel the suspicion of Padre Bracciano, Padre Colletto, even Padre Carlo, upon his spirit. And he was worried that it might be justified. He was worldly. He did love art, love the cities, love people: everything captivated him! Governments, reforms, proposals, everything about the earthly city. To build up everything that was truthful and was good, to conserve it. . . men in love and at peace, clear breezes, blue skies . . . these were what he wanted on the earth. Did he belong, then, in a cloister? Was there not a contradiction? Were his desires compensation for what he was not fulfilling in the seminary?

An ultimatum. And Father Milton leaving soon for England. What will happen then? Only this year to decide, once-for-all, for a lifetime. In June there would come ordination to the subdiaconate: the step was irrevocable. It would bind him to the clerical state forever. In the following December then, on a bright cold day as he imagined it, at St. John Lateran's or at St. Mary Major's, he would be ordained a priest. The priesthood! There was the prize. He looked at his hands again . . . hands that would hold the Body of the Lord, would lift His chalice . . . hands that would paint, would work, would bless . . . hands that would cease to be his and belong to all, forever. The ultimate vocation—it *would* be his—it *must* be . . .

But how? His mind saw only blackness and reeling lights behind his closed eyelids. How? What could he do that he was not doing? He tried only to be honest. His zeal seemed to lead him to a thousand faults, a thousand things that others around him didn't seem to do. But was it zeal? Or was it pride and desire? Was it his own secret manner of rebellion, hidden behind posturings of holiness and longing? One thing was sure: from now on, he would have to scrutinize himself. He would have to lay his motives bare, merciless in self-examination. The priesthood was too large a task to trifle with; it was forever, for other men as well as for himself. Himself a priest. Was he able? Did he desire it? What was true desire and what was false? He had always thought he knew who he was and what he wanted. He assured himself he still did. He wished to be a priest. That was definite. He had put six years into his choice already. He had been accepted by the order, taken his temporary vows year by year, even taken his final vows. Surely these were signs that he was right in his vocation.

Careful now, he warned himself. Doubts about vocation are subtle things. Self and Satan and the world—everything conspires to make a man take the easy way. Never entertain a doubt once vows are made. But hadn't Father Milton introduced the doubt? And, anyway, my whole restlessness induces it. I must speak to Padre Benedetto soon. A whole inner world is rising up against me. What am I supposed to do? I only want to do what is right. But what is that? Is it wrong, having taken up the plow, to turn away? Or is that precisely what the Lord is asking? Is it Satan? Is it myself? Is it only a moment of purification and of trial?

Lord, help me. Give me light; give me courage. How my parents will be disappointed, after five years of waiting. Not to make the trip for ordination! My relatives and friends . . . don't let me deceive myself! Keep away the secondary things! He looked silently at the tabernacle for a while. The Lord was there, but silent and unmoving. Richard heard the straining silence of the chapel. The benches creaked. He felt strangely cold and unprayerful. His thoughts had hardly been a prayer; they had been reasonings. He tried to find a moment's peace, but he tried to think when it was that he had last really prayed, without dry imaginations and quiet reasonings. Had he ever really prayed, gone out into nothingness with a call of the heart? Maybe all his prayer life was a sham, a legalistic ritual by the bell, an exercise. His heart turned cold with fear. Maybe here was the source of his doubts. He had been deceiving himself all along. No, he knew that wasn't true. But was it? He knelt in silence for a while. Then he arose, glad at least that he knew something of his task, genuflected, and walked slowly from the chapel, a little fearfully.

4

TWO HOURS LATER the bell rang for supper. The metallic clang sang through the corridors with a shrill, high whistle overriding its brazen raucousness. Young men in black cassocks hurried down the narrow stairs and along the gray corridors to the refectory, some fastening their leathern belts as they walked. Each moved in silence and stood, arms folded, at his place. Richard walked quietly, his thoughts still preoccupied. The refectory was not a large room; six tables, for eight men each, filled the room. Richard sought the second table on the left. White oilcloth covered the tables; simple dishes, silverware, and cloth napkins sat mutely and in order upon them. The wooden chairs were old and worn. Richard elbowed through the rows of cassocks. Padre Bracciano entered the refectory last, blessing himself with holy water from the little font at the entrance, as everybody had done. He looked around. He began the grace.

Richard could not help looking closely at the superior. Short, stocky, dark-haired—he was the one who held Richard's future in his hands. It was he who approved or disapproved of his advance to ordination. Richard found his hand coming up to cup his chin, as it often did when he was nervous and preoccupied. His attitude toward Padre Bracciano was ambiguous. As a superior, Richard tried to follow his wishes faithfully. As a man, he did not like him. He did not like his mannerisms. He could be the quintessence of suavity and diplomacy; he could give a rude command without concern for the tone he used or for the situation he might be disrupting. Still more, Richard simply could not like his ideas. Herbert had a word for them: they were "clerical." He seemed to see himself as an administrator in an organization to which men conformed, did as they were told, and did not gripe—except, of course, playfully, in the type of story that circulated among the clergy of Rome, the story of private inadequacy by which subordinates took revenge on the system and its rulers. Padre Bracciano was inclined to view the Church as always right. Subordinates, the laity, impractical professors, atheists, artists, Protestants, Jews, Communists, liberals, French theologians—everybody was mistaken. At first glance, and also from then onwards, he was prepared to see that the wisdom of authority was right, adequate, and beautiful. The grating of the machine, and its breakdowns, were due to insufficient loyalty or to lack of faith. Those who lacked faith sometimes saw faults where there really were none; they simply took a "human" point of view. Or, if there clearly was an incontrovertible fault, then the duty of subordinates was still to fall in line, to "wash the dirty linen at home," and to respect authority with silence and obedience. For him, the life of the Church could be expressed in a word: obey. Superiors made decisions. "Blessed," he would say, "are those not called to the difficult tasks of command, who eat their daily bread in simplicity." There was no contingency that simple obedience could not meet. Even liturgy, in his mind, lay chiefly in the dignified performance of the rubrics. No political problem, no social strain escaped the workings of his formula. He thought little about the extension of his pseudomonastic point of view to all fields of the Church's life; for, after all, his task was the seminary, and it devolved upon higher superiors to be concerned with matters of theory and general scope.

He was aware that human nature is frail and, hence, he could allow for the inevitable failures of superiors and for his own. His faith was never shaken by such things, once he had grasped the fact that the Church was human as well as divine—that is to say, ugly and conniving. He preached indulgence toward the frailties of superiors, and, hence, in this way, too, his security remained intact. He imagined somewhere, outside of any specific structure that anyone could point to, a vast hypostasis as vague as a ghost or a hovering cloud, and to this vague, imperishable, unassailable, unhistoric image he attached the name of "Church," or even "Mystical Body," and affixed there all his devotion. With such a platonic, abstract ideal, there could be no argument. Richard found communication with Padre Bracciano almost impossible. The concept of obedience and subjection prevented real give-and-take in discussion. The easy vision of "obey your superiors and be at peace" prevented scrutiny, criticism, and creative thought. Superiors had the "grace of state," the "guidance of the Holy Spirit"; what need had they of *your* opinion? To offer an opinion was an impertinence. Docility and humility forbade it; the "spirit of faith" obviated its necessity.

Richard blessed himself and sat down with foreboding. Is this what he must become? Is this what being a good religious meant? He saw clearly that he would have to distinguish with the utmost precision between rebelliousness and sincere questioning. He would have to find some way to be a perfect religious—the words gave his conscience pain—and a perfect man.

"Whether you eat or drink, or whatsoever else you do, do all for the glory of God!" said the lector loudly from the reading stand in Italian.

Since it was vacation time, Padre Bracciano tapped the little bell at his place on the table.

"Deo gratias!" said the seated religious, some thirty of them.

They reached for their napkins and turned over their plates. The buzz of conversation began to fill the high-ceilinged, dully painted room. A dark oil painting of a Renaissance cardinal looked down from one wall. A copy of a Raphael Madonna looked down from another. A large painting of Pope Pius XI rested above the superior's table.

Richard looked at Padre Bracciano; he was talking to Padre Milton on his right, and then to Padre Eugenio, a short, thin Italian, on his left.

"How are you today, Riccardo?"

The abrupt question brought him back to the table. Luigi Alessandro, his dark-brown eyes laughing at him, waited for his answer.

Richard smiled wryly. "Not too bad," he said in Italian. "Hate to start school, that's all."

"We have a week yet. Tomorrow . . . the new men."

"How many are coming?" Herbert asked, butting in on the conversation.

"Eight Italians," Luigi said. "How many from America?"

"One."

"Three Germans," Herbert said.

"*Allora,* twelve," Luigi concluded.

"Hope they are a lively bunch," Richard suggested. He didn't feel like entering on a conversation. He sat back from the table and began passing the bowl of soup that Umberto was filling. Umberto stood at the end of the oblong table, wearing a white apron, ladling the steaming soup from a tureen. Umberto was tall and broad; something about him suggested clumsiness and merriment. When he was finished serving he sat down. There were only five at the table: Umberto, Luigi, the silent Carmelo, Herbert, and Richard.

"It's too hot for soup," Umberto said, idling his spoon in his bowl. "Better Coca-Cola."

"With noodles?" Herbert asked, turning up his nose.

Umberto laughed amiably.

Luigi Alessandro stopped stirring his soup and looked up at Richard, who sat across from him. Luigi had very shiny dark eyes and straight black hair; his complexion was olive; his teeth were straight and white. He wore dark-rimmed glasses and was as studious as he looked. He had always wanted to be a friend of Richard's but had never been able to. In a way, he resented Paolo, Herbert, and Umberto, who had been able to attract him. Richard was merely kind to him, with a forced politeness. He seemed to imply that Luigi was not good enough, but there had never been anything harsh or definite in his tone. Luigi wanted to be taken seriously. French thinkers, German thinkers, American thinkers were taken seriously; Italian thinkers were not. He was a clever student; he knew that. Why then didn't Richard like him? Why did no one listen to him? He thought of something that Richard was enthusiastic about. He squirmed in his seat. He baited Richard by speaking of the condemnation of the worker priests in France. Censure, not condemnation, Richard retorted. The argument became bitter. Herbert, too, entered it—on Richard's side. Carmelo and Umberto listened passively. Luigi's image blended in Richard's mind with Padre Bracciano's and with his provincial's warning; a great wall of frustration seemed to rise before him. Richard flayed at it but felt cold and doomed to failure.

"We have got to take a modern point of view!" he argued.

"Conform, in other words," Luigi said. "You wish the Church to approve modern society; to give her blessing to usury and capital, to disrespect for authority, to political ideology, to social revolution; to yield divine faith to pluralism: you forget everything eternal, for the sake of earth."

"You come out with such stupidities!" Richard said. "You are so reactionary. You don't see what is happening. There must be a total reconstruction!"

"I only preach the Gospels."

"The Gospels! I can only say that you serve a different Church than I do."

"It is the Roman Catholic Church," Luigi smiled.

"I hate to think so," Richard said.

"You will be a priest in it."

"Not your kind of priest. I have ideas entirely different."

Luigi shrugged.

Umberto brought in the tray. He put a spoon in the warmed-over spaghetti and passed the platter to Richard. He had a bowl of boiled turnips and another of lettuce salad. He set a basket of rolls on the table, near the water pitcher, and set the worn silver coffeepot on a hot plate. There was a bowl of fruit already on the table. Richard helped himself to each platter and passed it on. He poured olive oil over his salad and salted it. He broke a roll and began to eat. He didn't feel very hungry.

"Luigi," Umberto asked. "The bread, please."

Luigi nodded and reached for the basket. "Here you are."

"Grazie."

Silence hung over the table until the current of conversation could change.

"Coffee, anybody?" Richard asked after a moment, lifting the pot.

"For me, please," Carmelo said, extending his cup. Richard poured.

"No, thanks," Luigi smiled, covering his cup with his hand.

Herbert nodded: "Later."

Richard poured for Umberto and then for himself. He watched the strong black coffee rise halfway in his cup; then he stopped. He had said things he didn't mean. He had not argued as Christ would have argued. Apparently he could do nothing right. And what if Luigi were correct, and he himself wrong?

"When does school start?" Herbert asked.

"Wednesday," Carmelo said.

"And we have a retreat before then?"

"Saturday and Sunday."

5

THE NEW MEN were arriving. It was October third and one of Richard's favorite feasts: that of St. Thérèse of Lisieux. The day was a Thérèsian day: bright, billowy, fresh. He had awakened with a song near his lips. His prayer at early meditation and at mass had simply flown to God. Now, in the afternoon, the sun spanked gaily on the Tiber. The sycamores along the riverbank flashed their peeling bark. The sky was a rich Italian blue, silvery with wind and light. The clouds were large, swift, fleecy. Richard drew a deep breath of the warm October air.

As Richard stood there in the front doorway, the sun lighting up the redness in his brown hair, his cassock falling neatly from his young frame, Father Milton drove up in a cab with the one American to arrive this year: "Conny" McInerny—Cornelius James McInerny. Richard had known him in the States; they had been together for a while in their college years. They had not hit it off. Now Conny was in Rome.

Conny was from Chicago. He was a great baseball fan, a volatile talker, and he purposely wore the pretense of being brassy and insensitive. Richard watched him step from the cab into the sunlight and look around. His straw-blond hair shone in the sun. Conny never wore a hat: he always carried it if the rule said wear it. The black suit and tie looked strange now to Richard, after having seen seminarians only in cassock in Italy. He stirred himself to cross the hot pavement, down the steps, to go to Conny's aid.

"Conny! Good to see you!"

"Ricky, old man, you look great! You wear that outfit on the street?"

Richard looked down at his cassock and the black leather belt that girded it in. He wanted to wince but smiled instead. "You know that, Conny. I wrote you."

"Just kidding, Ricky. Say . . . looks great!"

Richard, too, looked over the house. "You'll like it, Conny. It'll be tough at first, but you'll manage."

"Wait'll you hear my Italian. I've been practicing. *Gratzie*— that's the word for thanks, right?"

"Almost, Conny. You better stick to baseball slang for awhile. Anyway, the first few days there's 'per' to talk English. You can sit with Frank and me."

"Perrone! Where is the old Franker?"

"He's driving the superior. He's been *autista* almost since he got here. That's chauffeur. Really likes Rome."

"Should. He's a wop, ain't he? Oh, sorry, Ricky. Just kidding." He slapped Richard on the back. "In Chicago it doesn't mean a thing. I mean, we're mickys, he's a wop. So what?"

Richard had a wry expression on his face but hid it by turning to the street. Father Milton was calling from the cab.

"I'll take him up," Richard answered.

"Know his room?" shouted the tall priest.

"Forty-nine," Richard nodded, then pushed Conny through the door. "Padre Bracciano's out; we don't have to see him now. Here's our chapel. Want to go in?"

"O.K." Conny looked from right to left, then entered. He genuflected tiredly and put his chin on his hands at the last bench, closed his eyes for a moment, and then opened them for a look around. The chapel was grayish and dark. The altar was huge and baroque. Two giant angels stood poised in the shadows on either side, either just alighting or just taking off, each bearing a huge candle three inches thick. On each candle was an old electric bulb. The pillars of the altar were squat and dark. The candelabra were hideously ornate and unpolished. The crucifix was dark, Spanish, fanciful; angels danced at its base. A dark painting hung above the altar, which Conny was somehow glad he couldn't see. "Ugh," he thought, "art." Somewhere there nestled the tabernacle, his eyes finally resting on it; its stiff white veil seemed even to him not a little grayish.

"I don't like it," Conny said when they got out into the hall.

"Oh?" said Richard.

"Even the holy water's dirty. Gad! How old is that font?"

"Probably a century or two."

"Anybody ever clean it?"

"You'll get used to it. . . . Here, see that fellow? I want to introduce you. Come on . . . Umberto! Umberto!" Richard whispered the name loudly up the hall.

Umberto turned. He was tall and very heavy and had a jolly face. He came right over.

"Please, Umberto," Richard said in Italian. "I'd like you to meet our new American. We're three now. Watch out!"

"But God is on our side," replied Umberto, laughing. *"Piacere,"* he said to Conny, bowing and shaking hands.

"Umberto Carrozza. Padre Cornelio."

"Cornelio?" replied the Italian, smiling graciously. *"Il mio zio si chiama Cornelio."*

Conny stood there a little nervously. He was not quite in the mood for meeting people. "What did he say?" he asked.

"He likes your name; he has an uncle named Cornelius. He says it is a pleasure to meet you."

"Uh . . . tell him the same. The same to him."

Umberto nodded, laid his hand gently on Richard's arm, and prayed, in the delicate Italian fashion, to be excused; he had to help *fratello* in the refectory. *"Arrivederla,"* he concluded to Conny, bowing as he backed off. *"Auguri! Benvenuto!"*

"Grazie, Umberto," Richard replied. *"Ciao"*

"What did he say?" demanded Conny.

"He has to help set up the dining hall. He wishes you well. *Arrivederla* is the polite form for good-bye until later."

"Do they all bow and scrape like that?"

"He is a fine fellow. He graduated from the University of Rome. In medicine. There are two others here—one in letters, one in law. Paolo Veronese—he entered late, too. The other Italians are all little-sem kids."

"Who's this Paolo?"

"Veronese. A good friend of mine. One of the finest men here. Or anywhere."

"Oh."

They walked up two flights of stairs—worn marble stairs, worn by generations of feet treading in the same patterns on every step. Richard carried both of Conny's new gray bags. They looked so different from the artificial leather or cloth bags the new Italian or German men were bringing in.

"How many in the house now, Richie?"

"Forty-five, with the faculty. You and me and Frank—three Americans. Twelve Germans. The rest Italians. Three of the Germans and two Italians will eat at table with us tonight. They speak English."

They rounded a corner. Two black-clad figures, who had been laughing and talking, looked up, frightened a moment, backing to the sides of the corridor. When they saw Richard and Conny they relaxed again and hurried on talking.

"That gripes me!" Richard said quietly. Then he smiled apologetically, knowing Conny wouldn't like it. "They're discipline-conscious, Conny. Very strict rules, but they cheat on them. It makes me furious sometimes, but it's just different."

"Great. There's nothing like manly honesty!"

"They'll learn. They've been brought up in it. Those two have been in a seminary since they were eleven."

"I can see I'm going to like living with the likes of them."

"It isn't bad, Conny. You have to try to understand. Here's your room, Conny. Forty-nine."

"Oh."

The outside of the doorframe was nicked, old, in need of paint. The wooden indicator read: *occupato, fuori di casa, cappella, giardino, terrazza.* The two Z's of *terrazza* were broken out. A bit of broken chain dangled from the indicator. Richard pushed open the door and stepped in with the bags.

"Oh . . . thanks."

There was a single cot of white metal in need of paint, a small battered dresser, a green metal locker with door ajar and a square of old paper awry in its bottom and three old hangers askew on the loosened bar. A wooden wicker chair beside the bed and a small, square, dark-colored desk and white-painted chair completed the furnishings of the room. A small mirror hung on the wall near the locker. A sticky-sweet Magdalene face graced the other wall, and an ornate crucifix with two lengths of last year's palm leaves behind it hung on the far wall. The holy water font at the door was a gaudy blue Lady of Lourdes design, dirty and chipped. The one window at the far side of the room had a musty green blind on it, no curtains. Its view, small as it was, was into the center courtyard of the buff stone building. A few trees grew in the courtyard around an asphalt center.

"Well," Conny said. "Fine, fine. I'll make out all right. I can unpack now?"

"Sure, sure. You have three hours until supper. Frankie said he'd be back in half an hour to take care of you. I have an appointment, so I'll have to be leaving you. Anything I can do before I go?"

He stood looking at the sandy-haired Chicagoan, who looked for all the world like a little boy suddenly grown big and transplanted across the sea before he knew what happened to him. Conny had baby features, smooth skin, reddish-blond hair—the innocent, well-bathed "American look," as Richard was beginning to call it after three years in Rome. The English and the German sometimes shared it: the boyishness, the Nordic cleanness. But the Englishmen wore the most baggy cassocks and tattered hats, and the Germans wore bright-red cassocks and big shoes or, if from other colleges than the German college proper, at least the big shoes or some other indefinable Teutonic mark. The Americans wore new cassocks, had new brief cases, wore sturdy Oxfords, or were otherwise distinguishable from their poorer cousins.

"Not a thing, Ricky. Run along. I can take care of myself."

"It's good to see you, Conny. Best wishes for a good year."

"Sure, sure. Thanks. Yeah, thanks. It's good to be here."

Richard started to close the door behind him, then went back. "Uh . . . the head's three doors down. On the left. It doesn't look like much. No Chicago plumbing and all that sort of thing."

"Yeah, yeah, thanks," Conny flushed. He was already opening one of his shiny suitcases, but closed it quickly as Richard re-entered.

6

RICHARD CAUGHT the ninety-eight bus at Largo Tassoni. He entered at the rear, fumbled in his pockets for twenty lire, and laid them on the tray for the collector. The man listlessly thumbed off a thin green ticket to hand to him.

"Thanks," said Richard. "I save them."

"*Che cosa?*"

"I do. I save them. I have a whole trunkful of them."

"Nooo," said the black-haired collector, beginning to smile.

"I do. I send them to my grandmother in America. She collects bus tickets."

The fellow threw back his head and laughed. "*Si*, padre, *si!* I believe it."

Richard smiled as he moved to the back of the bus. The bus swerved through a narrow alley, rushed uphill to Lungotevere, and stopped. The ticket dispenser still looked at Richard wonderingly and affectionately, but new passengers crowded aboard.

"*Avanti, per favore! Avanti!*"

"*Permesso! Permesso!*"

There were old women with web shopping bags, younger ones with babies, young fellows, workers. Richard mused about their pasts and their secrets.

At the top of the long hill Richard pulled the buzzer. He descended from the back of the bus into the heat of the sun. He pulled his cassock about him to keep it free of the bus, clutched his *romano*, and straightened his leather belt. A small ravine stood at his

feet, green and luxuriant; rows of vines grew on part of it. Large buff
and cream and green apartments stood beyond the ravine and on the
hill. Down below, from where the bus had come, gleamed St. Peter's
dome above the other buildings. The sky hung a misty gray and blue
above it. Far off, unseen, were the purple Apennines. Richard drew a
deep breath, now that the fumes of the bus had had a chance to clear
away, and began across the grand artery that poured traffic into
Rome. He dodged Fiats and Vespas and Volkswagens and American
Chevrolets and three-wheeled Italian trucks, and they dodged him,
swerving as Italian traffic does to accommodate the situation. He
stamped his shoes to clear them of dust and headed for the tiny Via
del Torre Rosso that bore off to the left between two private walls. A
heavy grille protected a Madonna in the corner of the far wall.

He walked down the narrow *via*, A Vespa roared by him. A
truck drove a burst of hot air and traces of grit into his face. He
removed his *romano* and carried it in his hand. When he came to
the entrance of the yellow brick buildings of San Girolamo's, he
wiped his hand across his brow and stopped a moment. Work on
the new edition of the Bible had been going on here at the Benedictine monastery for many years now—slow work and thorough
work. And here Padre Benedetto lived. That made it, for Richard,
one of the most memorable spots of Rome.

A black-clad, smiling Benedictine came, finally, to Richard's
ringing of the bell. "*Buon giorno,* padre. Ah! Padre Riccardo! *Avanti!
Avanti! S'accomodi!*"

"Good morning, padre," Richard smiled back. "Padre Benedetto
is expecting me."

"You don't have to tell me! *Venga, venga.* You know the way."
Padre Francesco, tall, thin, balding, a Frenchman whose Italian was
thin and gallicized, bowed politely to Richard and turned off down
the corridor.

Richard thought how kind was the spirit of San Girolamo, how
happy and ordinary were the men of the household. In institutions
a gruffness can sometimes reign, or a mere cold politeness. Someone
hard to get along with can start a chain reaction of frayed nerves

and quickened tempers; the love of God can grow cool and only ordinary; the grips of melancholy and acedia can climb upwards in hearts like dank water and stifle mirth and joy. Here, at San Girolamo, it was a pleasure to walk in the warmth of charity, joy, peace, patience, fear of the Lord. God lived here. Men were ordinary, full of ordinary faults, but they loved.

"Padre Benedetto!" he called as he stood in the open door. "It's I, Riccardo!"

The wizened old man looked up from his desk, where he was tilting a New Testament awkwardly to catch the window's sun. His glasses were askew.

"Padre Riccardo!" The voice was full of joy. *"Avanti! Avanti! Figliuolo mio!"* He held up to Richard the little black-bound volume. "Come, come. See here: do you know the meaning of this verse?"

"It's in English, padre!" Richard said as he got near enough to see it.

"I always practice my English before you come. But the verse, Riccardo, the verse. Do you know it?"

" 'I will show you a yet more excellent way.' Yes, padre, I know it."

"What does it mean? Tell an ass like me what it might mean."

"Padre," said Richard, looking at him awry. "That's not a nice word in English."

"I lived with Benedictines, son, in England. My prior called me that three or four times. And I believe I used it of him once or twice myself." His eyes flashed a moment.

Richard laughed. "Padre Benedetto!" The old priest laughed with him.

"A *yet more excellent way*" began the priest again. "What is it?"

Richard shrugged: "Love."

"Be careful what you're saying."

Richard said: "Now I'm afraid to say."

"But what good are you if you don't know the love of God? Think. Think." The priest waited silently.

"He loved us before we ever were," Richard said, looking into the dark eyes.

"*Si,*" thought the old priest aloud. "*Si* . . . He first loved us. Before we were anything. He put us in the movement of time. And what does that mean?"

"That we don't have to prove ourselves to Him. That His love for us is not based on what we are but from when we were nothing."

"Some day those words will mean much more to you." The priest watched the youth shrewdly but with affection. "Remember them. That God is love. That He cannot do anything but love." The priest's voice was low. He set down his glasses. "God's love is constant. He cannot do anything but love. Love is His one necessity. He is love. You have no idea how that changes everything." The priest looked away for a long while. Richard enjoyed the silence of the white plastered room. A crucifix alone broke the whiteness of the wall. Low bookcases were filled with new books and old, even English pocketbooks.

"Padre?" Richard asked.

The priest turned to him.

"Why is it you make everything sound so simple? So many priests—" he bit his lip.

"Yes?"

"I don't want to sound rash."

"But you do that so well! At your age I knew everything. Why shouldn't you? You don't want to sound rash!"

Richard colored and laughed.

"You were saying about priests . . ."

"And religious! They get me all mixed up. Moral virtues, theological virtues, cardinal virtues, means, ends, vows, spirit, *prudence*—everything complicated and analyzed and put in impossible systems! It's like a net that won't let you move. It gives me a headache, padre. It sucks all the life and good will out of me. You are almost the only one who makes sense. I get furious when I listen to the others. I lose my temper. I sound like a heretic when I argue, and all I want to do is get to the truth."

"What do I say that is so different?"

"You talk of love instead of law and discipline. You make God seem so close. You make holiness seem so familiar."

"Is that so revolutionary?"

"No, but it makes you easy to talk to. You aren't interested in forcing things upon me; you want to—draw me out. I feel I don't have to say the right words, go along with a system. With you . . ." Richard shrugged. "It's—like talking to God. He knows what I want to say before I say it. He knows all my excuses before I can come to them. He trusts me."

The priest's eyes looked at him shrewdly. Richard rubbed his hands together in his lap. After a while Richard looked up and met his gaze. "I guess what I'm saying is that I'm in trouble again. The provincial is worried about my attitude." Richard said it with an edge of sarcasm. "Padre Bracciano has been writing him."

"Did the provincial himself tell you this?"

"Father Milton did. He just got back from the States."

"And?"

"He's sort of warned me. Decide now to obey. Padre, how can I be myself? If I say what I think, back it goes to the provincial. This year I have to keep my mouth shut, really shut! I hope I can do it."

Padre Benedetto sat back and looked at Richard from a distance. "You'll never do it. Not a chance!"

"Padre, I'm not joking. I *have* to."

"Riccardo, Riccardo. All this is silly. Religious life is not meant to be like this. You are a man. You must think. You must say what you think. You must go to God in your own way. And you must speak up. But you must know what you are doing. Why, why, why. You must be very clear on that."

Padre Benedetto got up and shuffled stiffly to the window. He looked out on the garden below and up at the blue sky above. Just then the droning roar of three jet planes split the air almost immediately overhead. Three silver jets, wing to wing, raced low against the blue and on over the city. They passed, but the roar lingered in the room. "How they love speed," said the priest. "The Vespa wasn't fast enough, so your government had to sell them jets."

"Padre . . ."

The priest turned away from the light to look at the young man. He shuffled over to him. "Come, Riccardo." He put his arm around him. "I will pray for you. It will be a hard year. We will walk every step of the way as the Lord directs. Do you understand me, Riccardo?"

"Yes, but you don't offer much help."

"What am I trying to say?"

"I—I don't know."

"Listen, then. Many times a young cleric almost quits just before the end. Everything seems to be going wrong. Don't take all these things so seriously. Who do you think you are? As for the provincial, well, we have all got to suffer, haven't we? It may get a lot worse." The priest looked into his eyes.

A new confidence entered Richard's mind with that look. From what his director was saying, he might just be undergoing a trial in the Lord's hands. His vocation might not be threatened at all. He felt a deep, comforting relief. He sat and talked with the priest for a long time. When he rose to leave, the priest motioned him to kneel and blessed him.

"Padre, I will try to learn."

"Whether you will or no, the Lord will teach you. But the Lord is cruel—I want you to know that. It will be with love, but He will take everything you have. You should know that. He will take everything."

Richard closed the door slowly. A premonition of his own inadequacy and immaturity began to slip its cold fingers around his heart. What if he were depending not on God, but on Padre Benedetto?

The blue October sky did not hold his gaze as he rode back to Lungotevere. Nothing did. His heart was relieved, yet preoccupied and troubled.

7

AFTER LUNCH on Saturday, Richard went to chapel with the others, reciting in the corridor the *Laudate Dominum*. Afterwards, each stayed a moment or two to pray. The superior and priests rose to leave, then the seminarians. At Padre Bracciano's office door, Richard pulled from his breast pocket a list of new library purchases. He promised himself to be meek and obedient. The door opened and Padre Eugenio came out. Without time to think, Richard was knocking on the open door and entering.

Padre Bracciano was turned toward the door, resting heavily upon the arms of his swivel chair. "Padre Riccardo?"

"*Buon giorno,* padre. I have another list of books for the library. May we have permission to order them? I checked them with Padre Carlo."

Padre Bracciano took the list and swung slowly to his desk. He set the list down and studied it. He set his chin in his hand and turned his head slowly from side to side against the palm. He totaled up the cost. "All right," he shrugged. "We are spending sixty thousand lire every year on books."

"A good library means a lot."

Padre Bracciano rubbed the bridge of his nose, lifting his rimless glasses. "These Americans! Money is nothing to them. Here is your other list," he said, reaching into the drawer.

"I'd like to continue stocking books. Padre Carlo approves."

"Provided we don't start reading everything but theology. Your obedience is to study theology. I cannot insist on that enough."

With that Padre Bracciano came back down on his chair and set his hands on his knees.

"We won't be wasting time. I only buy books that I think theology touches. . . ."

"Well, talk it over with Padre Carlo. Show me the list before you order them." He made a note on his pad. "We'll have to reach some policy."

"Thank you, padre." Richard creased the library list.

As he climbed the stairway to his room, Richard took two steps at a time. He opened his door and entered the room in one motion, without breaking his stride. Then he stopped, happy and breathless. He sat down heavily at his desk; a stack of papers waited there for sorting; a row of theology books stirred in him a strange repugnance. Perhaps it was only the normal reaction to the end of vacation: everybody felt it. He drew himself erect and began opening his cassock. A knock came at the door and Conny entered without waiting for an answer. He carried a basketball under one arm. He wore a tight-fitting yellow T-shirt and blue slacks.

"Want to play basketball, kiddo? Game of horse?" He was only one step in the room, with his head around the door.

Richard suppressed the desire to tell him to wait for an answer next time. "Not today, Conny." A surge of triumph at his self-control battled with the desire to tell him anyway.

"Just till four, Ricky."

"*Just* till four?"

"Sure, come on, Ricky." Conny stood erect and entered for good. "Say, I've been meaning to ask you. What's the rule on going into town? Can we leave the house any time?"

"You can go into town, O.K., but you need permission. And you have to go two together."

"Really trust us, don't they?"

"You can get into a lot of trouble going out alone, unless you have permission. But it's easy to find somebody. Just ask."

Conny pondered his plans awhile. Then he brightened and asked again: "Sure I can't talk you into coming out for a while,

Ricky? Just for an hour? I'm still stiff from the boat ride. Want to limber up my legs."

"It's too hot, Conny. And I have all this to do. Retreat tonight, opening mass on Tuesday, school on Wednesday . . ."

"Come on out now, while there's time!"

"Sorry, I better not. How's the old hook shot?"

Conny made a hooking motion with his arm. "Sharp as ever." He winked an eye and clicked his gums. "I've been perfectin' it. Had eighteen points a game last year. And we *won* the championship."

Ricky blushed. In his last year in the seminary he had had a chance to win the championship for his team with two foul shots after the final whistle. The score was 72–71. He had missed both of them; the last one had fallen short, not even touching the rim.

"I'll get you out there this year and make you run!" Conny warned. He ducked his head out the door. "Sorry you can't make it. Frankie's waiting for me. Be seeing you!" His new gym shoes squeaked in the corridor.

Richard shook his head, smiling. The immaturity that can perdure within a seminary! Conny and his sports; Conny and his smart remarks. It was always a problem for him to understand it and to cope with it. He turned and opened up his window. The leaves of the trees over Lungotevere were hard and turning dark. Traffic rumbled by. The air was warm. He began slipping out of his cassock, draping his leather belt over the chair. He hung the cassock in his narrow metal locker. He wiped his hand tiredly across his forehead and stretched; the straining on his limbs was delicious. He pulled out two wooden frames from behind his desk and reached again into his locker for a roll of canvas. He bent over his bed, unrolling the canvas across the top frame. As he worked, a knock came at the door again.

"Avanti!" he called. He was bent over the bed in white T-shirt and black trousers.

"Will you serve Benediction tonight?"

Richard clicked his fingers. "Is it my turn already?" He stood erect and faced Paolo.

"Rudolph asked me to skip him."

Richard nodded absently. "I hate to see retreat begin! I feel like some *excitement*, a carnival or something. I'm in an awful mood!"

"I know just how you feel. It's always hard after a vacation."

"Vacations usually bring me back refreshed. Well, O.K., Paolo, I'll be there. Eight-thirty."

Paolo nodded. "*Grazie,* Riccardo." He waved and left.

Richard bent over his canvas again. He began to whistle a tune from *South Pacific* very softly. They had used the tune in a seminary play at the college in Illinois after a summer in camp. He had helped write the play; Conny had been in it; sure, he was just a freshman then. The four of them, with Indians painted on their T-shirts and lipstick, rouge, and grease heavy on their faces, had danced across the stage and sung:

> *Camp Quicksand is as Indian as an arrow.*
> *Camp Quicksand has a layout to applaud.*
> *She is narrow where a jetty should he narrow*
> *And she is broad-where a hall field-should he bro-o-ad!*
>
> *Two hundred and one yards of shore,*
> *Twenty-seven acres more.*
> *Plunge your kids in Quicksand if you're sore!*
>
> *The sky's so blue up above.*
> *Everywhere fraternal love.*
> *Your kids'll fit in Quicksand like a glove.*

Richard chuckled to himself. They would have to organize a play in Rome, too. He pushed a tack into the side of the frame; it started to bend; he set it right and pushed more firmly with his thumb. Perhaps at Christmas. Or for the feast of the Annunciation, maybe. That gave them until March. But how would they get around the language barrier? Italian, maybe? Well, something to think about.

He wondered suddenly if he would still be in the seminary by March. The thought startled him because he thought he had put the matter to rest. He dismissed it as a temptation against persever-ance and a trouble to his peace. He turned his mind to other things and began whistling again. He had one frame finished.

PART II
Early Winter

8

IT WAS A GRAY November day, overcast but luminous. The
breeze was knife-cold. Richard and Paolo chose the Forum for their
weekly walk. Their spirits were subdued because of the news of the
night before. Richard had entered the recreation room; there had
been silence as the group leaned over the radio. The dull-green
walls echoed with the announcer's voice and occasionally with
static. Old dark canvases hung silent and unobserved upon the
walls. Faces around the radio were as stunned and serious as the
collegio had ever seen.

"What's the report now?" he had asked.

"Shhh!" came three or four voices.

"Aspetti," Luigi Alessandro had beckoned quietly. "Radio Budapest is silent now. The Russians returned with tanks during the night."

Johann had begun to cry and left the room. Herbert had said in
anger that the Americans were cowards, that the Russians meant
their revolution; the Americans had forgotten theirs.

"Herbert was pretty angry, wasn't he?" Richard said.

"Johann didn't sleep at all last night," Paolo nodded.

"Why was Johann so upset?"

"His brother is studying in Budapest."

Richard hadn't known that. His heart felt a new sympathy.

"I wish there were something we could do!" Richard said.
"This—cassock. I sometimes wish I didn't wear it!"

"Riccardo."

"It's true."

They shoved their student passes under the grille at the window. Richard said *buon giorno* and, hardly breaking his serious expression, smiled to the bored custodian. The man answered a dry *buon giorno* but looked after them as they walked away.

"Paolo, I don't understand our world. I'm free, you understand. I don't want money, or fame, or success. All I want to do is live as much like a man as I can. I want to throw myself against the things that hurt man."

"But you are, Riccardo."

Their footsteps fell steadily. "Am I? Is this the best I can do? Is this what I'm meant to do?"

Paolo didn't reply. He pulled Richard's arm to the right. "Come, see over here, the marks of the fire."

Richard walked slowly after him. He let go his serious thoughts. Enjoy the afternoon, he thought.

They stepped over pediments imbedded in the glass and walked towards the ancient marble floor. They pushed branches of a tree aside. Flashes of orange slept dully in the old marble, as though ready to regain the glory of old if the sun fell upon them.

"Do you really believe the fire made these marks?" He pointed to the streaks of green and little holes dug in the marble.

"Who knows? In Rome it's better not to ask too many questions. Don't believe or disbelieve. Just enjoy."

The breeze blew through the Forum, stirring the long gray grass. Beyond rose the arch of Septimius Severus, behind it an ugly baroque chapel, and then the Capitoline. The green-red-white flags of Italy snapped against the leaden sky from the Victor Emmanuel monument. Wisps of gray passed underneath the sturdy cumulus.

Richard tightened his field coat and dug his hands farther in his pockets.

They began to walk towards the Palatine. Richard nodded towards the Temple of the Vestal Virgins, a thin smile on his lips: "Our predecessors." The moist sense of dripping, collecting water rose from the underground passageways along their upward climb. He jerked his head backwards toward the white Victor Emmanuel.

"It fits Rome perfectly. Huge, overdone, commanding. The Palace of the Caesars must have been like that."

Paolo shrugged. "It will look better in ruins."

"Rome is an operatic city. Even the police direct traffic operatically." They reached the top of the hill. "Rome is like a dream: the falling water of the fountains, the smells, the crowding in the buses. It's full of form, and yet—chaotic. Rome is—Freudian." He scanned the gray, the warm buff and rust horizon. Domes, roofs, towers, tiny autos in the *corso*. The noises of the city rose, filtered by the distance. "I want to paint this view. I want to get the gray deadness, with the living warmth. I want to get the sadness, with the endurance and the life."

"You will," said Paolo. "You will. When do you miss? I only wish you had encouragement—a command from your superiors to do nothing but paint."

"I miss a lot. I miss more than I hit. I hit nothing. But you would be my favorite critic. At least you seem to know what I am driving at. Encouragement from up above? Nothing but paint? Impossible."

"You have the talent, Riccardo. It is a crime to waste talent. It is one sin for which I have no compassion." Paolo's voice was angry.

"Do I? I wish I knew. It is so hard to know. Where are my critics, my audience, my fellow laborers? I know no tricks, no techniques. I'm working in the dark. I wish I knew, Paolo."

"The dark is good for artists. It makes them find themselves and not someone else. Take a good look, Riccardo." Paolo nodded toward the city. "Paint it."

As RICHARD WALKED from the chapel two weeks later, Herbert pulled his sleeve and led him into the parlor. It was a gloomy room and smelled of old furnishings and little use. In the poor light Herbert turned to him: "Can I see you in your room?" His eyes searched Richard's eyes, then looked away, full of trouble.

"Sure," Richard said. "Right away?"

Herbert wouldn't look at him. "In a couple minutes. I have to see Padre."

"I'm going right up. I'll wait for you."

"Thanks." Herbert squeezed his arm and left.

Richard stood at the door a moment, then walked slowly to the staircase. He climbed slowly, cautioning himself to restrain his imagination. He opened the shade in his room and sat down at his desk. He pulled in front of him an outline of a thesis he had to learn. Then he pushed it back. He rose and stood by the window. After a while he came back and sat down again, stretching his long legs. He looked at his watch and sat absently, strumming on his desk.

Finally a knock came at the door.

Richard stood up. The door began to open. "Come on in. I've been waiting for you."

Herbert brushed a hand through his long hair and sat down on the bed. He rubbed his hands together. "Sit down, Ricky," he said with a dry throat. Richard pulled the chair over and Herbert looked up at him but then away. He tossed his head. "I'm leaving," he said. "Hungary was too much. I'm going home." His eyes glanced over Richard's face and then darted away. His voice was full of emotion, and he sat in the abjection of one who has bowed to the inevitable. "I have to, Riccardo! I have to! I can't stay here." He held his hands before him and looked at them. "These, Ricky, these were made to do something! They were made to fight, to work. This cassock—it restrains me. I have got to go, Riccardo!"

Richard overlooked the passionate tone. "I know that."

"Believe me, I have struggled with it. I'm not leaving just in haste. I'm not emotional about it. I'm clear on it. I've never been so clear in my life. I've thought of nothing else for two weeks, prayed over it. I haven't slept. I *must* go, Ricky."

Richard was distressed but didn't contradict him.

"I begged Padre Bracciano to let me go. He wants me to wait a month or even six weeks." Herbert fixed his hard blue eyes on Richard's for a moment. "I told him I'd leave on my own if he didn't let me. He didn't like that. Neither did I." Herbert smiled. "He was frightened. He sent in my papers, and they came back this morning."

Richard saw that it was all decided. "When will you leave?" His throat was dry.

"Tomorrow morning." Herbert tossed his long hair. "I'm nearly all packed."

Richard felt very sick at heart. But he thought it was the right decision, even if its manner troubled him. "I'm glad you came to tell me."

"I couldn't have left without telling you."

"And now you're sure, aren't you?"

Herbert's voice quavered. "I've never been so sure about anything."

"You've always wanted to enter into things." Richard looked at the wall.

"Always! I can't stand this 'prudence,' this 'restraint,' this 'decorum.' I want to labor. I want to roll up my sleeves and get to work. There is so much to do. So many changes are taking place."

"You'll do great things, Herbert."

"I'll do something! I may only be a local hack, but I'll do something." Herbert spread his legs on the bed and put his hands on the mattress. His smooth face showed nervousness and pain. "Now I'm so confused! Where will I go? What will I do? I only know that I *must* go."

"It's always like that, isn't it? Out into the dark." Richard thought of himself.

"Yes, it is very dark. Riccardo! There must be many of us who will work together, you in black, we who aren't."

Richard looked steadily at him, half nodding, half abstaining.

"We have been very close, Riccardo. Remember the talks we have had?"

"On the Adriatic . . . on trains . . . on the way to school in the mornings. A lot of talks, Herbert!"

"I'll miss the old Greg, much as I hated it. I'll miss it."

"You're always like that. You chastise the things you love."

"Riccardo, how is it you understand me so well? How is it the two of us became so close?" He thought a moment. "And then . . . I don't understand myself. I don't know where I am or what I want."

"You are emotional, Herbert. You have imagination and energy. You go where you feel you should. Those are the things I . . . like about you. I think the Lord is taking care of you."

"He better be."

"He is."

The bed creaked as Herbert shifted weight. They sat awhile.

"I wonder," Richard said absently, "what will become of *me?*"

"You will become a priest, Riccardo. You will become a splendid priest."

"I wish it were so clear." Richard's tone was wry.

"You are kind. You are steady. I always wanted to model myself on you."

"Steady? If you only knew!" Richard played with the fingers of his left hand. "If you only knew."

"Riccardo, we'll continue to be friends, won't we? We'll write? I will need your support for a while. I have nobody. My mother will be disappointed. I have no work. It will be a long climb until I get where I wish to be."

"You'll make it. You will start as a local party man and you'll be premier of Germany."

Herbert laughed. "I will try to be."

"You'll make it. You have the courage. You have the ideas of a leader."

"We'll see," Herbert smiled.

They stood.

"I almost wish that I were going with you."

"You must stay here. There is more to do here."

"But if I am not meant to be here?"

"Not. . ." A look of trouble came into Herbert's blue eyes.

Richard nodded.

"You must become a priest."

"Why, if it is not right?"

"Because . . . because I am sure that it is right. What could be more clear? You, Riccardo." He looked at Richard searchingly.

"Nothing definite. I have taken no steps."

"Don't! For my sake, Riccardo . . . be ordained."

"For your sake?"

Herbert colored. "You are meant to be."

Richard smiled. "Time will tell, won't it? Is there anything I can do for you? Packing, messages?"

"I am almost finished. Only the good-byes. I cannot face them all."

"They'll understand."

"In my place in chapel, there are two library books. You can return those."

"Anything else?"

"Nothing. Pray for me."

"Will I see you in the morning or tonight?"

"I'm leaving during mass. Tonight I'm going to the station with my trunk. I'd like to make this . . . good-bye. It is hard enough, once."

"Then this is the temporary end, to part one at least."

"To part one."

Herbert held out his hand. Richard grasped it and pressed it. Both tested their strength and their affection. Herbert's eyes were restless and full of emotion. Richard looked into them steadily. Herbert's eyes were a bright blue, thin and light.

"Well, good-bye."

"Good-bye, Riccardo."

"Good luck. Many blessings."

"Many blessings to you, Riccardo."

Herbert broke the grip and went to the door. His step was precise and German. He turned again, as though to store up Richard's image.

"Ciao, amico."

"Ciao, amico."

He closed the door.

The room was very silent. Footsteps faded from the hallway. The click of the latch rang on and on in Richard's mind. He walked slowly to the window. He looked up to see the pale sky and the thin clouds. His hand lay upon the frame. His fingers curled a little, until his nails rested on the wood. His inner world came tumbling down again. Leaves blew against the sky. He was tall in the window. But he felt like an ant who labors again and again to build himself a hill, which is then crushed by a passerby.

He had none of the spirit of the monks of old. None of their calm, none of their prayer, none of their penance. Then what was he doing here? Wasting days like the present one? When he should be out underneath the sky? Monks strove for a victory over self, for independence and yet brotherly love; they asked nothing for themselves, no human comfort; they gave everything to God. Friendships, dreams, ambitions, yearnings. On the contrary, his dismal life was a wallowing in his own emotions. He wanted what he wanted. He wanted his will, his way, his reward. He wanted friends; he wanted companionship; he didn't want to be alone, not alone against the blue sky. He wanted affection.

He turned from the window. He felt a sudden fear of losing everything. No matter which way he turned, he was inadequate. He shouldn't want affection. He should control his emotions. Suddenly Conny's head poking in the door flashed before his eyes. He seemed suddenly to hate Conny. No, that wasn't true! But he felt a strong rush of hatred. He thought back over Conny's coming in. Yes, it had been annoying. Shallow, careless, easygoing Conny—he didn't *dislike* him. A fugitive thought glimmered on the edge of his mind. Richard tried to find it. He had seen something rising in that thought. The thought refused to come. Richard's heart was beating now. What was going on inside him?

How can a drip like Conny want to be a priest? He wished to disown the thought; it frightened him and sickened him. How could he think it, when his own heart was in confusion? The vision of his secret thoughts was too repugnant.

He turned back to the window and ran his nails on the glass. Herbert? I'll be looking for you, Herbert. Prime minister of Germany! I'll be looking for your name.

Herbert was his problem now. If he could get Herbert from his mind, he could be happy. He wanted to turn from the window, but he couldn't move, and so he continued to stand in it. What would become of him? He squinted up at the sky. In his mind's eye he saw himself squinting up, brown-haired, tall, in an adolescent pose. How did you flee away from self-awareness? How did you grow up and live as normal people live? Conny had it so easy! Conny desired nothing but his sports news, his recreations, and his duties. Richard's hands, fingers, heart yearned for so much more! He wanted to tell himself that that was the reason for his troubles. But he felt a fallacy in that. He had such huge ambitions! That's where his sudden, abrupt movements sprang. He was being held in, and then for a moment his inhibitions would be relaxed, and there would spring into his conduct a silly swipe of the hand, an operatic gesture, a burst of speed on the stairs. He was holding himself down, buckling himself in. Why? And what if some day he should explode?

Do I really want to be a priest? There was that specter again. Herbert had driven his specter away; Herbert had answered his specter: no. Isn't that what he should do? His fingers played slowly on the glass, up and down. Isn't that what he should do? Up and down. Wasn't he like Herbert? Active, aggressive, energetic? Maybe he was only cowardly, unable to face a decision. What would someone else do in my place? he asked. He didn't know. He felt very much alone, with no sense of perspective any longer. Where was the truth? Sometimes his emotions responded: you do want to be a priest. Sometimes they said he didn't. Sometimes he feared the future as a priest; sometimes he looked forward to it. There was no use making a decision on the basis of emotion. He would regret it endlessly. His intelligence then? Mentally he tried to line up reasons for and against the priesthood logically, geometrically. But his head began to ache. He knew few of the consequences of either choice. How could he know what would seem right in the future? Was he really meant to be an artist? Or in art would his life be simply thrown away, his efforts third-rate or worse? Maybe his entire doubting was only due to immaturity and crazy confusion. But he suspected that no one else could help him. And his intelligence was overwhelmed. His mind was a tiny light reaching out into the darkness. The darkness was immense. His life was out in it, tiny and insignificant, yet longing for love and for vitality, alive like an exposed nerve to every painful touch of the night. Night, night. That is what he felt beating on his head. He could not control his destiny. He was a prey of forces. Even as he was free, making a decision in which all the risks were his, in which not even intelligence compelled him to take one course, even so, he was in the night, where consequences of action are not seen, where motives are unknown.

Herbert, Herbert, how lucky to have chosen! Conny, how lucky to live unthinkingly! He would have added: Richard, how wrong to take your life so seriously. But he saw in a discouraging flash that all his reflections were but an excess of self-pity. It became impossible for him to find a beachhead of truth within himself. Delusion and double-motive seemed to wash over every part of him.

He said a prayer for light, looking out of the window. The leaves were hard and old, brushing against the sky. He hoped *God* could figure him out. He hoped *God* knew. Then he thought that that was unfair, too—to hide behind God. He turned from the window and sat heavily on the bed to untie his shoes. He would take the nap that Conny had suggested. He kicked his shoes under the foot of the bed. God, he thought, easing himself down; God, what is the right thing for me to do?

He couldn't sleep. The pillow felt cool, but then hot. He got up, dressed again, and went to find Paolo. He warned himself not to count on other men for comfort, but on the Lord. But underneath the warning he was set on human consolation. He moved swiftly and with activity. He hurried down to Paolo's room, finding things he had been meaning to ask him about.

9

IT WAS DECEMBER. Richard had been sick a few days after Herbert left; he ran a high fever. Umberto Carrozza, the infirmarian, thought it was a virus. But today Richard sat in the classroom of the University, the days of sickness long since forgotten. Outside, the day was beautiful and fresh; he would not have worn a coat to school today, except for the Roman rule that clerics always wear one overtop their cassocks. It was like April in the States. Inside the University, the classroom was gray and dark. The lights above were barely yellowish. The big windows all along the rear wall caught only dull reflections from the narrow courtyard. Hundreds of seats rose in semicircular rows from the teacher's rostrum. A baroque IHS was carved in a wooden sun above the high-backed chair in which the Jesuit professor sat. The lecturer was an American; his Latin accent was abominable, his vowels flat and Midwestern, as the microphone only emphasized. Richard nudged Frankie, who happened to be underlining something in a textbook.

Below them—they were sitting in nearly the top row—seminarians listened, dreamt, or read surreptitiously the European edition of *Time*, the Rome *Daily American*, or Italian, German, French, or Spanish equivalents. They took notes, twiddled pencils, whispered together. Four or five hundred young men, from all quarters of the globe: black faces, yellow faces, white faces of olive or of Anglo-Saxon fairness, coming to the centuries-old institution founded by and beloved of the Jesuits on the Via della Pilotta. There were the national cassocks of all countries and the religious cassocks of many centuries: the red of the Germans; the brown wool of the Franciscans and Capuchins; the flowing black of the Augustinians; the striking white cincture of the black Franciscans; the red, white, and blue of the Trinitarians; the black of the modern congregations. There were the shaven heads of the young monks of the older orders—a Chinese, American, and French Trappist sitting together. The many cassocks covered the young bodies of fatigued, long-suffering students, not quite so interested in books as in expressing restlessness and boredom, divided in opinion as to the best of their lecturers, undivided as students everywhere in assessing the dryness of sitting hours on end in droning classrooms.

"Did you get that?" Richard was asking Frankie.

"Missed it," said Frankie, looking up with a finger still on his text.

"Pretty good. I missed the first part. Listen."

They pushed down the aisle after the first class—and were pushed. They greeted friends from other colleges. Even before they got to the door, Richard asked Frankie again if he'd got it.

"He made a neat distinction between philosophic thinking and logical thinking. The Scholastics are mostly logicians. He didn't say that; I am. He said the philosophic mind has understanding. The logical mind merely manipulates, countering objections with counterarguments—you know the way they do."

"What's that philosophic mind again?" Frankie was interested but tired; just interested enough to keep Richard's ardor alive. Richard began to feel a little silly.

"It's not so interested in proving or manipulating; it's interested in seeing."

"I may be dumb this morning, Ricky; I don't see much difference."

They were walking on the second floor of the University, on the balcony around the inner court. Richard fingered in his pocket a five-hundred-lire note with which he was supposed to buy some post cards for his aunt. Above them the skylight was open and the December sky shone glassy-blue and cold. Below, the marble court was filled with peripatetic talk, laughter, gesticulating—men learning languages from one another or simply exchanging news. Knots of students surrounded professors who were trying to make their way gradually to elevators at the end of the hall.

"The logical mind is trying only to *prove*. He's not looking for anything new or even to see what the old definitions really mean. He's trying to defend a system. He quotes, he invents new distinctions, he gets very sharp and subtle. He's impossible to talk to because everything has to be in his terms for his system. It's what makes him seem so narrow."

"Ricky, you ought to write a book."

"Do you see the point, though, Frank? I was so glad to hear him make it."

"In a class in theology? Isn't that philosophy?" Frank scanned the crowd.

"It's *important*. Like he said. If you get an adequate idea of God, false dilemmas disappear. The whole key to his course is trying to understand what God is like, how God acts, how He knows, how He loves. Then all the logical business falls into place. You need the insight first."

"Well, Ricky, that may be. But the big thing is to get these notes." He tapped the large sheaf of mimeographed notes he was carrying. "It's all here. I have to save the speculation until later. I'm not very good at it."

"But it isn't speculation! That's the whole point!"

"There goes Sandy!" broke in Frankie, reaching out past Richard. "Sandy!"

"Oh, hi! How're you? How're you, Ricky? I hear you fellows beat the Augies."

"No, they beat us," Frank laughed. "You're rubbing it in. We only have five fellows in the whole house who know the game."

Sandy's eyebrows were very orange; his eyes were pale blue. "You give us a pretty good game."

"When you use your third team," Richard smiled,.

"Can we get a game with you soon?" Frankie was Annunciation's captain.

"Be hard before Christmas. Play practice, football play-offs, a lot of the guys getting ready for the kids' Christmas party in Trastevere. Seems everybody is busy from now until Christmas."

"Well, after Christmas?"

"Sure thing. I'll talk to you later about it, though. I have to see somebody about mimeographing Lampada's notes. He's pestering me about it. See you later? Take it easy now. See you, Ricky." The second buzzer sounded. Sandy flashed a busy, affable smile—an American masterpiece—and hurried through the press of students, his orange head towering several inches above the others. He pulled the long, flowing ribbon of his traditional North American coat to keep it from getting tangled in the mob.

"We better get our seats. Keep thinking of it, Ricky. Sounds good." Thanks, Richard thought to himself. But he knew he had something nearly in his grasp.

AFTER THE FOURTH class, the mass of students hurried down the broad marble stairs, out the great studded metal doors. Richard blinked as he met the sunlight. His brown hair shone for a moment, almost red, before he put on his *romano*. The hat shadowed his slim face. He turned round in the crowd of jabbering, hurrying seminarians, looking for a companion, but saw none.

Traffic lined the narrow *via*. A tourist bus honked and honked; German tourists pointed and smiled from its windows. A tiny Fiat led a wedge against the bus but couldn't pass because of a parked Renault. A motorcyclist pushed his way through the jam, hurling an insult at the bus driver as he slid underneath the window. A Vespa tried the same but couldn't make it. More insults. The noon heat filled up the *via*. A *carrozza* with an impatient horse and cursing driver now blocked the way behind the Fiat. The gray and olive buses of the North American College sealed one end of the passage irretrievably. Horns blew. Tempers soared into satellitic orbit. Hands waved *scemo!* and *stupido!* while their mates pressed on horns. Two light-green uniforms were finally pushing down the *via* from the wide Via Nazionale, where traffic was also beginning to be snarled from the overflow. Seminarians streamed by, filling in all the empty spaces between the vehicles, in a sea of cassocks, black and brown and white.

"Parasites!" shouted the driver of the Fiat, totally engulfed.

"Fools! Pumpkin heads! Stupids! Idiots!" The words sailed serenely in the sunlight over their unconcerned youthful heads.

Richard smiled. Every day was the same, and no one had yet thought of making the *via* one-way for the half hour that school let out. The two *carabinieri* stood idle on the corner until matters reached the state of homicide; though probably no one in the crowd could have faced the sight of blood on such a lovely day.

Richard enjoyed walking slowly past the store windows, and posters on the walls, and movie ads. He enjoyed the people in the streets, the continental suits, the briefcases, the mustaches. The way the women dressed, impeccably, in fashion smart as possible—in dresses doughty, tight, showy. The women of Rome, he thought. He did not like them and thought of a remark he had heard: the wise young man goes to the little towns of the *paese* for a wife and picks a fresh and unsophisticated flower . . . or to the north for a cultured gentlewoman . . . but not to Rome. He laughed at himself for thinking it. Out of the running, *Deo gratias!*

He loved Rome, the sky, the thick grass-green leaves of the perennial trees within the park overhead. He waited on the corner of the neighboring university, a couple of blocks from his own, for his college bus and for his fellow religious from both universities.

After watching him a while, a begger stepped towards him from the wall. "Padre."

Richard turned.

"Padre." The man thrust a soiled note into his hands.

Richard smiled hesitantly. In the end he would be able to give him nothing.

"Read, padre. Read." The man was very modest and afraid.

Richard opened the soft paper carefully.

"Francesco Bottini, bearer of this note, is one of my parishioners. Help him if you can, for the love of God and the Madonna. His wife and child were taken from him three weeks ago."

Don Tommaso Cristino, parish priest
Milardo, Apulia Prov.
The 7 October, 1956

"I am poor. I have great hunger, padre."

Richard looked into the young man's troubled eyes. He fingered the five-hundred-lire note. It wasn't his. "You have come all the way from Apulia?"

"To work, padre. There's nothing in Apulia."

"I'm sorry to hear about your wife and baby."

Francesco winced. The sun was on his face.

"Where are you sleeping?"

The man's eyes avoided Richard's. "Places." Francesco tried to look him straight in the eye.

Richard smiled. "Under trees? Along the Tiber? In the Forum?"

Francesco smiled. "*Si,* padre."

Richard took a deep breath. "Francesco, I'm very sorry. I want to help you. My vow . . ."

"*Si,* padre, I understand," the man said, embarrassed by the gathering seminarians. "I'm sorry. I understand." His eyes shifted to the note.

Richard's heart tightened. How will I explain? He silenced his fears by acting quickly. "Francesco, I was given some money for some business. I'm not supposed to, but I will. It's not much." He pulled the bill from his pocket. "Here."

Francesco reached out very slowly. He had the eyes of an eight-year-old. They were filled with tears.

"Many good things," Francesco wished him, nodding his head. "Many good things, padre."

RICHARD FOUGHT against the fumes of the bus. He crowded himself into one of the narrow seats, his knees against the picture on the seat in front of him. Luigi and Cesare and one or two other ones looked at him as they passed. He paid no attention. He looked out the thick window.

Francesco stood near the wall again, out of the way. He looked for Richard. His face brightened. He had the money and the soiled paper in his hand.

Richard turned back to the books on his knees. His heart went very cold at the difficulty there would be in explaining.

10

RICHARD WAS AFRAID he might be too late. Padre Bracciano would be taking his siesta. But the door opened and Conny came out just as Richard got there. Conny winked, but Richard hurried in the door without responding.

"*Buon giorno,* padre," he said as he advanced across the floor.

"*Buon giorno,* Riccardo." The superior sat with his elbows on the arms of his swivel chair and had just been getting up. He sat back down to listen.

Richard stood before the short, stocky man and gathered his thoughts. "First, padre, may I have permission to visit my director?"

"Oh, a list, eh?" Padre Bracciano chuckled. "*Si,* Riccardo."

"And, second," Richard nodded, "it's not so easy. I . . . the five hundred lire I had for my aunt's cards . . . I gave it to a beggar. He needed it. He was very poor. He—"

"I see." Padre Bracciano covered his mouth with his thick, clean hand. "Five hundred lire." Richard waited. "The money was given you for another purpose. It wasn't yours to spend."

"*Si,* padre."

"And you know the vow of poverty does not allow you to spend such money?"

"*Si,* padre."

The priest removed his hand and continued looking steadily at Richard. "You realize this house gives five hundred dollars every Christmas to the St. Vincent de Paul Society, where it can do some good? Many people say that I am foolish; but, give generously and the Lord returns."

"*Si,* padre.

"Riccardo . . ." the priest paused, "Most of the beggars in the streets are racketeers. The beggars are shameless, full of guile, intimidating. You know that even the government is calling it a national disgrace?"

"*Si,* padre."

"And you know that we are living on charity ourselves? That we have no income here? That good people all around the world are keeping us in food and clothes?"

"*Si,* padre."

"Of course, when I was a young student in Rome, the beggars used to hand us little notes from some parish priest. 'Please give, for the love of God and *La Madonna.*' Girls hired little babies to carry in their arms, after streaking them with dirt and grease. Ah, Riccardo, I used to feel sorry for all this. You are young. You have a soft heart. You are not—shall we say—prudent. *Va bene,* you will learn. . . . I'll give you the money when you need it again. I have the drawer locked."

"I need forty lire for the bus, padre."

"I have that here." The superior handed him four light coins from his blotter. "Ask your director about the violation of poverty. I know you did it with the best intentions. But we must learn prudence, Riccardo. What will the beggars think if they find we have five hundred lire to give away every day?"

"*Si,* padre. I'm sorry. *Grazie,*"

Richard had gone to his room and napped a little. An hour later, in the brisk, graying afternoon, he went to see Padre Benedetto. He found the old man in his white cell, red-faced and coughing.

"'Tis nothing, nothing at all!" the Benedictine said, wiping his mouth and nose with the slow, deliberate movements of an old man. He was caught by a sneeze again. As he rubbed his nose and folded his handkerchief, his eyes flashed. "Just a common cold."

"Better be careful, padre!" Richard expostulated, but then held himself back. He was afraid today of feeling as boylike with Padre

Benedetto as he usually had. In times past, he had felt surrounded by a warmth and superiority that melted all resistance. Even then he had felt tempted to be careful not to reveal too much of himself, so that Padre Benedetto would always like him. He had recognized it for that and had tried to take advantage of Padre Benedetto's goodness and to be as limpidly honest as he could. He was not sure, now, he had been really honest. He was uneasy. He controlled his feelings and his words. "You're getting old, padre. The winters are tricky here. You must be careful."

A strange ambiguity flashed in Padre Benedetto's brown eyes. He seemed merry and jocund, serious and reflective. "In the Lord's good time, Riccardo, in the Lord's good time!" he laughed. He slipped his handkerchief into his tight sleeve, under the outer one. "How about you, Riccardo? Are you over your sickness?"

"I was playing basketball three days afterwards!"

"I mean prudently, *ragazzaccio*! Prudently. . . . *Si*, you do look better. A little pale. Turn there, to the light. That's it. . . . *Si*, a little pale. A little thinner. But ready again to get down to work."

"Ready again."

They sat there in silence for a while. Richard played with his fingers. For the first time he shrank before the thin old face of the man he considered a saint. He knew that at times Padre Benedetto prayed all through the night and that there were secrets among the Benedictines about him, as if Padre Benedetto had sworn them to silence. And he knew that the townspeople came often to him to bring their babies for him to bless, as well as their miseries and crises for him to share and give counsel for. A group of young men from the University of Rome, students in medicine and letters and law and engineering, came to him for guidance. They spent one day a week, quietly, in Trastevere, hunting out the most rejected poor and bringing them foodstuffs, clothes, and word of work and lodgings that were available—all in the secret tradition of Philip Neri's Rome. How all these things got started around Padre Benedetto, nobody knew. He seldom left the monastery. His task seemed academic. He never spoke of these activities; he probably believed that Richard knew none of it.

But knowledge of who Padre Benedetto was gave Richard the sense of his ability and practicality, which otherwise might have escaped him. He was dealing with an ardent and accomplished man, and his own doubts seemed more and more ridiculous.

"And how are you and Padre Bracciano getting along?" asked the old man quietly, to break the silence. He was beginning to circle in on the point. Richard knew that his nervousness was giving him away.

"I just came from him," Richard answered slowly. He felt fear rising within him, as if the conversation were threatening. "I had to report a violation of poverty. I gave five hundred lire to a beggar without permission."

"Where did you get five hundred lire? Did you steal it?" Padre Benedetto asked, covering a smile.

Richard smiled wryly in return. "Almost. I was supposed to buy cards with it."

"And what did Padre Bracciano say to that?"

"Oh, all the usual things. Did I know the money wasn't mine, that I needed permission, that the college gave to the poor every Christmas, that I was immature and softhearted and not very prudent."

"And?"

"Well, he said he'd give me the five hundred lire when I needed it. I was afraid he wouldn't. And he said to speak to you about it."

"And?"

Richard didn't know. "And . . . what?"

"What did you say?"

"What did I say? "*Si,* padre, six times."

"You agreed with him then."

"Well, he was very nice about it. He could have—"

"So you stood there saying *si* to him. I see. An obedient, mechanical soldier."

The words cut. Richard was silent.

"But in fact you didn't really agree with him."

"No."

"But you were too cowardly to say so."

"Padre! He's the superior . . ."

"Yes?"

"One doesn't talk back to superiors."

"No?"

"I mean, hasn't that been my trouble? Talking back too much?"

"Has it been?"

"Well, what *am* I supposed to do?"

"Hm!" The priest paused. He looked away and then at Richard. "Do you believe a student should give to beggars in the streets?"

"When we have the money, yes."

"Should you have the money, even if it meant an expense for the college?"

"Well . . ." Richard started to smile.

"Should you?"

"Well, yes! Now that you ask. I think it would do us good, even if the college were impossible. It would change everything, break down the—institutions around Rome. Make us all—really poor. Really beggars. Ourselves."

"But you didn't say this to Padre Bracciano! Is that honest?"

"But he'd just laugh. *'St. Francis!'* he'd say."

"And?"

"Padre! I'm no St. Francis!"

"Then why do you talk like one? Riccardo, it is good to talk like one or not to talk like one. But you must be honest. Are you on the side of St. Francis or are you not?" The priest changed his position in his chair. "You have a valid point. Love is greater than anything— love and Lady Poverty. Poverty is like a gift and a dependence. Everything for God and others. That's above institutions, above permissions, above constitutions, and we need a taste of it; somewhere, somehow, we have to feel the ardor of it again. But it won't be done as you are doing it Riccardo, you have a point . . ."

After a while, Richard said in the silence, "And I understand that there have to be institutions . . . like the community. Even the Franciscans had to . . . institutionalize."

"They fought over it a long time. It almost caused a schism," Padre Benedetto nodded. "Institutions are necessary to human nature, but they hurt human nature, too. Institutions do not move as fast as love. Young spirits are needed, young hearts, to renew old institutions. Institutions are like the flesh; youth is like the spirit. Only youth must be courageous and honest and wise. But youth so seldom is. Reformers are not pretty characters; hopes for good are always slim. The race gets by from age to age, never changing much. The reformers don't reform themselves. They remain proud, and the new corruption is soon as widespread as the old, but men believe that a new age has really come."

"I should have argued with Padre Bracciano. I knew it. I should have!"

"Perhaps. It is done now. It is probably for the better." Padre Benedetto pulled his wrinkled handkerchief from his sleeve again and dabbed his nose. "I am glad you did what you did, for the beggar. It is good to see a young man with a soft heart. And it is good to see you hold your tongue, even if I prefer to see you bold. As things are, it may be better to be silent. But never worry about a soft heart. Never call it immature. If you are sincere, no one can take advantage of you. They can take your money and seem to deceive you or make a fool of you, but they can't take away the impulse of generosity. That is a treasure that is yours and dear to the Lord. Never do anything to kill compassion. Stir it always, for it dies easily. There is much sorrow that will try to choke it."

"I don't like to call him a beggar, padre. I can't do it when I see him in my mind. He was Francesco. Francesco Bottini. And he had a real sorrow."

"Francesco!" smiled the priest, with emphasis. He stirred himself. "Well, now, how are other things with *Padre Superiore?*"

"He was . . . good to me when I was sick. He came to my room every day. He used to stay and talk for a while, though we really couldn't find much to say. But he meant to be kind, sincerely. He brought me his radio to listen to." Richard felt himself trying to become enthusiastic over his relations with Padre Bracciano, and he knew he was hiding from something concerning them. He didn't see what it was, and as he spoke he was afraid.

The priest took a tangent. "I hope . . . the radio didn't keep you from your sickness and your prayers. I hope you didn't have it on all the time."

"I—I don't like to listen much. I suppose I did use it for escape. It is restful when you are sick."

"What could do more harm to your spirit? You must have silence if you wish the Lord—long, deep silence. You must be lonely and turned back upon yourself. You must be tired and suffering. That is where joy is, Riccardo, in the self where the Lord is."

"That is hard."

"Very hard." Padre Benedetto watched Richard playing with the fingers of his left hand. "Keep your spirit free, Riccardo. Keep your heart soft and joyous."

There was a long silence. Richard was uncomfortable.

"My heart is not very soft and joyous, padre! That is what I wanted to see you about." He forced out the words, shifting his weight on his chair. "I am very tired inside, padre. I don't have many friends, many joys. Conversations are so difficult. I—I like to talk about painting, or philosophy, or—people, or politics, or things. Frankie and Conny—well, they just don't. And the Italian fellows—well, they like to talk ideas, ideas, categories, things I don't agree with at all. I'm always arguing or holding my temper. Their minds aren't very free; they've got all the answers, right out of medieval books. It's a different world, padre! Then Herbert left: I didn't realize I was so close to him. I thought Paolo was my best friend, but I guess the two of them were. Paolo's the one I told you about, whose father is a journalist in Milan. But I can't always be running to Paolo the minute I want to talk. And I want to talk lots, padre, more than I ever did. I feel all pent up."

"Hm. No, you can't always be running to Paolo. What was this Herbert like? I don't believe you've spoken much of him."

"He was from Hamburg. The Hungarian Revolution shook him very much. He's always longed to enter politics. He remembers the Nazis. He's convinced that the main battle of our world is political: Communism and liberalism and Christianity."

"And what do you think?"

"I didn't agree at first. I told him that only Europeans worried so much about ideology, that that was their trouble. But he showed me that America has an ideology, too, but won't admit it, and that that infuriates the world without anybody's knowing exactly why. But it is—it's an ideology."

"So you are engaged in political problems, too?"

"No, padre, not like Herbert. I only want to see what is going on, because I don't want to place my preaching on the wrong side. I don't want to miss the real course of events. I keep thinking, what if Pope Gregory and the others had preached against the barbarians instead of sending out priests to convert them? I think the Dark Ages are the most creative ages earth ever sees, and I think it is a matter of vision and charity."

"I see."

"But, padre . . ."

"Yes?"

"I realize I'm not being honest. It's not Herbert that's been upsetting me. Or friends. I don't—"

"Let's just keep going on, Riccardo. Just tell me more about the way you think."

Richard thought for a moment, lowering his head. Nothing would come to mind. "I—I hate the recreations, padre. The walks aren't so bad. But even then there are so many things that I want to talk about—"

"Things? What things, Riccardo?"

"The way—the sun turns the buildings to gold about four o'clock in the afternoon. The way the dust turns the color of the olive leaves. The patterns of gray and yellow on the roof tops in the rain. And people. There are so many touching people in this city! The poor. Honest suffering. The young people, so full of lustiness. The old chestnut vendors, with such long memories."

"You see the city as a painter."

"My heart is full of this city, and I can't talk about it"

"Why not, Riccardo, why not? I confess I don't see that."

"It sounds—awful, padre. Snobby and pretentious. I'm not a painter yet. I've no right to pretend to art. But my companions think little of painting and of painters. They don't see all these things that I think are beautiful. It sounds silly to talk of them. Oh, beauty—they know a lot about that—architecture and museums and that—a lot more than I do. But out of books. Ideas. Words!"

The old priest was silent. Richard didn't know what more to say, afraid somehow that he was gushing out uncontrollably, though the speaking felt good. It was lancing a sore that he didn't know was there. He didn't know what the sore meant, or how much more he should say, or how much of the hurt he should struggle to master and conceal; he was afraid, in the relief, that he might actually cry. He felt very strange and hoped it wasn't foolish. He longed to continue, but pride, or dignity, or deception, or *something* pleaded with him to say no more, to let nothing more escape.

"And the recreations, Riccardo. You mentioned recreations."

"Padre, it is so *hard* to go into a room, at a certain time, and to be told to 'recreate!' You look around. Some of the fellows are reading magazines. Some play on the ping-pong table Frank built. Some talk or argue. Some listen to the news on the radio. I go in. I look around. I don't know quite where to go. I want to see Paolo, but that's not right—at least not all the time. It's so hard to talk with most of the others! We know each other's ideas already. There's so little small talk available to us, since we're all in the same environment all day. I smile. They smile. There's a kind of superficial charity that makes me sick!"

The old priest looked out the window. He nodded his head, put his chin on his hand, then took his hand away. Then he looked at Richard and made contact with him again. "What is it, Richard, you are seeking when you talk with others?"

"I—I don't know, padre."

"Think for a moment." The voice was severe.

Richard was uncomfortable; he didn't know what the director was looking for, and obviously he had given something away. "You shouldn't seek yourself at recreation; you should seek others."

"And what does *that* mean?"

Richard began to feel afraid. "Not—to be selfish. To look out for others' happiness more than your own."

"Is that what the books say?" smiled Padre Benedetto.

Richard smiled back. "I think so. It isn't easy!"

"What makes it hard? What do you suppose you are looking for in recreation that makes you unhappy when you don't get it?"

"I don't know, padre. I don't know." He turned his head and thought back over the countless times, in America as in Rome, he had entered the community recreation room. The image brought with it the familiar sense of boredom and uneasiness he knew there. Sometimes there was great fun. Often there were pranks or skits or exchanges of stories and laughter that brought real release. But, more often, the ordinary day was ordinary. And the heavy, trying days colored the mediocre ones with somberness.

"Riccardo, trust me," asked the old man suddenly, looking into Richard's gray eyes.

Richard tried not to move a muscle or betray an emotion.

"I have a search to pose for you," Padre Benedetto began. "I am your spiritual director, not your emotional director. My task is to talk to you of prayer, and charity. But there are always the prior difficulties, always the abysses and lacunae and darknesses." The priest's thin face was very serious, looking away now from Richard's. "Always the ambiguities. Riccardo, Riccardo *mio*," he looked back. "I want you to promise me to be honest with yourself. Always do that. Always be honest. Do you understand that?" He waited until Richard's eyes met fully with his and held there. "Will you promise me to be honest with yourself, always?"

He shook his head, slowly, yes. He had an alarming presentiment of fear.

"I want you, Riccardo," the priest said, relaxing and sitting back now, "I want you to think a great deal about what you are really searching for from people. What makes you happy, what makes you sad, in your reactions to others. I want you to separate emotional needs from the needs of charity. I want you to understand yourself, as clearly as a bell. *Ut cognoscam Te, Deus meus, et meipsum.* That I might know Thee, my God, and myself. Riccardo, there is the secret of everything. There is the prayer of Augustine." The priest stopped, his fingertips resting on fingertips in front of his face, his eyes looking absently away from Richard. "To know God. To know yourself. One without the other you cannot do. But, Riccardo *mio,*" he began, his eyes flashing again. "It is a long, long task. It is a circle, a spiral. Learn a little about God, then you will see yourself. Learn a little about yourself, then you will see God more objectively. Climb!" He said the last word quietly.

A cough caught the old man as he whispered. Richard waited.

The coughing overcome, they talked some more. Richard told him of his difficulties at prayer: His mind wandered, his heart was dry, he seemed to get no light or warmth and to offer no steadiness or success in keeping out distractions. "I repeat and repeat and repeat my thoughts, padre. Sometimes I am tired, and even the repeating is just a gesture, not very strong. There is nothing there. I am not very successful."

"Recreation, prayer," sympathized the old priest meditatively. "Where do you find your joy?"

That precise sympathy touched Richard very deeply. "You are right, padre! Where *do* I find it? Just now, nowhere. I am very dry."

"Ah, good. It is the Lord's time. I told you, Richard, several weeks ago. The Lord will ask much of you. Here is a little of what I meant."

"A little, padre? I have been very upset."

The priest laughed long and warmly. "Ah, Riccardo, little do you know how much the Lord can ask! He will ask *everything*! I tell you that now. Be sure of it. If you are faithful to Him, He will ask everything." The priest's good humor, his smile, his shining brown eyes and mild white hair almost belied his meaning.

Richard turned away in pain. "But I am already dark, padre. I don't know whether I believe. I don't know whether I love. Or if I want to be a priest." He looked back again. "Everything is all mixed up."

"I know that, Riccardo. I saw it long ago."

"It's like a great, vast night, an immense blackness. I'm empty. Very empty. I'm like a little . . . thread of tangled root, phosphorus maybe, glowing in the dark. But that's all the light there is—that little bit in so much darkness." Richard shuddered from the cold. "I'm so empty and alone."

Padre Benedetto waited.

"I'm here in Rome all alone. I've moved away from my friends. I don't know anybody any longer. I'm not trusted here. I can't put down roots. Herbert left. Paolo has his problems. Padre Bracciano . . . he's nice, but . . . I'm lost, I tell you! Padre, I feel lost. I'm faithless, loveless . . . I've no energy. I wish . . . I were dead."

Richard blushed. He wished he could wipe out those words, though he felt relieved. "That's how I feel. It's horrible to feel that way."

"What's so horrible about it, Riccardo?"

"To find life meaningless. To be out here alone and dark. And not be able to believe there is anything but the night. That is horror."

"Yes, that is horror, when you're young." The old man drew a slow breath. "Riccardo, if I burnt a piece of root to turn it into flame, it would turn black, and shrivel, and give off ugly rolls of smoke."

Richard sat in silence, nervously fingering his left hand.

"When have you ever been more humble, Riccardo? When have you ever been so concerned about your motives and the perfection of your actions? When have you ever been more sensitive to others or prayed with more intensity? I don't see it all so black, Richard. I see small flames."

"But there is nothing there . . . nothing there. . . . That is horrible!"

"Yes, of course. Nothing there. What is faith, Richard?"

"An act of intelligence, moved by the will."

Padre Benedetto smiled. "Is it? Yes, it is. But it is a naked act. There are no thoughts, no emotions, no feelings. You can't touch God with your fingers, or feel Him with your emotions, or imagine Him, or think Him. Of course there is nothing there."

"So cold? So empty?"

"Often. The Holy Spirit blows fresh dews and joys sometimes. Sometimes He does not. Then there is a desert."

"A darkness, a darkness, not a desert."

"A darkness, then. In which prayer is impossible."

"In which the soul is restless and life is—intolerable."

"Perhaps."

"I am afraid."

"Of course."

"I have to trust you, that you see what I see."

"No, you must step out alone. I don't see what you see. You must identify the landscape for yourself. It's your voyage. I can only say what I know in my own spirit, and have learned from others, in reading and in life. But you must take only what you need for yourself."

"Alone, and dark, and cold."

"Yes."

Richard shook his head and tried to smile. "It is hard!"

"Yes, it is hard. You have not been honest. You have not been mature. Now you will have to suffer the pains of growth."

"But what if—what if it is more than growth? What if, really, I should not be a priest? What if I am suffering because I am out of place?"

The priest shrugged. "We shall see as we go on." The old man looked at Richard sharply. "Do you want to be a priest?"

"Y-yes."

"Why do you want to be a priest?"

Richard thought a moment. "To help men. To teach them about immortality. That's all that is important. Christ is so beautiful."

The priest nodded, warmth coming to his eyes. "But you must have determination. Do you know St. Teresa? Of Avila? *Determinación*. You cannot be half in, half out. You must have a single decision, the sort of thing you make every day. You must stand by it, come hell or high water."

"*Sí,* padre."

The priest winced to hear these words. Richard, too, sensed something wrong in them. Was he deceiving the old man and himself? The black waters closed over him again.

11

THE ROOM was full of laughter. Eight or nine fellows sat in the darkened recreation hall, at the foot of the temporary stage, howling into their hands. On the stage, Conny, Frank, and Richard danced with hands on each other's shoulders, lifted their cassocks, kicked. They wore their birettas rakishly on the back of their heads. To the tune of a Gilbert and Sullivan song, they sang in mock high voices like the Andrews sisters:

Three old apologetes are we,
Pride of the university,
Full of the air of certainty—
Three old apologetes.

We can explain every mystery;
We can refute every heresy
(Up to the nineteenth century)—
We three apologetes.

Three fundamental theologians
Free from all nasty modern notions.
We may not move hut we go through the motions—
We three apologetes!

Up pops an error fresh or stale.
What on earth shall we raise for a wail?
Cite the decrees that never fail
Us three apologetes!

Bending down very low, Conny sang secretively:

Do you know the inquisition tricks?
Well, down in the basement just for kicks,
Fridays we burn three heretics.

And he was followed by Frank and Richard, who joined in for:

We three apologetes.
Three old apo-lo-getes!

Paolo played the last chords on the piano with a flourish. The dancers stopped for breath. The listeners were laughing.

"But do you think Padre Bracciano is going to let that go on?" Umberto asked.

Richard was breathing heavily. "I think so. I hope so! It's naughty, but it's just in fun. He knows what we mean."

"I'm not so sure!" Luigi said over a smile.

"Did you show it to him yet?" Johann asked.

Richard was standing at the front of the stage. The responsibility for the show was his. Paolo swung around on the piano stool to watch. "No."

Umberto shook his head. "It's your neck."

"I'm a little afraid of it," Frank Perrone admitted.

"Aw, it's just for laughs," Conny said. "Keep it, Ricky."

"Well, I intend to show it to him first. But I think it's good to laugh at serious things. God knows, everybody criticizes apologetics. Nobody laughs."

"What's the other number like?" Umberto asked. "You have two, don't you?"

"I'm afraid to do it now."

"Go ahead. It's really not that bad. Maybe they'll both go over very well. It all depends on whether people laugh or not. If they take you seriously . . ."

"They'll laugh," Conny said. "With us kicking and singing high, as though we'd been knifed, they'll laugh."

"They'd better," Richard said, gritting his teeth. There was a lot to do in the two days before the show. "Let's do the other one, then move on. It's in the other book, Paolo. It's marked. Follow Conny. O.K."

Conny stood at a speaker's stand, gripping its edges and massaging his teeth with his lips. Paolo played softly. Conny pulled out his pocket watch; he brought it directly up against his eye to see the time, as one of the old professors did. Paolo laughed and had to stop playing. He began again. Conny looked at him sternly, again as a professor might. Umberto and the others were tittering with pleasure.

"Thank you," Conny began, "thank you, thank you." He then intoned a sweet note for some duration: "I'll-l-l—" Paolo held the tempo for him, and Conny broke into the song with a soft toe dance around the rostrum. Poker-faced, Richard and Frankie sometimes sang with him:

> . . . *be the very model of a Doctor of Theology,*
> *As positively certain as a Doctor of Biology.*
> *I'll catalogue the Summa with new IBM machinery*
> *And pop statistic certitudes like buttons in a deanery.*
> *I'll study probabilities and probably pontificate*
> *On what we'll find in outer space or on the moon (at any rate).*
> *I don't think evolution's true but will not try amending it:*
> *To make a monkey of myself has few points recommending it.*
> *I've figured every problem out from books and texts*
>   *and manuscripts*
> *Until the year twelve thirty-one (when Thomas reached*
>   *the age of six).*
> *I've only seven centuries more to add to my anthology.*
> *1 am the very model of a Doctor of Theology!*

While Richard and Frankie whistled, Conny danced back and forth before the rostrum, fulminated, pointed up like Plato, down like Aristotle, and rose to his full height to sing the second verse.

Johann roared in his seat. "That's hilarious!"

Umberto laughed. "If we could invite some guests from the Greg."

"I have a feeling this show will never go on," Luigi chuckled.

"Is it that bad?" Richard asked, stepping downstage for the reaction.

"These guys are afraid of their shadows!" Conny said. "Let's do it, Ricky. Nix on the pessimists."

"I hope it's going to be amusing," Richard said. "I really hope no one takes it seriously. I mean, I appreciate all the great men we have and all that. But I still think the old theology deserves a ribbing."

"Old-time religion!" Conny hooted. "That ole-time religion!" He clapped his hands. "I think we ought to help kill it."

"Just don't make it our suicide," Paolo smiled.

"Well, I'll show it to the boss," Richard said. "Hope he doesn't object. We have to give this day after tomorrow. You have your number ready, Johann?"

"Almost."

"Only have two days."

"Well, see, the thing is, we need some props. We can't do without a couple of items."

"Like what?" Conny asked.

"Well, four horses and a carriage."

"What?"

"I'm just kidding." The others were laughing at Conny. "Just a couple of things."

Richard looked around the stage. "How about you, Umberto? Ready with *radiodiffusione*?"

Umberto shrugged.

"Want to try it?"

Umberto rubbed his hand across his large nose. "As you wish."

"Go ahead."

Umberto, Luigi, and Cesare climbed to the stage. The Americans jumped down and found chairs at the card tables.

"This is a kind of take-off on the Italian radio," Umberto said, gesturing with his large olive hands. "We—haven't written out an introduction yet, but—Cesare here, see, he's trying to get some music on the radio. He wants music for listening to while he reads. When he—turns the dial, here's what happens."

Umberto nodded to Cesare, who was sitting by an old cabinet radio, his feet propped on a chair, a large volume of Migne's *Patrología Graeca* open on his lap. Cesare turned the radio on. There was no sound. He puffed on his pipe. He reached over calmly and pounded on the radio. Umberto and Luigi began to drone the call theme of the Vatican radio: *"Christus vincit, Christus regnat, Christus, Christus imperat!"*

The door at the back of the recreation room opened and Rudolph came in. He looked over the backs of heads.

"Professore, you say the word *uc-cello* is pronounced sometimes *uc-cel-lo?"*

"That depends. In Tuscany . . ."

"Padre Bracciano wants to see you."

Richard felt the tap on his shoulder, but the words took a moment to register.

"O.K.," Richard nodded to Rudolph and arose. "Keep going," he said. "I'll be back."

He hurried up the stairs, wondering what could be the matter. All the way down the hall reasons and explanations flew into his mind.

"You sent for me, padre?"

Padre Bracciano stood at his bookcase, writing on its top as he sometimes did. *"Sì,* Riccardo. *Padre Generale* will arrive tonight. He will only be here two days, and tomorrow night he will be at a reception. So he asks if he can speak to the students on Tuesday night."

"But that's the night of the play."

"Yes, that's why I sent for you."

"Can we schedule it some other night? Saturday? Or next week?"

"We'll see."

"You're not in favor of it?"

Padre Bracciano waved his pen. *"Veramente,* Riccardo, no. I said yes, I know that. You told me how easily it could be done. Against my better judgment . . ."

"The practices have not been long. We're almost ready."

"No, but there have been several. And all the extra work—writing, memorizing. There is always more than is tabulated." His eyes smiled.

"Especially when young enthusiastic people do the tabulating. I've reconsidered. I don't want any more time used for it."

"Does that mean—it's all off?"

Padre Bracciano shrugged. "For Tuesday certainly . . ."

"We're so nearly ready!"

"*Beh,* let us say—we shall not have it."

"Not in a week or two?"

"Not at all. That would be the simplest."

Richard hesitated a moment respectfully. "No more at all, padre?"

"No more."

"Did we do something wrong, padre?"

"No. I merely repented my decision."

"Not even with all the effort?"

"I'm sorry." The superior's eyes were friendly but firm.

Richard heaved a light sigh and tried to smile. "Well, that settles that. Some problems I won't have to solve now." He caught Padre Bracciano's eyes. "*Va bene,* padre, as you say."

He turned and headed slowly for the recreation room. The superior went back to his writing.

As Richard came into the room again, faces turned. "Well!" he said, running his fingers over the backs of the chairs he passed. "We won't have to worry about any censorship!"

"You mean he doesn't even want to read it?"

"It's all off."

"All off?"

They crowded around him.

"Padre Bracciano just called me in. The General wants to speak to us Tuesday night."

"What about tomorrow? Or Saturday?"

"We could never have it tomorrow," Johann said. "Our part won't be ready."

"I asked him."

"No?"

"No."

'What's up? Why the change?"

"I don't know," Richard said. "Interferes with studies, I guess. It's just no, that's all. Solves a lot of problems, though."

"It sure does," Umberto said wryly.

"Nuts!" Conny said, slapping his belt on a table. "I really liked those songs. Just as I get a good part!"

"Detachment," Frankie laughed. "The superior has spoken."

Richard shrugged, looking at the temporary stage. 'Well, we had a lot of fun practicing. And I won't lose my neck for those lyrics."

"It was a lot of fun," Umberto said. "Maybe next year or in the spring."

"Next year, when Padre Milton's here maybe," Richard said.

"I wish he were coming back soon," Frankie said.

"The very model of a Doctor of Theology!" snorted Conny, slapping his leather belt on the table.

12

THE NEXT MORNING at breakfast, after five o'clock rising, meditation, and mass, Richard was tired and despondent. The squelching
of the play seemed one more in a series of arbitrary constraints. He
broke a roll over his white plate. He forced into it some of the apple
jelly the sisters served almost every day for breakfast. He sipped his
hot, strong coffee and bit into the fresh roll. Stiff crumbs fell to his
plate, surrounding some drops of coffee. The lector read from the
Imitation of Christ in Latin. The phrases seemed distant, and the voice
seemed to be in another world. Richard gestured to Umberto across
the table whether he wanted to take half of another roll. Umberto
rubbed the back of his hand across his nose and nodded yes.

The lector closed the book. A knife clanged on a dish. The
silence made Richard feel more cold than he had before. He tried to
recollect himself and pray. But thoughts and affections refused to
rise. One by one his companions rose as they finished eating, blessed
themselves—some slowly, some carelessly—and carried their plates
to the pantry. Richard followed them. Antonio, Alfonso, and Dante
were not there yet, and the dishes piled up around the machine,
exuding the smell of crumbs and jelly and coffee.

Richard visited the chapel. The morning light was just coloring
the amber windows; the sacristans walked silently around the altar,
removing missal and cruets, covering the altar, dusting; the acrid
smell of extinguished candles was in the air. Richard left and went
to the library to catalogue some books. Twenty minutes later, to the
sound of brooms banging on the stairs and dustmop handles falling

on the floor, he went to his room, brushed his teeth, and made ready for school. The bell began to clang and whine in the corridors and stairwells. His heart felt equally metallic and clangorous. He hurried down the stairs, books under his arm, for the bus.

Outside, the air was sweet and the sky was blue. He climbed into the atmosphere of upholstery and fumes, hopeful of a rise in spirits as the day went on. He sat with Paolo. For the fifteen blocks or so to school they spoke Latin, preparing each day one of the nearly two hundred theses they would have to defend in the exams. They went over the definition of the terms, the history of the thesis in the great councils, the principal heresies, the Scriptural basis. They took turns interrogating and answering.

They arrived at school a little early. Paolo took Richard's books upstairs and promised to save him a place. Richard slipped out into a tiny patio in the right side of the building and opened up his new breviary. He had a new holy card marking his place—a picture of a cross upon an Alpine peak, with other peaks in the background— and it said in French: "If you wish to love like Christ, extend your love to the whole world.—St. Augustine." He made the sign of the cross and began saying tierce, a section composed of three psalms and a very few short invocations and colloquys. Sounds of voices from the classroom windows hovered above him. He walked silently and found his attention held by the psalms. They were almost always prayers of a suffering man, and so he found them refreshing even when he was as dry and empty as today. The buzzer rang insistently. He finished his prayer slowly and walked back into the cool, dark corridor. The stairs were crowded with students now, rushing and laughing. He climbed to his large classroom on the second floor. He kept his heart to himself.

After the first period, Richard had a free hour. Paolo went to a special course, in which Richard went to the alternate on a different day. He decided to go for a lazy walk. He sauntered to the great metal doors of the University on the first floor. He looked out over the sloping cobblestone piazza. Parked Fiats and Vespas gleamed in the piazza. The old stucco buildings across the way, with their old shutters, looked yellowish and peeling. He thought of the fragility of his life. He saw himself tall, young, full of energy, sorrowful and heavy for a moment, but alive. He was alive to the tips of his fingers. He knew his hands—small hands with hard, masculine nails and heavy white hairs growing on them—his own active hands, his own body. He liked his brown hair and his gray eyes; his nose was a little large; he wasn't particularly handsome or noticeable, but he was alive. He was alive, yet the buildings were so much more enduring, had seen so many like him grow old and disappear.

Richard stepped down the few wide concrete steps of the University. A short Negro student, in straight black cassock, stood nearby; he held his books crooked in his arm.

"*Buon giorno,*" Richard said. The morning was still, except for two German seminarists in red who strode past them quickly, talking in excited guttural accents.

"*Buon giorno*" replied the Negro, turning to him with hesitance. His dark eyes were full of intelligence and life.

"Do you speak English?"

"Yes," smiled the African.

"Good!" Richard said. "I'm an American." They shook hands.

"Are you? I'm George Bulakaba. I am from Kenya." He spoke a very precise English. His vowel sounds were rich and full.

"Glad to meet you, George! McKay. Richard McKay. Are you with the White Fathers?"

"Ah, no! For my diocese. Are you going for a walk?"

"Would you like to? To the Fountain of Trevi?"

"Is it far?"

"Two blocks. Come along."

They began walking in the narrow cobblestone street.

"So you like Rome?" Richard asked.

"Very much. Different from Africa. I've only been here a month."

"It's different from America, too."

"Rome is full of extremes. You see, perhaps I notice it more, because I was not always a Catholic. My people, they were savages."

George laughed. "Rousseau wrote of savages, but I have to laugh. Rousseau didn't know. It is horrible."

Richard listened as they walked in the shade of the narrow *via*. The smells from the buildings were sour and damp; sawdust lay on the cobblestones; a melon rind gave two flies a feast. They smelled the wood crates and the fruits of a public market in the next street.

"European civilization—all this," George said, "owes everything to Christ. You can't understand that, because you are in it. I have never met anyone who understood. There is savagery where there isn't Christ, no matter what kind of civilization develops. The notion of *history* is inconceivable; it's always the same old thing, the old natural rhythms of death and sex. That's all there is—the cycles on and on—and people don't mean anything. I know, because that's the way my people always lived. That's what I've been born from. People who knew about life and death and about fertility and pain. They had a very simple life, but exceedingly cruel. You have no way of knowing, Richard. But when I think of all my ancestors . . . the horror! The horror!"

George's lips were twitching and the edges of his eyes were lined. "It went on for thousands of years. They put babies to death. They made one another suffer. But, most of all, they didn't know what for. There was only sunup and sundown. And new life was always like the old. Even the stories my grandfather used to tell as we sat in the grass—the heroes were always people we were supposed to . . . not imitate . . . well, *be*. The hero would come alive in us again—the spirit of the tribe. Do you know what that means, Richard? Life goes on, around and around in a circle, and at its best it only comes back to a point. The best we could ever do was to see that point for an instant in our lives, usually in war and killings. Isn't that an awful way to live?"

"I don't see how you think Europe has avoided that."

"Oh, it hasn't. The strange thing about Europe—I mean the strange thing for an outsider—is that Europe doesn't know what it is. I mean, it has Christ, and it took the notion of progress from the Jews and the Christians. It took a kind of optimism and hope, and it really tried to make a world of justice and peace. You don't know how unbelievable that sounds. My people . . . we were brought up in a civilization—and we have a civilization, we endured, and we made some great men, and poetry, and music—you have to understand. We were brought up to think of bloodshed and privilege as normal. We never questioned that. Who ever believed that human life could be just and peaceful? Who ever brought such a dream? Who ever changed the idea that history was meaningless, that the best we had were our ancestors and other previous worlds? Who ever changed it all and gave history impetus? It happened only in the West, Richard. It happened only where Christ has touched, as he touched the lepers. I think of it as yeast in dough. It takes time, and it is quiet, and you can deny it if you wish. But the dough puffs up. There it is." George laughed. "You see how I love to talk. You are sorry you walked with me now."

"No, I am flabbergasted. I'm delighted. I think that's a beautiful thing, and I haven't heard a non-Westerner explain it."

"Well, don't think that I love the West. How could any African or nonwhite love the West? But I do love Christ. I owe the West that. What an unbelievable man!" George blushed. "I mean God— but it is funny: I like to think of him best as a man. Not gentle, by the way. But fierce. I like the mosaics here, you know."

"The Byzantines."

"Yes, they have something. They have something honest and strong."

"I like them, too."

"Not the pretty Italian statues."

Richard laughed. "No, not very much."

"That's what I mean about the West. And, you know, our missionaries were that way. They brought us Christ, I won't take that away from them. But such strange ideas! Different churches for the whites and colored, and no revolution. Peace, you know. They stay out of politics. It's a strange kind of religion, which I can't understand. Say your prayers, have the sacraments, but no more. Keep things the way they are. Isn't it peculiar? I ask myself. You know, I don't understand some things very well. Do you get confused about religion?"

"Sometimes."

"I do!" said George, rushing on. "It confuses me terribly. I can't understand the Western church, and I can't understand the West."

They reached the corner of the Fountain of Trevi and crossed the street after a black Fiat darted by. Very few people stood around the fountain. The sun fell brightly on the gray twisted forms, the huge inscription, the tumbling waters, the green pools. They walked along the side of the fountain, where they could sit on the railing in the sun.

"Take this," George laughed, "this looks like the front of a church. A pope built it. It could have been a church. But it's only for the water. Strange things happen in the West."

Richard laughed. "How big is Kenya, George?" he asked after a little while.

"Oh, not very big. About six million people—about that, I think. But we are a great country. We will have our independence soon."

"What about the Communists?"

George didn't like that. "Why blame our desires on the Communists?"

"I didn't mean that."

"Africa is like a field of grass. Our people know very little. It is not like America, you must remember that. For them, issues are very simple. But I will tell you something. It helps the colonial governments to say that Communists are causing the trouble. But the flame that is passing through Africa," George said, "it is here." He touched the breast of his cassock. "Christ put it there. The Communists are making it known best of anyone, but Christ put it there. We owe the Communists a tremendous debt of gratitude, because they are teaching the people what they can do, better than the missionaries."

"I don't see what you mean, 'Christ put it there.'"

"The meaning of Christianity is freedom—that's what I discovered for myself," George said. "Here you seem to think it means law and order, priests and churches. All these moral books, all these dogma books—that's what the missionaries thought. But that isn't Christianity. Christianity means life has a meaning; it means men live forever. It means men can change things, change the whole course of history, and above all themselves. It means men have room inside to be what they want to be. Christianity . . . makes men miniature gods."

"Humble gods."

George talked with a kind of intensity; the sun shone brightly on his black face. He watched Richard as they talked, to note his reaction.

"Not really humble. Just—perceptive. They admit that they are basically unlovable at one point or another. That's a miracle to get men to admit that. That's one thing men won't face. But that's what it means to be a creature, a black creature or a white one or any other kind. At some point you stop being lovable and become unnecessary, limited, and even ugly. But that's not really much to admit. It's so evident."

"It's hard to face that evidence," said Richard. "It's a steep road down. It's a never-ending abyss, truthfulness."

"It's hard. Freedom is the great idea."

"Or self-knowledge."

"Maybe we come to the same goal in the end."

"Maybe."

"Hell, for example. I think hell is the most passionate symbol of liberty that mankind knows. Only Christ had the courage to announce a freedom that included the ability to damn oneself. Without hell, there is no final value and no final responsibility. Hell is a mature man's notion—a man who is not afraid. Hell is only the choice of self against existence. It is the affirmation of selfishness. No one is sent there; you have to choose it. But you can't get away from the alternatives: you choose the whole meaning of existence or you choose yourself. And the choice lasts forever. I think that's powerful! I think that's the dimension that makes human life what it is!"

Richard looked out over the fountain. "There's a lot of good everywhere. People want mostly good. Words aren't important. I don't think there are many people in hell."

"But there is a hell. Or there is if men choose it. Men cause it to come to be—the real, concrete flames of self-consuming egoism. There has to be a hell for freedom to be valid."

"I hear people making fun of God. But what they're laughing at isn't *God*—it's somebody's caricature of God, somebody's illusion. The most terrible power men have is to make God seem as they want Him to seem. I'm tempted to argue, to say, 'You don't understand; you're not mocking God!' Then I think: But you are right; God is not like that, and so you may as well mock it; now, let us see, what is God like? George, it is so hard to know. What is God like? A whole life is worth the attempt to see."

"All my life has been the same quest."

You, too? Richard thought, looking George in the eye.

Richard looked away. The green and gray gods of the fountain were motionless in the sunlight as they had been for hundreds of years. "I take hell as a symbol of self-knowledge rather than of freedom, and its pain as the pain they write about in psychoanalysis, when the whole soul turns itself over and judges itself as inadequate. I think hell hurts as the truth hurts. Or maybe it is as a lie hurts when it is discovered but can't be undone."

"You know," said George, after listening to the water for a while and then wishing to resume an earlier point, "the missionaries did not teach us how to be men. They did not teach us human dignity and freedom or how to change the whole pattern of our lives. They found us savages, and they changed all that. And, as I said, they brought us the seeds of an idea. But the religion they brought us—it was such a strange thing. They taught us to be submissive and humble at the very same time they said we were the equals of all men. It was a strange experience, being taught by the missionaries. It was a strange religion, transcendent, impractical, ethereal."

"But sometimes I wonder. Shouldn't it be strange? Did St. Paul try to free the slaves? No, he merely preached equality and peace. Time did the rest. Perhaps the Church should be on the side of peace, avoiding the conflicts of parties and reforms. After all, aren't these things secondary? Isn't life too fleeting? Isn't life for heaven and hell—and there's suffering involved no matter what we do? Should the Church wish to have a social impact?"

George became excited. His dark hands flashed out, exposing their lighter side. "I only know that in Africa she must! Africa is not looking now for salvation. Africa wants an earthly life fit for free and Christian men. And if it can't have the two together, well, the *Christian* will be forgotten. The Irish got support from their clergy. The Tyrolese here in Italy get leadership from their clergy. Well, what about the nationalism of Africa? Is that any different? You know, the missionaries work hard. But it is not enough just to work. They can't be nationalists—not when they are not black. But they aren't even interested in politics! How can they understand what is going on in our souls?"

"But you have other leaders, young people, laymen."

"Ah, yes! But too few. And they are not understood. The priests discourage their political interest. You see, I, too, am young—and suspect. If I spoke out, it would be said that I am 'infected.'"

"We have to catch something!" Richard exclaimed in pain. "We have to catch some fever." His own disappointments and con-straints were coming home to him. He was beginning to confound them with the nature of the Church.

"In Africa," George began, "they wish to build churches and schools; they wish to administer the sacraments. That is their Church. Government? I think they would prefer to deal with the Europeans. They don't care about the educated Africans among us. They call them atheists and let it go at that. They want obedience and peace. They will get bloodshed and upheaval."

"The revolution will come, whatever happens."

"Yes, because Christ is a witness against the whole former world, and his witness has not had effect in Africa as yet. Or in Asia. Or in Latin America."

"Latin America? How can you say that?"

"It is a strange type of Catholicism in Latin America. It is—like the missionaries taught us."

"I think you are wrong. I think it is the Enlightenment that is bringing these revolutions on."

"But you do not understand! The Enlightenment is the West without Christ. It has nothing that it did not take from Christ— neither freedom, nor individual value, nor the idea of history and progress. It has nothing without Christ; only it has abandoned Christ. This is the most terrible irony in history. Just as the world began to progress, it lost its inner source and impetus. That is why the West seems so confused, why her words seem so hypocritical. It is also why the Church seems so strange. The Church cannot exist apart from the world, and the world cannot live without Christ. Or, rather, it cannot live as human beings live. It will relapse into the ages of the jungle and the ages of cyclic history and personal death. Isn't that what is happening in the West? What does conscience mean? Does it mean anything? What does human dignity mean? Inside the Church it means nothing, because the Church has lost culture, the Church is no longer the Church of this world and its problems. Outside the Church it means nothing because there *is* nothing. There is only relativism, and there is death. These are the inevitable facts of a world without Christ."

Richard rested his hands on the gritty banister. The sun felt warm on his cassock. "I'd be more sympathetic to what you say," he began, "if I hadn't read so many really good things by those who hate Christ or count him as just another among great men."

"But they don't really know. They never really stop to tally up all that the Middle Ages meant. Only in Europe, Richard, did the Enlightenment occur. Only in Europe did progress begin. All the ideas I am telling you about in Africa—all of these come from the West. But the fallacy is this: The young Africans studying in the West are coming back to say that Christ is old-fashioned, coming back as atheists. And so they are bringing Africa a contradiction. They are teaching human dignity without Christ. As if man had some meaning, as if man were not some beast, as if man were not meant for death and corruption without Christ! I can't understand it. Maybe I am a peculiar type of fellow, but I can't understand it. I can love man when I think of Christ. I can see beauty. But, otherwise, there are too many contradictions; it is all too ugly, too hopeless. There is too much pain and irrationality. There is Christ, or it is meaningless."

"What does your bishop say about your ideas?" Richard asked.

"He doesn't know all of them," George laughed. "Once I told him that we can't avoid risks by clinging to the *status quo*. That's the biggest risk of all. I told him that was really reckless." George chuckled.

"What did he say to that?"

"He didn't know what to say. A month later he wished me success in my studies and packed me off to Rome. He said to think about it more and to study all I could in Rome about policy for Africa. He was pretty good about it."

"But afraid."

"Yes, afraid. For thirty years he was just a simple missionary. He did his duties, baptized thousands, built six schools, was loved. He never had these other problems."

"Never once *thought* of them?"

George smiled, his white teeth flashing. His eyeballs were yellowish above his smiling cheeks. His hair gleamed black and stiff in the sun. "Do they teach politics in the seminary?"

"Where did you learn yours?"

"In two places. Books and life."

Richard smiled. The people of the future, he thought, the leaders of the future. Then he thought of the time. He felt a moment of fear and saw Padre Bracciano's image before his eyes. He looked at his watch.

"George! It's eleven-thirty already. We've missed our fourth class. In fact, it's almost over."

"Eleven-thirty!"

"We've been here for an hour and a half."

George shrugged sheepishly. "Was it worth it?"

"Very much so." They began rising from the cement wall.

"It's what we came to Rome for—to learn."

"Only I have to go in and report it."

"Pardon?"

"Oh, nothing. I just have to tell my superior."

"You do?"

"Yes. We can't cut classes."

"Maybe I should, too. I don't know."

They stretched their tired legs and slapped out their wrinkled cassocks. They took a last look at the gray statues and the sparkling water started up the cobblestone *via* alongside the reddish stucco buildings. They didn't talk much, rather gathering their thoughts. Richard hated the thought of facing Padre Bracciano again with another exception to the rules. But he tried to push the thought from his mind. George had given him a vision of Christianity again, as Herbert used to do. Only George was very different from Herbert, much more ardent, much more—religious. He felt with George a sense of urgency and dedication for which he was searching, and a kind of sympathy in many ideals. He felt a kind of strength in that sharing and had new things to think about. But he felt uneasy, too. African bishops seemed to match his superiors. He felt as if he were fighting something vast, and his own search for freedom and self-discovery became confused with the crises of the world. Massive walls closed in all about him. Shouts and drums pounded in his ears. He had the sensation of trying to fight outwards, trying to gasp for air.

That's silly! he thought. Really silly.

They agreed to meet and talk often at the Greg.

PART III
Christmas

13

"THESE ITALIANS! God. They don't know nothing!" Conny talked disgustedly as the three of them walked, dodging, down the sidewalks of the Via Nazionale. "Excuse me, Paolo; but it's true! Frank and I had to do the whole blame crib ourselves. But we showed them. They never saw a crib that big!"

Paolo shrugged his shoulders merrily. It was Christmas. Richard, as usual, was embarrassed. He tried to smile.

"Maybe they don't like big cribs."

"They don't even like beautiful ones. The gaudy little things they build. My God, were they all brought up as schoolgirls in those little sems they have?"

"Almost," smiled Paolo. "It is a beautiful crib. *Good job!*" he said in accented English, smiling broadly. His cheeks were very red in the cool air.

"Go easy on them, Conny," Richard said more harshly than he intended. "It's a different country. You've got to understand it."

"They could try to understand us!" returned Conny, his short blond American hair to the wind, his hat in his hand. "Christmas! Does it seem like Christmas to you? They laughed because we wanted to decorate the rec room. A whole week's vacation, and what do they do? Read St. Thomas and take walks. These guys are dead. I mean it. Dead."

"Not a bad day today. Nice sun. It'll get warmer," remarked Paolo lightly, after a while, to no one in particular. He looked up at the sky through the overhead wires and the buildings. The flow of people on the sidewalk separated the three of them; they came together. No one greeted them or tipped a hat—nowhere hostility exactly, only cold-ness. They were clerics: Theirs was a different world.

"It is nice," said Richard. "It's a beautiful Christmas." He was determined to enjoy the cool air, the very light blue sky. There was joy in that if he felt it nowhere else. He didn't—and Conny only intensified the struggle. Why had he had to come? Why couldn't Paolo and himself have had the walk to themselves? Charity, he thought. Charity, charity, charity, charity, charity. Love your broth-ers. It is Christmas. It ought not to be too hard.

After a while he laughed a little. "Conny, cheer up! You'll live through it."

"Don't feel sorry for *me*!" Conny retorted. "It's these guys. *They're* the ones I feel sorry for. Studying *today*!"

Snatches of ". . . and I said . . ." caught and stayed in Richard's ear. A kaleidoscope of sounds, colors, and passing persons pulled at him.

At midnight mass the night before the *collegio* choir had sung Italian Christmas hymns, lilting and sweet and tender; sung them in strong young voices, quickly and not heavily. Richard had been inwardly frayed and exhausted, after matins and lauds sung in choir, midnight mass, and two low masses. During the low masses he had knelt or sat or stood, his thin-echoing thought rising no place. Only the music had stirred his mind, carrying it where it was too cold and worn to go of its own. *Bambino mio divino!* had tripped and rolled through the early morning air of the high chapel. Inside, his heart was cold. Cold as the stable. As it had been for weeks. Come, Lord. Come, *Bambino*. Only cold, naked will reaching up toward God in faith.

What made him happy? What made him sad? Richard remem-bered Padre Benedetto's words. He asked himself what he was look-ing for from Paolo and from Conny. Why was harshness eating like acid into his response to Conny? Entering Santa Maria Maggiore minutes before, he had stood beside them in the vast cold church, walked the porticoes, trod on the uneven stone floor, looked up at the mosaics caught in the bright, cold light of the morning. The massive spaces and silence that he ordinarily so loved spoke to him only of stone and chill and distance. *Bambino mio divino!* The marble and bronze of the main altar twisted down into the confession, down, down underground, and the great baroque side chapels were golden and dead in commemorative silence. The admiration of tourists and the noiselessness and the quiet walking of Paolo and Conny only impressed on him that he was so cold. Then there was the sun again out in the square as they came out from the side door, the red Egyptian obelisk standing into the sun. The three of them walked devious shortcuts under the thick-leaved green trees on the hilly streets till they came to the busy Via Nazionale and the bustle and the brightness.

"It's eleven," said Paolo, looking at his cheap wrist watch. Conny checked him by his own.

"I'm hungry," Conny confirmed. "What are we going to have? Spaghetti?"

"*Pastasciutta?*" laughed Paolo. "What would you have in Chicago?"

"Turkey! Lots of turkey. And stuffing. Potatoes: creamy, rich mashed potatoes. Gravy. Sweet potatoes—candied. Peas. Cranberries. Whole-kernel corn. Celery stuffed with cheese. Ah, everything, Paolo, everything! We know how to live!"

"I never had turkey," said Paolo.

"Never had turkey!" Conny was stopped. He tried to conceive of it.

"We'll have lots of *panettone*" Richard suggested.

"*Panettone?* What's that?"

"The stuff that's advertised on all the posters."

"Like we had after midnight mass?"

"Uh-huh."

"Great."

"That was a good *réveillon*," Paolo remarked. "I enjoy that. Candlelight, greetings, good spirits. I sort of look forward to it every year."

"Cocoa and *panettone?* Are you serious?"

"You should have stayed in Chicago!" Richard chided him.

"I wish I had, I'll tell the world."

Paolo tapped him lightly on the shoulder, resting his hand there a moment. "Conny, someday you will show me Chicago. It must be a great city."

"It is a great city."

"And you must show me some gangsters."

"Gangsters! This whole city is full of them. I've never seen so many pickpockets and crooks. Why, every taxi driver in town is a thief."

"Do you ever ride taxicabs?" asked Richard.

"No, but I heard. Anyway, what do they know about Chicago? Couple of movies. I wish I was back with those gangsters. Honestly, I wish I was."

Incredible, Richard was thinking. He is a kid. He is a kid. He can't find himself.

Paolo pulled him to a stop outside the Palazzo Esposizione. They saw posters for an exhibition of masterpieces from the 1400s: *Il Quattro Cento*. Conny stood there impatiently.

"I was supposed to tell you, Riccardo. Umberto says there is an exhibition at the Villa Borghese for young painters. It sounds like an ideal thing for you to enter."

Richard's heart leapt quickly, though he was in a dismal mood. "Open to students?"

"No qualification. Just present your work to the committee at the Villa. It's all free."

"When is it?"

"In March."

"You're sure it's open to everybody?"

"That's what Umberto told me. He has a brochure; he'll give it to you. I was supposed to tell you to see him yesterday."

Richard had visions of his own paintings hanging in a gallery, his first exhibition, his first contact with other artists, his first taste of criticism and competition.

"You're not afraid, are you? You have the paintings."

"No, not that. Permission."

"You'd get that! The exhibition costs nothing. It wouldn't take time. And it would be an honor for the house."

"I'd love to enter! What a difference it would make. I'd like to see how I would do."

Paolo watched his enthusiasm grow. "You should enter."

"I don't see what you get out of all this painting, Ricky," Conny contributed. "I mean, it's all right. But how can you spend all that time just—painting? You go for hours on one painting, and it looks like a—like a kid could do it. Maybe I'm stupid, but I just don't get it."

"You'd like it if you knew more about it."

"Maybe."

"To sit down with paints, or with charcoal, and your surface, and to make things you see come to life. You'd like it, Conny. You used to be pretty good at cartoons in college."

"Cartoons is different. I couldn't paint to save my life. Or draw something really actual. Fooling around, that's different." Conny looked up and down the street as he talked. He didn't like talking art.

"I'm going to think about that, Paolo. I don't think there's a ghost of a chance. There's not. He'll say no, sure as shooting. It seems I go in to report something wrong or ask something new every day. He's already told me I ask for too many exceptions. I should be just like everybody else. We're going to have a red-hot interview one of these days as it is."

"I still think you should try."

"No use."

"It'll be just like the play, Ricky."

"Oh, that. Forget that."

"He can't do any more than say no, Riccardo. Have you done any painting since the vacation began?"

"We only got out of class the day before yesterday. I haven't done a thing; haven't even got my paints out. Tomorrow, maybe, or the next day. I've wasted a lot of time. My fingers are itching. And yet I don't feel up to it. I feel played out."

"We have a basketball game soon; don't forget," Conny said. They were walking down the street again.

"Never would be soon enough for me," Richard replied wryly. *"What?"*

"I don't enjoy it so much any more. Oh, I do, but . . ."

"Aw, don't go high-hat on me, Ricky. Come off it! This crazy Rome's getting into you. Come off it! Come off it!" He shook Richard's arm.

Richard pulled his arm loose. "Conny, it's childish."

"What is?"

"Sports all the time."

"Childish? What about your painting? Making marks all over paper like a six-year-old! In sports at least you get exercise. Judas priest, Ricky, are you going egghead! A real squirrel."

"Forget it, Conny."

"All right, all right, *don't* talk to me. I probably wouldn't understand. I'm not an artist. I'm not an intellectual. Go ahead, you and Paolo talk about your painting. Don't let me break it up. I don't want to interfere with—culture."

"I didn't mean it that way, Conny. You know that."

"No, not that time. But you sure can talk down to people. That makes me sick. Go ahead, talk about your painting."

"We weren't talking just about painting. We were talking to you."

"I didn't mean now."

"When did you mean?"

Conny hesitated. "Often. You two go around like two squirrels. Always together. Always big ideas. The rest of us aren't good enough. And don't think I'm the only one that notices."

"Conny, that isn't true!"

"No, I guess not, if you say it isn't. You're always right. Big-deal!"

Conny began walking just a little in front of them. Richard dug his hands futilely into his pockets. Christmas! he thought with dismay and bitterness. Pretentious, talking down, superior! He shook his head to clear his thoughts and took a breath of the cold air. They walked on in silence, isolated by their argument. Via Nazionale curved. The three went straight ahead, down an ancient staircase and into Piazza Venezia. Mussolini's far-off balcony was empty, as was the square. The breeze whipped cold across it in the sun. They crossed to the set of stairs that led up to the old Franciscan church of Ara Coeli. Hawthorne's tale of this church and a horrible murder came back to Richard as he climbed the worn stairs. Tarpeia had plunged to death from the same cliff. Murder, horror—he was in the mood for that. Michelangelo had stood on this hill, had designed the Caesar on Horseback that strode the center of the Capitoline piazza next door. He was in no mood for Michelangelo. He lifted his feet slowly, step by worn step. Men and women descended and ascended, children ran up and down. The women's bright skirts and petticoats quickened his heart—their legs were pretty as they climbed above him. He murmured a prayer and tasted in that, at least, a mite of joy. But a kind of heaviness matched the slow tread of his steps up the ancient stairs. He needed breath when he got to the top, and he was sweating.

In the confusion of the much-trafficked church they tried to pray for a moment. Richard rubbed his head in his hands. He pushed his fingers on his eyes. Paolo lay his hand on his shoulder. "*Guardi!*" He gestured with his head toward the rear of the church.

A small crowd was gathered at a miniature pulpit. The three seminarists genuflected toward the main altar, Conny carelessly and hanging on to the bench with one hand, Paolo and Richard a little more gravely. Slowly they walked to the pulpit. Richard rubbed his right eye. Close up, they saw a boy of nine reciting a poem. His hands moved in practiced stiffness. Uncles laughed. His mustachioed father smiled with amusement and pride; his mother's eyes shone; his demure older sister smiled behind a glove, a lovely girl of fifteen or so.

As the boy finished, the crowd applauded. The boy gazed triumphantly at them, intoxicated with the sound. He didn't want to leave. He wanted to grasp the rail and begin again and hear the applause again. His uncle's strong arms pulled him and embraced him, and again he was in the family circle and petted and moving away.

A newcomer of five faced the crowd from the back of the pulpit. The voices of strangers encouraged him. Timidly, step by step, he advanced. He had his finger at his lips. He removed it. He opened his little mouth, shrank back, opened it again. He put his hands at his sides. He wanted to run and for a moment teetered on the edge of tears.

"*Parla, Tommaso! Eh, bravo, eh?*" a woman's voice came to him over the abyss.

"O beautiful star!" he began in a voice thin and coached and childishly regular:

> *O beautiful star,*
> *O beautiful light,*
> *How lovely your flight*
> *Through sky of the night.*

The thin voice faltered but gained new courage:

> *Come thou as thou art,*
> *Come shine in my heart.*

A woman wiped her eyes. The child fled the pulpit, swept into his mother's arms, held away from her for admiration. An older brother pulled at her arms for attention; she embraced him, too. Richard loved to be with people. He wanted to know them, to share their lives and their ways, to learn of them and talk with them. He wanted to know their sorrow, the limit of their abilities, the beginning of their boredom and loneliness, and the lancing finger of fire that supported them. He wanted so badly! He couldn't. His cassock. His flesh.

A little girl slipped into the line among the boys. Her gray skirt was too short, crisp and fluted over several petticoats; her small legs were plump and babyish.

> *Gesu, I love you,*
> *God of love, I love you.*
> *God become baby—*
> *Baby, I love you.*

Conny was bored and tapped Richard's shoulder that he was leaving. Richard looked back at the little girl. He hesitated. Reluctantly he followed. He pushed through the crowd.

"*Bello!*" he whispered to Paolo.

"*Beh!* Children!" Paolo smiled and shrugged.

They genuflected and found their way out the great doors. The piazza of rushing cars and climbing people seemed like an image of the whole world. An airliner flew overhead. The sun fell and shone on everything. The breeze blew fresh and cool. O beautiful start. They walked to the steps and started down. *God of love, I love you.* For Richard, contrary emotions of joy and love and restless desire and frustration spun in the sunlight and scintillated on the roofs of the passing cars.

"I'm sorry, Conny," Richard said, leaning over to him.

"I got hot. Forget it."

They walked silently down the steps.

14

THAT NIGHT, after a dismal Christmas day, Richard hadn't slept for hours, and then he had dozed. His sheets were hot and resistant. He awoke with a start. He had had a dream. His mouth tasted bad, and the room was dark and spinning. He remembered little lights sparkling, two little lights, many little lights, answering like signals. Answering what? He sat up. Only darkness. He had lost it.

His head ached. Inside, the coldness of St. Mary Major's greatness came back to him, the stupidity of Conny's chatter, his own harshness and bitterness. The little girl recited a poem again. A choir sang *Bambino mio divino*! He rubbed his head. He threw his legs out from the covers and sat on the edge of the bed, hands dismally between his knees. The room was dark and rang with the silence and pounding of his dream. He ran a hand through his hair, then pulled his blankets over his lap again. The air was cold. He lay down again. He tossed.

He threw off the covers and sat up. *He dare not do it!* He didn't want to argue it, so he quickly slipped his trousers on—over his pajamas; that would be best if he were caught. He pulled his pajama shirt over his head, clutched up a white T-shirt and a sweater. He fumbled in the dark for socks and shoes. He grunted. His heels hurt from forcing them into his shoes. He stood, breathing heavily. He leaned against the wall and thought out what he would do. He wanted to take a walk, anywhere, just to get away. He knew what the risks were. It was against the strictest rules. They would treat him as a runaway religious, dismiss him in disgrace or give him heavy penances. . . . He *had* to walk! He wouldn't think of the consequences. He was sleepy and the room seemed unreal. The walls seemed to be closing in on him. He had to walk.

It was dark in the room. He tried to get a glimpse of his watch in the dark. It was supposed to be luminous. 2:35. If they caught him outside, they might think he had spent the night away. They might think that he had done it often. His cassock? He held it up. That would make it worse. He let it fall. He clutched his blue jacket and a cap and stepped to the door. He pressed the brass handle, turned it, looked out in the hall. The night light was dim. The pipes groaned somewhere in the wall. No one stirred.

He stepped out into the hall. . . . The priesthood! The priesthood. . . . His steps went quickly down the hall. He gained the stairwell. He listened. Not a sound anywhere. He tripped lightly down the dark steps. Second floor. He rounded the stairwell and started down the steps again.

A door opened somewhere. He shrank against the wall. He clutched his woolen cap more tightly in his hand. He heard a switch click, heard steps, heard a wooden door slam. It was the third floor. He breathed and started down the stairs again quickly, then up the dim hall past Padre Bracciano's room, past the office, past the parlor. The hall had never seemed so long before or so reverberating. The corridor seemed filled with drums. He paused at the vestibule door. He opened it carefully, without a squeak.

The air was colder in the vestibule. He zippered his jacket. He fished in his pocket to be sure he had a key. He turned the latch of the heavy metal door. The brass hurt his fingers. The lock twanged open. He pulled on the door, and moonlight fell through the gap. He slithered through the doorway, pulled the heavy door behind him. It closed solidly. He was out!

He covered his tonsure with his cap, looking left and right under the sycamores. He descended the steps and turned up the street to the right. His steps rang freely in the cold beneath the trees. The moon flooded everything beyond the shadow of the trees; the shadows moved quietly. He put his hands in his pockets; he shivered. He wanted to whistle or to sing. He wanted to cry out: "Hello, everybody!" He asked himself if he were dreaming. He couldn't believe the night and its sounds were real. His past life seemed a dream far away from him. He couldn't believe he came from Gary and had lived in Rome for two years. Waking moments of the past seemed vague and distant, blended with fantasy. As though suddenly he saw a sweet secret—sweet and frightening.

An amazing sense of freedom gripped him. The city—the city now was his! The immensity of the city comforted him—the darkness, the silence. He reached the first corner. He crossed, to walk another block. Then another. The sidewalk pavements were uneven underneath his feet. A taxi sped by in the dark. The dim lights fell on him; the taillights blinked in the wind stream as it passed. Little papers blew and nestled further along the curb. He stopped and looked at the bridge that loomed before him. Its lamps were soft and luminous. Across it, some distance, lay St. Peter's. He began to climb the slight incline, out under the sky.

Somewhere a boy shouted. The sky was crystalline. Richard leaned against the cool cement balustrade. The moon was full, brilliant, serene, like a luscious fruit. The stars were pale: lesser lights, answering to the moon, as in his dream. Black cypress trees stood against the sky on the Gianiculo. Sycamores waved coolly along the Tiber. The ancient river lay in the black pit of its banks like a silver thread. Steps in the concrete banks cast abstract patterns in the moonlight. The island in the river seemed like a looming battleship. Two cars rang spinning over the cement. Richard turned. A fellow and a girl walked, embracing, on the other side of the bridge. He watched and then looked back at the water. He watched the silver water. Barbarian hordes poured down from the city walls on the hillside. Knights pounded, kicking sparks, over the bridge and shouted out a challenge. Garibaldi's legions marched black-shirted and singing, bearing torches, along the river front. Cleopatra floated on a silver barge, breaking the stillness of the water in the moonlight. History was dissolving. There was only one moment on the Tiber.

He ran across the bridge. His footsteps rang hollow in the night. His shadow penciled out angularly before him and leapt over the opposing balustrade. He reached the rail and grasped it with his hands. Across the way, Castel Sant' Angelo was solid in the night. It seemed to have Hadrian's marble siding it again. Gold gleamed from its statues and lancing torchworks. He felt the terror of frightened popes, heard the screams of prisoners, and saw the writhing of those who died of poisons in dungeons and in chambers. He heard somebody pray. The figures on Bernini's bridge seemed to yield their hair and garments to the wind and seemed to be singing in the breeze.

He looked towards San Pietro to his left and hurried from the bridge. The night was dark and quiet, darker, more quiet in the narrow *via* along the Tiber. The Tiber fascinated him. He didn't want to leave it. Trees waved against the sky. His footsteps sounded on the cobblestones. The lights from the lamps were dim. He wanted to reach the other bridge, ahead, and approach the dark basilica through the long Via della Conciliazione that Mussolini had built to it. His shadow moved along the ancient walls of the *via*.

When he reached Mussolini's broad approach, he walked resolutely to the center of the empty avenue without looking toward San Pietro. His eyes down, he imagined the lamplights like milestones leading up to it and the dark buildings channeling his gaze like canyon walls. He turned and slowly raised his head. In the moonlight San Pietro floated like a monument of ice. The cold dome was brilliant on one side, gray and green on the other. Perfect silence enfolded the front columns, the black statues on the roof line, the milky piazza, the obelisk. Bernini's columns spread out of sight. The fountains were stilled, too far in the distance for him to hear. The sky was glassy-clear. The pale stars sparkled. His breath hung cold before his face. He walked slowly toward the basilica.

He never took his eyes from it, though he seemed living a dream and not reality. At last the columns of Bernini embraced him. The sound of fountains filled his ear. The water leapt like silver in the moonlight, sprayed like foam into the sky, fell like crystal glass into its bowls. He walked the milk-white stones of the piazza. Every movement made a sound. He touched the cold red marble pediments around the obelisk. His eyes searched the white detail on the surface of the dome, the ball, the point. He sat against a marble pediment and gazed. The silver fountains fell and rose again in the silence.

His soul was now quiet and there was nothing left except to pray. But his heart was dry and barren. No words came from it, no affections stirred within it. It was as if the moonlight made a desert, a thin and insubstantial light in which nothing earthy could grow. There seemed no contact possible between him and God; heaven and eternity were too thin for him to reach. God did not exist. He stood in the great piazza but was alone, and no one heard. There was not a sound, only water falling musically. He wished to scream, to kneel, to tear aside the curtains. The water fell. His eyes searched the piazza, columns, temple, night. *Has all of civilization come to this: I cannot see!*

He rose. Slowly he turned and walked again towards home. His eyes did not look up again. His shadow fell beside him step by step. He was cold, and his hands went deeper in his cotton pockets. By the Tiber it was very dark. He thought he heard the river talking as it flowed. It was only the voices of others out in the night. He reached his bridge.

He walked along it. He paused and touched the concrete rail, though a better voice told him to continue on. The Tiber was silver. The moon hung overhead, luminous, silent, still. It was a perfectly white ball, deathly still. White light screamed from it. Trees rustled in the night. The dark masses of the city lay in silence. Richard was responsive to the silence, cold and bare as the moonlight. He was not sure he believed in God. He looked and could not find Him. There was not a sound, not an intimation, only mockery. He had been going to serve Him as a priest! His love, his energy, his art—he had trusted them all to Him, to a God who was mocking him. If there was no God, his life was disastrous. His life was delusion. It was wasted. His mind reeled off among the cold stars. He felt as if he would choke for want of air. He wanted to breathe. The moon hung over the city, mocking him. The moon and the stars gave the city beauty in the silence.

Richard turned away. Where could he go? His eyes sought out the moon again. Where are you, my God? he asked. Where are you?

An unseasonal shooting star broke from the heavens, fell long and peacefully, burnt away. He stood statuelike in the dark. His heart bounded with joy; his sides expanded. But icy fear chilled him instantly, and his excitement fell like ash to earth. Coincidence meant nothing. He couldn't base anything on pseudo vision.

The pale stars sparkled, the moon shone quietly. There was silence and distance. Time was ringing in his ears. It could have been any year, any era, and the moon and the stars would have been the same. He was angry that God could be so cruel. He was angry that God could toy with him. But he had his freedom. He could curse or he could love. It took him a long time to say.

I believe, he said. I accept creation as it is.

He walked back through the night. His heart was neither heavy nor glad, only empty. Perhaps it was his tiredness. Perhaps the high pitch of his emotions had snapped. The heavy door of the *collegio* twanged closed behind him like the doorway of a tomb. A sudden fear chilled him: that, to accompany his inner dryness, he might now have jeopardized his advance to the priesthood. The deed was done. If anybody had seen it, or were later to hear of it, he was ruined.

He climbed the stairs, sick with lack of sleep and with alarm at his foolishness. He dropped fitfully into a doze between his cold sheets. Almost instantly, it seemed, the bell clanged.

15

CONFESSION OF THE INCIDENT became inevitable. All that day he felt guilty and afraid. He assuaged his fears by telling himself that he would explain his feelings first to Padre Benedetto and then, if necessary, to Padre Bracciano. The accumulation of things he would have to bring up soon to Padre Bracciano troubled him. He still debated asking him about the Borghese exhibition. All day he busied himself with the base coats and sketches of a painting. That night he had a good sleep.

The next day he was himself. He got permission to go to the dentist alone. Padre Bracciano seemed very friendly. The trip to the dentist took all afternoon; his office was on the far side of Rome, far out in the scores of new green and buff and pale-blue apartment buildings on the north flatlands of the city. On and on forever the bus had seemed to grind, on wide expressways and into piazzas with new fountains and trees and statues, and on out trolley-lined streets and turns. Coming back into the city was more tiring still: twenty minutes with the doctor, an hour and a half of travel each way. But Richard decided not to catch his second bus after traveling as far as he could on the first; he wanted to walk the narrow streets and enjoy the gray windy day. He liked to watch the night coming on. He liked the pleasure of walking, not because he was tired of riding in the bus or waiting for the dentist—who was an hour late for his appointment even though not another soul was waiting—but because it was not often that he got out alone. How strange! A life dedicated to God, and yet so seldom real solitude. Days harried from one exercise to another; and everywhere he went, someone else along. Sometimes it seemed that all was "community this" and "community that" and then ever more complaints that what was needed was more "community spirit." He craved solitude. It became almost an ache. Not merely the solitude and silence of kneeling in prayer, no matter how many were around—for here, too, there was a profound solitude, if all too rare, too rare because too rushed: so many religious exercises that they did not refresh, but fatigued, the spirit no matter what his good will. He longed, too, for the solitude of thought, of feeling, of wonder. Of simply standing before a sunset, or under the stars, or in the midst of people: solitude to observe and to be grateful and to learn. So seldom did he encounter anything alone. Always at his side the interminable small talk of a companion, always chatter, or scheduled timing, or the weight of highly patterned reactions: a good religious should . . . this isn't part of our . . . our community does not.

Do you know what it is? he often thought. We are not monks, and we are not philanthropists—and we don't know what we are. We hide our loss of identity with vain efforts to achieve a perfect community spirit in which to find a pattern of happiness. And so we watch one another, and in our bad moments snipe at one another, and think of certain most affable and easy ones among us as the ideals, "real community men"; the others are a little odd. He breathed the clean, cold air as he walked. Like a cocktail party or a country club or a faculty bar.

He had the whole city to himself. He couldn't really wander about—they were told always to come directly home—but, relatively, all the city was his. To be out in it like this—and to belong to God—was to own it. No corner of it was his, and therefore all of it was. He sought nothing, so his spirit took all. Rome was his, without a lira or a love or a self-determined residence. He hadn't really permission to be walking through the city. But he had an hour yet before he was required home. He *was* going directly home. Surely there was nothing he wasn't taking into account—scandal to be seen abroad alone? A longer time in the city? No, surely, it was all right. He had to argue with himself to enjoy it.

So something took his liberty of spirit, too; something came and stole it from his grasp as a pelican swiftly slips a fish from the whole wide sea. And the sea churned and reached but could not recover it. He exhaled his breaths slowly, and it was cold enough for them to come back as vapor over his face. *Oh, it is so wonderful! Something is wrong, dreadfully wrong, with me or with something.* Like counterpoint the two themes played in his heart. His buoyancy won out: He would enjoy himself! He dug his hands deep into the rubbery pockets of his dark trench coat; his cold nails pushed down the doubled seam. He fingered a bit of softened old paper—a theater ticket, from New York still, from *War and Peace*, which he had seen before sailing. *War and Peace!* Natasha came to his eyes, and Pierre and his search for God. Natasha danced at the ball. And they rode into the cold night over the snows in a happy sleigh. And Andrey lay wounded and looked up at the stars and found God.

Tolstoi, he thought. And who in Italy? James. Hawthorne. Thomas Marin. Did they see *these* streets? What did they think of them? He walked along a cobblestoned alley, past nondescript apartment doors and closed shops and rubbish in barrels or not; and his footsteps sounded alone in the alleyway. A shutter closed above him and startled him. Light came through its slats: warmth, a family, affection—and quarreling and difficulty and sickness. The slats of the shutters yielded an orange light. The sky seemed violet and brownish from the twilight and the cold. Around the corner an old woman burned two crates in the alley, and the little yellow and blue flames licked speedily up into the night and colored maroon the side of the dark building. *"Buona sera!"* he found himself saying joyfully as he passed, but the old woman merely looked at him.

He came out suddenly on a thoroughfare. Traffic was brisk, the sidewalks were crowded. Lights shone in modern store fronts and in others not so modern. Business would go on until late. He felt the warmth of the light and the companionship, although of course the night was every bit as cold as before. Rome at night! The little Fiats had their parking lights on, and their taillights blinked red as they passed on and away. A policeman waved and whistled at the distant corner, his huge white gloves showing like dull phosphorus in the dusk.

He would have liked to go into one of the stores. Some excellent post cards caught his eye: masterpieces of painting, some of the ones he loved so much, from Florence and from Venice. His aunt's money burned his pocket; Padre Bracciano had replaced the five hundred lire he had given to Francesco. It was a neat-looking store. He stepped back to look at the window but didn't see the name. It seemed to be a religious store or an artists' shop. He stopped for a moment, thinking. He had time. He had permission to buy the cards. He pushed open the door and stepped in. He waited, for all was silent. The girl at the counter had her head down.

"*Buona sera,*" he said, loosening his coat in the warmth of the store. She had light-brown hair; she slipped cards into little packages at the rear counter. She was slender, perhaps twenty, he thought, by her frame and bearing. She was rather tall, but shorter than he. She looked up and smiled. His heart jumped.

"*Buona sera,* padre." She had a pleasant smile and a gracious appearance. Her pink dress was cut neatly and smartly. It was open at the neck in a modest square; it was gathered at the short sleeves, to puff a little; the skirt flared out in graceful folds. "May I help you?" she asked in Italian. She looked fully in his eyes with innocence.

"I'd like to look at some of your cards," he replied in Italian. "The masterpieces set."

"Oh, you like those?" she said, sliding around the counter and stepping briskly to the window. Her movements were light as the spring as she passed him. "*Mi scusi,* padre," she said. She moved softly in a pair of low white sneakers. "They are lovely. Considering they are post cards." She reached over the curtain of the display, stretched, and brought in a pile of cards. She realized they were too few and looked under the counter for more. She blew the dust off the top one, looked up laughingly, and handed them to him. "They aren't appreciated." She raised her blue eyes, full of intelligence and warmth.

He smiled back. "*Grazie,* I'll do what I can."

"I think we have some more. Yes. In back. One moment, I'll bring them."

"Don't bother. These—"

"*Niente,* padre. *Un momento solo.*"

She was back as he looked through the cards, "Here, padre."

He looked at the cards. Giorgione. Tintoretto. Tiziano. Michelangelo. He lingered over a Fra Angelico.

"You like that?" she said. "It's one of my favorites."

"It's the one at the head of the stairs," he said absently, as if to himself.

"I like it better than the one in the cell."

"You know them well!" he said.

"I spend a great deal of time in Florence."

He kept shuffling through the cards, laying some aside. "And, I suppose, in Venice," he replied. "And Rome."

"And Assisi. And Ravenna."

"I spent most of the summer near Ravenna."

"You loved San Vitale then!" Her eyes radiated sympathy.

"Very much."

"I would love to paint like that some day. Strong." She said it, not quite to him—to herself.

He glanced at her more intensely. "You are a painter?"

She flushed. Her eyes said for a moment: Why did I say that to you? "I try." Her eyes flashed and she smiled.

"I paint, too," he said. Her eyes were light blue, clear, and deep. Their conversation was marked by hiatus and lingering, and what they said didn't matter—they were communicating a certain sympathy. She is a lovely girl, he told himself, be careful.

"Padre," she said after a moment. "You are not Italian, are you?"

"*Americano.*"

Confusion clouded her face. She drew back, smiling, laughing. "Where are you from, father?" she said in English. "Buffalo, by chance?"

"You mean—and you're an American all the time!" They laughed together, both blushing. She covered her mouth with her hands.

"You speak Italian very well," he said.

"I wish I spoke it as easily as you; I have to think all the time of what I'm going to say next."

She studied his face. "I should have known by your reddish hair! You're Irish, aren't you, father? Where are you from?"

"Not father. They give us Mister for a formal title. Just Richard. Richard McKay. Noboby uses titles on us, really. I'm from Indiana—Gary. And Irish, but I don't admit to it."

"Gary's a steel town, too, isn't it?"

"And not much more, I'm afraid. It's good to talk English again!"

"Don't you get much chance?" She looked up at him.

"I don't look for chances. I've wanted to learn Italian very well."

"You speak it marvelously. I live with an Italian family for the same reason."

"Ah, no wonder you speak so well! That must he splendid, right with a family."

"It is! It's my second year with them. It's wonderful."

"It's my third year. May I ask you? What—brought you here? Painting?"

"A-hum. Painting." She paused, holding other notions back. "Painting—and travel. A little independence. And to help out with the Students' Program."

"And the store here?"

"I'm a busy little girl. It's better that way. You see, father—Mister—," she flushed.

"Richard," he said.

"Richard," she nodded. "This is one of our stores—the Program's. It's not much." Her eyes looked around the shelves at the wooden statues, the rosaries, the books, the stationery, the paints. "But it's a start. We can't stand the religious art shops in Rome. Or anywhere for that matter. So we're starting our own. These statues are carved in the Tyrol or in Germany—mainly by students. Off-beat stuff they couldn't sell most places. Our artists can experiment. They can copy forgotten things. It's a good outlet for them. The paintings, too. And we make enough on the post cards and stationery to keep going."

He looked at the slender statuettes and a few grotesque, tortured ones. He recognized Byzantine forms, even African forms, and many new experiments—in tapered lines and interrupted lines and mixed forms. The human body suffered countless convolutions and distortions, squares and circles and cylinders. Some of the art seemed very ugly. Some of it was very good—a spark of suffering, a spark of pity, a touch of reconciliation.

"Everything is kept very well. Except the dust on the post cards. I wish I had known about the place before." They laughed.

He walked over and looked at the books. He pulled out a Cardinal Newman, a St. John of the Cross, a Baudelaire in French. He saw Thomas Mann in German and in English. Shakespeare, Péguy, Goethe, Kierkegaard. "A fine collection."

"We try to keep it good. There's enough junk around."

"Who's we?" He looked over at her.

"Angela and I. She's the international secretary, an Italian girl. I wish you could meet her. She's quite a girl. She speaks about six languages fluently, organizes like an American, knows more about art than a library of books. She has a degree in philosophy, too, a doctorate."

"You know, I didn't ask your name," he said suddenly.

She blushed a moment. "Maria." Then she laughed. "I mean Mary. Mary Coleman. Only now I like Maria better."

"I—I like it better, too. Maria!" He smiled. "How much are the cards?"

"Twenty lire each," she said, looking at him with a little trepidation.

"That's robbery! No wonder you're making money."

She put her hands over her nose and mouth and laughed. Her blue eyes flashed clearly and intelligently. She counted the cards. "Seventeen." She looked up at him. "I think every one of these is a favorite of mine."

He felt that the quality of their minds was strikingly similar. "Do you do abstract work?" he asked.

"Almost all kinds. Traditional. Abstract. Impressionist. I like to try everything. I'll—if you stop by again, I'll—show you some of my things."

"I'll stop by if I can. I can't promise anything. I'd have to ask permission."

"And bring some of your own?"

"I'd like to." He handed her three more cards and the five-hun-dred-lire note. "I may be back for more. My aunt wants scores of them. I pick them slowly."

"Little by little," she laughed softly, walking lightly to the money drawer. "You learn that here, don't you?" She brought back his change, counted it out with her small fingers into his hands. She looked up at him, contentedly, hesitantly. "Good luck, Richard."

"Good luck in your work."

"*Ciao!*" he added as he went out the door.

"*Ciao!*" she replied, looking out after him as he left.

His steps were light in the street. The air was cool and clear. The shops seemed brighter, though now the dusk had gathered very heavily. People seemed happy and in Christmas joyousness. What a lovely girl, he thought. What is she doing here alone? His heart was warm and light from the pleasure of the conversation. To talk with ease and seriousness, to laugh together and to speak of one's love for art, to find one working so happily for her ideals: It restored his vision, sharpened his perception, awakened his sensibilities again. The buildings of the street towered into the dark above him. Dim light shone through curtains and shutters. Buses passed airily and noisily in the street; Vespas sped loudly in and out around them. But his heart was confused, too. All sorts of emotions played there, knotted up, vaguely disturbing. Lord, allow it to straighten out, he said. Help me to love you. Help me to understand myself.

He walked on in the dusk down the busy *corso*, and the image of Maria's slender but strong figure, and the pink dress firm over her breasts and flaring out from the waist, and her pretty smile, or her hands up over her nose as she laughed, or her quick clear eyes, or the toss of her light-brown hair filled his heart in spite of himself.

He did not try to hide her attractiveness from himself, nor the wistfulness, the very clear wistfulness he felt deep in his heart. At last the great dark front of the *collegio* loomed before him, and he approached the heavy door, rang for it to be opened from within. Rosetta peered out through the peephole.

"Ah, Padre Riccardo!" her eyes said, though she was evidently angry about something—her husband Giacomo again or "that good-for-nothing son of mine." The door opened and he went in.

16

HE WOKE UP in the morning very tired. He sat on the edge of his bed, head hanging sleepily, then forced himself to say *Deo gratias!* and stand. He fumbled for the light switch on the wall and bent over twenty times, slowly at first, to touch his toes. Six o'clock. It felt like five. Vacation. Free time in which to paint. And images of Maria came back to him. He saw her raise her head and say *"buona sera,* padre!" He saw her casual wave and heard her pretty *"Ciao!"* as he stood at the door and she looked after him. He smiled to himself. Dear Lord, I've got it bad.

He thought of the mass to come and began to recollect his thoughts. His heart now was warm. He prayed easily, though he knew that the joy sprang from the sympathy of Mary Coleman. Pink dress and brown hair spun through his mind. She had taken his hand and they had walked and then run through a meadow, against the sky, as light and free as Botticelli's *Spring*; and a chorus, from Botticelli's canvas—no, from a post card—sang to them. He sat down on the bed and pulled on his shoes, lacing them. He laughed at himself. He stood, wanting to whistle. To know myself, Lord, to know myself! He dressed swiftly, calmly, putting away his thoughts of Maria, and hurried out to the common washroom to brush his teeth, shave, and comb his hair before coming back for his cassock and descending for mental prayer and mass.

After breakfast he ascended quickly to his room and closed the door. He pulled on old clothes and tied an old blue apron over them. He sat and painted all day. He stopped for meals and long enough to pray his office and his rosary; he took a forty-minute nap. By six-thirty he was tired and his back was stiff. He had red and blue and yellow streaks of oil paint on his arm and dark smudges on his hands. He was content. He had a powerful canvas, he was sure of it. He had forgotten everything else today in that painting. He stepped back and looked at it. He glanced up at the bulb above his head. He set the picture over on the window sill at a new angle. He realized now he had had to work the last two hours with electric light, and he grimaced. He hadn't the free time to be choosy. Four canvases in three years: No progress like that! He wiped his fingers reflectively. He would get a good look at his new child in tomorrow's daylight. It was a good canvas; he felt it, rather than judged it with his eyes.

Slowly, in cassock and freshly clean, he walked down the stairs to the chapel. He prayed reflectively, withdrawing himself from the world of painting to the presence of the Lord. He had given himself too much to the painting. It was hard to re-enter the familiarity of His presence. On the other hand, his heart was still; he was tired; he was content. Finally his mind and will responded to his effort to be present to the Lord. Fingers interlocked with each other, quietly placed between the bench in front of him and his chest, eyes closed, lips still, his mind and heart silently lifted themselves to a sense of eternity, recalled that he was seen and loved and heard, and called before his imagination the young man of Galilee, Rouault's broken Christ. His heart took wing a moment to believe and to love. It was as peaceful a moment as he had had in many weeks. He was sorry he had given himself so utterly to painting all the day; tomorrow he would keep his heart nearer to the Lord. He thought of Fra Angelico. He would like to be as prayerful and contemplative as he. Not rash, headlong, ponderous, bitter, as he often was.

At supper, part of Richard's peace continued with him. But he was pensive. He knew that much of his peace came from work well done and that perfect prayer does not depend on peace. His tiredness was overcoming him. His mind was on his painting. He tried to enter conversation with Umberto, Johann, Carlo, Rudolph,

Attilio, who were at table with him; he tried to keep a smile on his face. He would have loved to tell someone about the canvas, to explain how he had tried piling up the reds, catching the lines of shadow in their sweep. He wanted to ask someone if he grasped the eye pattern he had left, if the impression was as integral and honest as he had labored to achieve. He wanted to test someone's reaction to its power, to see if he understood it as he did—or if, for his seven hours' work, he had been talking in the dark. But who was interested? He would see Paolo again after supper. Always it was Paolo for any serious talk. Conny's accusation hurt. Around him they discussed the death of a bishop in Apulia, and a new appointment in Calabria, and the play at the North American College due later in the week. His food tasted dull in his mouth, his bread was dry, the coffee was too strong. He ate his apple and his few grapes quietly, responding to the play of conversation politely—faraway.

He got hold of Paolo almost immediately after supper in the recreation room. He had found him at the far end of the noisy room, reading an American journal for which Richard had a gift subscription from his parents.

"I want to show you something. Come on up to my room."

"Painting again?" Paolo lay down the magazine. He smiled with wry amusement.

"You'll see. Come along."

They climbed three flights of stairs in the semidarkness and walked down the eerie corridor. As they entered his room, Richard said: "We have night prayer in private, don't we?"

"*Credo di si,*" Paolo nodded. "Always during vacation."

"Till ten-thirty then."

Paolo walked over toward the painting as Richard stepped aside and waved him on. Richard stood there. Paolo smiled slightly. He was pleased and studied it seriously. He backed up again. Richard noted with pleasure that Paolo picked out the proper distance. Paolo squinted up at the electric bulb.

"Powerful canvas, Riccardo! That bulb makes it too white. It is powerful even so."

"Where does your eye go?"

"The center, of course. That clearing. But it does not want to rest. It spirals and returns to the buildings and then out again into the sky. It spirals but cannot get away."

"Splendid! Splendid! Paolo, you are a marvelous audience."

"You are a good painter."

Richard's heart expanded with hope and joy. Communication was complete. Circuit was closed. If everyone in the whole world hated the painting now, it would stand and he would pride himself in it. Yet he was troubled that he needed to be spoon-fed all of Paolo's praise. Was it cheap to be like that? He walked over and lifted his canvas gingerly by its sides.

"It's so strong, Paolo, it's so strong, I'm really pleased with it."

"It is. You should be. . . . Where do you get such ideas? A city that is falling apart, that is splitting apart and opening out to the sky but never sailing loose."

"The collapsing buildings? You like them? All in black, yet edged with deep red." His eye followed them about.

"The red light on the foreground. Are the skyscrapers on fire?"

"No . . . I don't know. But red is right. The intensity and horror is exactly right."

"Will you paint *Abbandonare la Speranza* over the gates on the city?"

"I thought of that," Richard said, eyes flashing. "Do you like the pale blue of the sky?"

"It surprised me. . . . It seems so tranquil, so breezy, while the city seems furious. And it is not reddish but pale, serene blue."

"It was hard to render. It is reddish, but you don't see it. I had to blend it, to make it seem bluer. The plain blue looked too white."

"What started you?"

"I don't know. I've felt it growing for weeks. The blue sky. Jet planes. Perhaps it was the streets last night as I came home, the high buildings. Dark against the sky. And the orange light of the windows. Only in the picture it's red light, and like a fire . . . I don't know. Today I saw it and I finished it. That's all I know."

"I like it, Riccardo."

"I hoped you would. Your judgments are always generous."

"Beh."

"Want to go up on the roof? It's nice tonight. I'd like to talk."

"It's cold!"

"Get your coat."

"I want to say office before—"

"We have till ten-thirty. We'll come in at ten."

"Nine forty-five."

"O.K., nine forty-five. Get your coat."

Richard pulled his dark raincoat out of the closet; It felt rubbery. He reached in and found the worn-out theater ticket in his pocket. He turned back and set his painting on its easel and put the easel in the corner, out of the way. He brushed his hands and turned out the light. He found the dark roof-top stairs and climbed them slowly, waiting expectantly for Paolo to be following him. He reached the top, felt for the handle, and went out. The breeze met him—and the sudden movement of a black figure.

"How did you beat me?"

Paolo answered him: "I don't know. What kept you?"

"You're the one who always tells me *piano*. You must have flown."

"It's cold. Come on out. Shut the door."

They walked along the roof. "Look at the stars. A good piece of the moon, too," Richard said. Leafless branches waved in the dark. The young men could hardly see the Tiber as they came to the parapet. In one little break in the trees and shadowed bank they saw a silver ribbon moving slowly. Lights glimmered on the far bank in Trastevere. Richard wanted to talk. He wanted to soar out and be as big as the sky. He wanted to relieve his dilemmas. "The *campagna* is so huge," he began.

Paolo waited.

"From an airplane it must look very strange. Thousands of people under their little lights."

"So . . . you paint a picture of it? Of yourself, trying to break away?"

"Of what? I paint a picture of what?"

Paolo shrugged in the dark. "The city. The city holding some-one in, the buildings thrown aside, a path cleared out into the blue sky . . ."

Richard leaned upon the parapet. "I didn't know I was painting that." He was careful of his words. "I do want to get free. But of what? Of what? It isn't here, this place. I don't think it is. I've cho-sen it. I love the life." He laughed softly. "I don't understand myself—not at all."

"No one understands himself, Riccardo. We're mysteries."

"You know what I would like to do, Paolo?" asked Richard sud-denly. "I would like to go out in this *campagna* for a month, for two months, and get to know the people. I would like to take this thing off. Paolo, I have come to hate this cassock!"

Paolo answered quietly. "Be careful who you say that to."

"I am."

They started walking up and down. The breeze moved the palm branches. Their steps rose and fell. Richard heaved a sigh.

"I don't know how to express myself. What I said isn't it. It's all so confused." Their footsteps fell awhile. "Honestly, Paolo, I am very much confused tonight—lately." The image of Mary Coleman forced words to his lips, but he held them back. "Seriously. I don't know what to do. I don't know where I am or where I've been. My head is spinning."

A car spun over the pavement far below. Silence.

"You've talked to Padre Benedetto?" Paolo asked finally.

"I will."

"He's the one to help you. . . . What can I say, Riccardo?" His friend turned to him in the dark. His cheeks shone a little from the street. "It's your voyage, isn't it? I have mine."

Their footsteps rose and fell. Richard agreed with him. "I didn't realize, exactly, that I was painting *this*."

"I have always told you your painting is powerful. Your feelings are strong. Your intelligence is active. Perhaps . . . your work is undisciplined. That will come."

Richard walked on in silence. He would have preferred no criticism at all—all praise. He looked up at the sky because the sky was
free. He found the North Star. He picked out Cassiopeia's Chair.

Paolo gave him an American slap on the back. "*Amico mio,* you
think too much."

"I understand too little."

"But what you want to understand is too big. You want to do it
all at once."

"You're right," Richard said, half wryly and half with earnestness. "We only have one life."

"Don't take it all so seriously!" warned Paolo. "Become *Romano.*"

The door opened on the roof. A dark figure stepped out on the
terrace. He walked along the roof.

"Oh!" he said when he saw Paolo and Richard. "I didn't know
anybody was here."

"Hello," Richard said.

"*Buona sera,*" Paolo added.

It was Frank Perrone.

"Nice night."

"Yes, it is. Nothing doing in the rec room?"

"I just thought I'd take a walk."

The three fell in together. While Frank and Paolo talked,
Richard's thoughts wandered. Mary Coleman would be such a comfort to him now. Her intelligence and vivacity—that's what made a
woman so attractive—the daily sympathy and receptivity; men
couldn't match it. He felt young and strong; he had many energies
and all the saps of life. He longed for a companion, for a heart to
cling to, for an embrace. His arms almost ached. He hadn't felt so
young before. He hadn't felt so virile and desirous.

The conversation of Paolo and Frank was tedious to him, and
he longed for it to finish.

17

PADRE GIORGIO Bracciano leaned over his white sink and spat out the tooth paste, turning on the flowing water as he did so and brushing vigorously. With one hand he gathered the front of his cassock to keep it from getting splashed. He stood, rinsed off his brush, cupped his hand, wiped some of the paste from his burning lips, and filled the glass with cold water. He rinsed, gurgled a little, spat. He took a long, cold drink, sighed, wiped his lips and hands, saw in the mirror that his hair was straight, turned out the light, and entered his office.

He picked up his breviary from his desk, looked about the room with his index finger to his lower lip, and, strangely ill at ease, walked to the door. Out in the hall, he closed the office door, locked it, slipped the keys into his pocket, and walked towards the chapel. His mouth felt enlivened and fresh. He had a half hour yet. He would say two nocturns of matins before Richard McKay would be coming to his office.

In chapel he noted that the sacristy light was on, then was relieved to hear someone moving around in there. Probably Cesare. He bowed his head, to clear distractions from his mind, and began his prayer. In a short while he opened his breviary. He would offer matins for young McKay. He was going to have to administer a warning he did not relish.

It wasn't that he didn't like McKay. It was rather that there was something there he didn't understand. He wasn't sure what the fellow's motives were. He was talented, no denying that. He was faithful to his religious life, to all appearances. But . . . something else was present . . . some indefinable something that the father superior's long-practiced sensitivity detected.

Padre Bracciano had spoken to Richard's provincial about it in the summer. "I intend to ordain him," he had said. "I find nothing wrong in his conduct. But he seems—restless. I can't tell what he is thinking. I don't know." He had shrugged.

"I think I know what you mean," Father Provincial had said. "I know Richard pretty well. You talk to him. Challenge him. See what he's made of. Perhaps that's all he needs."

"He's got talent and ideas, so he has got to know what he's doing."

"Hmm . . . yes, he has always struck me as somehow immature."

"Exactly! He's untried, idealistic, oversensitive. And very strong in his thinking. I feel he'd do anything I asked him to, but—"

"I'll write to him myself, father. And I'll trust you to do the rest." Ordaining young men was no joke. It was Padre Bracciano's word that in actuality swayed superior officers and, through them, the ordaining bishop. Men who received orders from Collegio del-l'Annunziazione received the approval of the Church through him. The powers of the priesthood, eternal and irrevocable, came to whomever he approved, were in practice refused or delayed wherever he wrote the hesitating word. Padre Giorgio thought often of this immense responsibility, not only to the men involved, but to the Church. He prayed for his own prudence and for his young men. He prayed for their future and for the work that they would do in Germany and Italy and America—wherever they would be sent. It was a mighty thing, the confessions they would hear, the young people they would counsel, the masses they would say, the instructions they would preach in their accumulated lifetimes. By the formation he was trying to give them, he would share in all of it. Thousands of men and women around the world would be affected. His was a frightful task. An unfaithful priest, an unhappy priest, an incapable priest would cause indescribable sorrow. Some of his boys would be in that number. It was inevitable. . . . Which? If only there were a way of knowing!

He would see them walking into mass in the morning, see them kneeling in prayer—sometimes in drowsiness—at thanksgiving after mass, watch them stream into the refectory for meals or enter singly into his office for some trivial permission. He would correct their reading aloud in the refectory, their errors serving mass, their general household spirit. He scrutinized their class marks, talked to them about their courses, got to know, briefly, their dreams for the future. Along with the pride he felt in looking on idealistic, fine young men, there was the fear. Which one? They were full of faults. Hindemann was no student, DiGeraldo was forever careless, Carrozza resented authority, Peregrino was a griper, Baldini was frankly childish, Schwartz was a stubborn German. But you couldn't keep a man from the priesthood for being human. You gave him a chance, to test his good will and to assure yourself of his basic qualities, above all of good judgment, and then you watched him for improvement and watched him at his critical points. Finally, you left him in the Lord's hands, a piece of straw ready to be used. He might break or he might hold. As best you knew, he'd hold. Some would not.

Padre Bracciano had lived these thoughts so long he didn't think them consciously any longer. Consciously he only knew regret that he never had all the time he wished for talking with his boys. He tried to see them privately at least once a year, twice if possible. They could come in any time if special problems should arise: "My door is always open." But he had work with the Holy Office, with the Congregation of Religious, and with the Secretariate of State. He made up the community's *ordo* and handled numerous affairs for Father General and the Procurator. He was confessor to a convent of Italian nuns and helped out with confessions at two colleges. He was writing a book on the Church in Italy under Napoleonic rule. He met occasionally with consultors who were preparing the cause of canonization of the Venerable Alessandro Mantella, founder of the Fathers of the Annunciation, who had died in 1903. He got stuck with a great deal of "dirty work" from higher up, which he accomplished patiently, though not without jocose complaining. There were also the constant receptions and anniversaries of visiting prelates and superiors general, at which he was obliged to represent his own community. The work of the Lord, he often thought, keeps a man busy twenty-four hours in the day! A thousand cares pressed upon his mind, details an administrator dared not forget—details Padre Bracciano, who was not an administrator by temperament, had to key himself up to remember.

And, throughout all of this, his prayers, his office, his mass. Good example for the boys. The Religious Spirit maintained within the house. "You are in Rome. The center of Christendom. You must turn out the best. The best. Beacons to the world." So he unconsciously, now, frequently admonished himself.

Padre Giorgio's historically trained mind could be very sentimental. Large images attracted him—bold strokes that a more delicate sensitivity would find jarring or unworthy. For all his administrative closeness, Padre Bracciano was amazingly idealistic. He spoke to his men of grand themes: the cultural advantages of their stay in Rome, painting, sculpture, the Holy Father, churches, monasteries, architecture, currents of history. He announced once, on a house trip to St. Benedict's first monastery in the West at Subiaco: "The birthplace of modern civilization." He considered himself a model churchman, active, broad, cultured, fervent, disciplined, competent, prudent. Humbly he thought of himself as inclined to self-esteem, to a certain coldness, to an occasional feeling of antipathy towards one or another of the boys—which he speedily stifled and countered by some kind deed or word for the unsuspecting one—to a certain tendency to be caught up in affairs at the cost of long distractions when he tried to pray. Perhaps, too, he was a little soft—he sat in an easy chair to read in the evenings at his hardy age; he liked good dinners; there were the receptions which he partly loved, for the people he met there and the importance he felt, and partly hated. He felt he was frank and hated pretense, yielded only to prudence and diplomacy and the demands of social intercourse, and otherwise never violated truth.

And this afternoon, after matins, on which his attention was trying to concentrate, he would have a conference with another of—how many boys now in these fifteen years? Faces fluttered through his memory: teachers now, preachers, pastors. They sent him Christmas cards and mementos on his ordination anniversary. Many of them remained close friends, became even closer friends. These were his joy. All remained warm, all recalled with pleasure the splendid days of youth and Rome. They wrote little catch phrases in Italian in their letters—or in English or German—the things they had learned from one another in Rome and shared with him. It was a real fraternity within the larger fraternity of the community and the still larger one of the Church. *Romani!* His heart thrilled to the name and its significance.

There were two who had left. Had left the priesthood—and one of these the Church. Padre Bracciano still prayed for them. Someday they would come back. He devoutly hoped it. He was certain of it. They had been good boys under him. Who could have known? Then one had run off with a woman only eighteen months after ordination. That cut Padre Bracciano, personally, to the quick. It was a sore he dreaded to remember.

At the end of his second nocturn, Padre Giorgio rolled his thick wrist outwards and looked at his watch, which he wore on the inside of his wrist. The watch had a black face, gold hands; it had a gold band. His arm around it was hairy. Five minutes to six. He closed his breviary, brushed his eyelids closed with his right hand, then rested his forehead on the hand and prayed. He was nervous. He never liked these confrontations. He prayed for light, courage, meekness, understanding. Finally he arose, dismissing his restlessness, genuflected erectly in the aisle, and walked slowly, superiorly, to his office. McKay would be in at six. He sat at his desk, fiddled with a pencil, pulled at some notes on Cavour, shoved them aside, put his chin in his hands.

A knock came at the door. He lay down his pencil, folded his hands in front of him, his elbows on the arms of his desk chair, and shouted: *"Avanti!"*

The knock came again.

"Avanti! he shouted louder, a little off balance now.

The door opened slowly.

"You wanted me at six?"

"Come in, Padre Riccardo. You're just on time. Come in. Be seated."

"*Grazie.* Did you say *'avanti'* twice?"

"I certainly did," said Padre Bracciano agreeably, with a nod.

"I thought so. I wasn't sure." Richard had his hands on his knees, then pulled them up towards his lap. They were moist. He lifted them near his face, resting his elbows on the arms of the chair—a low, soft one, Padre Bracciano's reading chair. He would much have preferred just now a straight wooden one. He tried to sit erect.

"How are you, Padre Riccardo? Your classes interesting? It's been a long time since I've had you in to talk to you, hasn't it?"

Richard inwardly relaxed. Umberto had come to find him after lunch to tell him the boss wanted him at six. His heart had gone cold. All afternoon he had been restless. He knew it could be nothing; his turn was coming round. But the episode the other night frightened him. Or could it concern Mary? Had someone seen them talking and twisted things? Maybe some conversation had been reported—that had happened. Maybe Father Provincial had written something. . . . His painting? All morning Richard had worked with charcoal sketches in his room. Then he had turned to pencil. He designed cylinders, squares, tried to work in depth and arrangement. He had started on human figures, sketching muscles, cartilage, and bone. He had turned to drawing nudes. A female figure escaping from his pencil had, at first, embarrassed him. Then he kept resolutely on, drew a second, a third. He was going to be a painter. He knew what he was doing. Then thoughts of Mary Coleman came to him—her small, petite figure. The whole idea began to trouble him. What was a seminarian to do? Certainly no one would understand. . . . He continued, determined to conquer foolish fears. When he was finished, he tore up his sketches, the female ones in the littlest shreds, to make sure no one would misunderstand. Perhaps Padre Bracciano . . . impossible!

"I haven't really talked to you for six months, padre. Since last spring."

"Since last spring! You are right. And your classes now?" Padre Giorgio aimlessly twirled a yellow pencil. Richard watched it.

"Just fine." Richard tried to sit up more comfortably. He mentioned with ardor the professors he liked, to make up for naming the ones he didn't like. Padre Bracciano coughed at his criticisms, mild as they were.

"Hmm. Bottmann? His reputation is great, padre. Isn't he a consuitor for the Biblical Commission?"

Richard colored. "He's very conser—very old, padre."

"Well . . . mmm . . . yes. Good to make room for the younger men. New ideas, new approaches. The times do change."

"But always with prudence," Richard added, biting his lip.

"Yes, yes, prudence! Key to all the virtues. My, yes." Padre Bracciano was obviously disturbed. Richard felt the storm clouds gathering. He sat and waited. Padre Bracciano twirled his pencil more rapidly. He cleared his throat. "Padre . . ." He hesitated again. "I'll come directly to the point." Richard heard someone walking far down the hall. Night had fallen heavily outside. There was only the light overhead. "Your class is about to be ordained subdeacons this year, isn't it?"

Richard's heart fell, plummeting down. "*Si*, padre," he said.

There was a long silence while Padre Bracciano framed the words. No ordination? thought Richard. A delay? A refusal?

"And you'll be making petition then in March or April."

"*Si* . . . padre." Richard's breath was very short.

"Do you intend to make petition?"

Padre Bracciano was himself very nervous. Richard feared the worst. Involuntarily he swallowed; he couldn't answer.

"*Si*, padre."

"What I'm getting at—" Padre Bracciano tapped with his pencil. Richard looked into his brown eyes, at his cleanly shaven face, at his curly, wiry hair. Padre Bracciano chose his words and turned to Richard. "I'll state it frankly. Father Provincial and I talked last summer. He thinks it would be a good idea if I laid some things before you . . ."

Richard tried to look him straight in the eye.

"You are very talented." Padre Bracciano tapped once with his pencil.

Richard almost imperceptibly nodded. Then he tried not to blush.

"You have many ideas. Good ideas. I don't mean to say anything against your ideas . . . or your good will. I know you have good will." Padre Bracciano, looking away, nodded as if to say: that's the second thing. "I believe you would do anything I asked you to do." He tapped the third thing with his pencil and looked at Richard again.

Richard met his eyes but waited.

"But the priesthood is a tremendous step."

Richard swallowed.

"The priesthood is a tremendous step. You like to paint. Good. Good. Nothing wrong with painting. You do some writing, too. Fine. All this love for art is marvelous. It belongs to the Church. Why— look—look at all the things in Rome. Art belongs to the Church; we need more of it. But which is it—art or the priesthood? Now, I don't mean to be laying down an ultimatum," he added, waving the yellow pencil to clear the ambiguity. "Not at all. But you have got to be clear in your mind, Padre Riccardo; you have got to be clear."

"I know that, padre." Richard brushed a nervous hand through his hair.

"You have got to be clear. All the more so because you are out-spoken and have strong feelings. You are a very positive young man —sometimes when you talk to me it is as if *you* were the superior."

Richard tried to retain his composure.

"You are so very sure of things—that's what I told Father Provincial. . . . Will you obey? What would you do if you were for-bidden ever to paint again or ever to speak your mind?"

Richard assumed the question was rhetorical. Should he answer?

"Padre Riccardo, think of what your later life will be like." Padre Bracciano lay down the yellow pencil and leaned forward with his elbows on his knees, very low and familiarly. "We have a small community. Very small. Our needs just now are many. What if we could never free you for your painting? Oh, I know, Father

Provincial plans for you to study. But what if in the actual doing he cannot arrange it?"

Can you obey? Can you obey? The words rang across the silence and on down the corridors of Richard's tired mind. Can you obey?

"Look at Savonarola, Padre Riccardo. Look at all the great men of the Church. Fra Angelico. Fra Filippo Lippi. St. Thomas. Newman—there's a man for you. So what happens to them? The die is cast. What do they make of it? When the command is given, how do they react? Even if they are geniuses, do they rebel or do they obey? Some go one way, some go the other. Not that I'm saying you are one of these. I don't know what your talents are. You probably have too swelled a head already. But I want to use examples you will know. History is full of them. Now think. Subdiaconate is the final step. Irrevocable. I don't want you to make the step—"

Richard's heart began to freeze.

"—unless you've thought this through. . . . You're what? Twenty-four?"

"Twenty-five."

Padre Bracciano nodded. "Very young yet. It is a huge decision for a man of your abilities to make. I want you to know that. I think very highly of you. I told Father Provincial that. I told him I wanted to ordain you. I think you'll make a fine priest of the Annunciation. We agreed you should be faced with the alternatives."

"I'm grateful for your telling me."

"I would do it for any of the boys." Padre Bracciano sat back; his chair squeaked. He picked up his yellow pencil and fondled it. Richard stirred, then was still.

"Padre—have you any complaints against me? Anything specific?"

Padre Bracciano sat up. His brow was furrowed. "Umm . . . no, nothing specific. I hadn't thought of anything. No. As far as I can see," Padre Bracciano opened his hands and shrugged. "You observe the rule. You come to chapel, to meals. Your studies are satisfactory." He was in one of his enumerating patterns again. "I—I find you, as I say, a little difficult sometimes. I—can't say I agree with all of your ideas." He swung his head around to look at Richard, then away. In that moment Richard saw the secret. He grew both to sympathize with Padre Bracciano and to hate him.

"I'm young yet, padre."

"That's what I say," the superior took up quickly. "You'll change a lot of your ideas. You need experience yet."

Richard sat back. His superior was defensive. He wondered now whether to reveal what was troubling him most. He began to speak, but his lips closed again without a sound. He determined with his will.

"I have something to confess to you," he said very quietly.

"Um, what's that, padre?"

Richard looked away. He searched the window, but the night had closed it off. He bit his lip. He looked back at Father but didn't know how to begin.

"I was—very nervous the other night." He looked away and began talking rapidly. "I couldn't sleep. I—I went for a walk. Outside, in the city. Across the bridge to St. Peter's."

Padre Bracciano sat perfectly still.

"Without permission?"

"Yes."

"What time was this?" The chair creaked again.

"Two-thirty. I—I was back in less than an hour."

Padre Bracciano shifted weight. He swallowed, playing with his pencil. "You know the scandal possible from this? Cleric out at night, alone, without permission. You know what the vicariate would do if they heard of it?"

Richard nodded.

"Were you in your habit?"

Richard dropped his gaze. "No, padre."

The superior sat erect. "You know the seriousness of this or you wouldn't have come to me about it. I'm—grateful that you told me." He drummed with his pencil. Richard even heard the pencil's movements in the air. "Not—many would have done that. Yet if anyone had seen you and reported it! Not only you, but us, the whole community . . ." Padre Bracciano looked at Richard, long, into his eyes.

Visions passed before both their eyes. Padre Bracciano shuddered inwardly. Dreadful newspaper accounts framed themselves before him. The gossiping clerical tongues of Rome clacked in his ears. "I'm—I'm going to give you a penance, even though you came to me yourself. I want you to realize . . ." He shuddered. "I want you to say the Stations every day for a week. For two weeks. Will you do that?"

"I often say them anyway."

"No one will notice then. And—don't—do that again."

"I won't."

Padre Bracciano leaned back. "Well, then, padre, is that all?" He felt somehow closer to the young student than he had before. He felt better.

"There is . . . one thing else, padre . . ."

The superior sat in lazy silence for a moment. "What is it, padre?"

Richard shifted in his chair. The springs creaked. He thought. He knew it would descend like lightning. It was the one thing Padre Bracciano would shudder to hear. It was the one quality on which he prided himself above all others. Richard bit his lip. Out it came. "You don't really understand me . . . do you, padre?" He asked the question very softly.

Even so, the words hit Padre Bracciano deadweight. Richard felt the pain. He drew a breath and watched the older man's expression change from surprise to pain and then to pride and composure. The older man breathed quickly.

"I don't mean it as any offense, padre! We're just different. I don't feel trusted. I feel there are some things . . ."

Richard wanted to fend off the rising pride. But he didn't know how much to reveal. He didn't want the superior to know he had talked to Father Milton or that Father Provincial was in touch with him.

"I don't mean ancient troubles. They're past: the permission about the North American College, my friends at the Academy. They're past. I don't mean those. . . . What do I mean?" Richard looked for words. He plunged blindly ahead. In a crucial moment he might make or break the year. *Be honest!* Padre Benedetto said. *Speak up!* Richard swallowed and continued. To hell with consequences, *speak!* "Maybe, maybe it's our culture. Maybe Americans are just—different. Odd and different. *Pazzi americani,* they say everywhere. . . . Or maybe it's our personalities. . . . Please, padre, let me be frank and open. I can't stand not to be trusted. Maybe that's my fault. Maybe I should be bigger than that. But it gets me down. When everything a fellow does is made to look like cheating somehow, or as if disapproved, or out of the ordinary and not conforming, it's—very hard. You don't know where to turn. Are you right or wrong? You don't know. All you know is the trouble and suspicion. That's why I . . . thought it would be good to talk. That's it—just talk and get it said . . . then we're better off. Even if you don't like some things. Even if we argue."

Padre Bracciano had regained the mastery. But a hurt rankled him and, in spite of himself, he said: "You don't feel I trust my students?"

"Oh no! I don't mean that. Not that way. I mean . . . I don't feel that we're communicating. That you understand me or I you. I want to be like water for you to see through—I don't mind that. But I feel as though there's something in me you can't put your finger on—that worries you. I feel a—suspicion."

Padre Bracciano flushed a little. He looked at Richard cautiously. "I—it's not that at all. I do find . . . moments . . . when . . . I'm not sure what you're thinking. When I know you'd obey, but just *something* about . . ."

"I've felt those moments, padre. I've felt them! But what did you expect of me? I can't possibly be expected to agree with you on everything."

Padre Bracciano flushed, and Richard felt as though the words might have landed on him like a lash.

"You can't demand my mind, only my obedience."

"But you must strive for obedience of judgment, too. That is the highest—"

"Only of the practical judgment," countered Richard, sitting up. "To *do* what the superior wants, and to know that *that in particular* happens to be the Lord's will whether it happens to be the wisest thing or not. *Not* of the speculative judgment . . ."

"You needn't instruct me in obedience!" rose Padre Bracciano's tone to silence him.

"I'm sorry." Richard lowered his voice and eyes.

"That's what I mean—that—that *rashness*. You sit there and tell me. I can't understand that! When we were seminarians. . . . You're the subject, and you talk to the superior. . . . I don't mind, you see, but what is going to happen to you in the future?"

"But how can frankness hurt? How can it hurt if I speak man-to-man to you and then obey anything you decide?"

"Religious life is not democracy, remember that! There's none of this man-to-man, none of this naturalist, humanist . . ."

"I don't mean democracy, padre; honestly I don't mean that. Politics is one thing, religious life is another. Americans are the same as others in religious life. But you have to admit we must live in charity. It's father to son, sons to father. How can we do it if we don't speak up? How can we do it? How can we do it if the sons are not allowed to be men? How can we do it if there's authority and distrust but never love?"

Padre Bracciano was silent. He was silent a long time. The discussion had taken a new turn, a turn he could not oppose. He didn't speak. He rubbed his eyes beneath his rimless glasses. He lay his yellow pencil down upon the blotter on his desk. Richard wondered what all the notes were on the desk, if Padre Bracciano really enjoyed writing his books on history. He even found himself wondering about the light-green color of the walls in the office, when they had been painted. The ceiling light shone down on Padre Bracciano's curly, stiff hair and on his shining forehead. It made his skin seem darker than it was. All the while, underneath, Richard knew the tenor of the coming year was being decided, there in the heart and mind of his superior. He wondered what was going on there, what memories lived there, what pains. He suddenly wondered where Padre Bracciano had been born, and where his family was, and what they were like, and if they were proud of him. He was basically a humble man . . .

Finally Padre Bracciano spoke, nodding slowly. " 'Not like the rulers of the gentiles.' "

Richard sat back. "Like—the monks, and St. Benedict, or like Teresa and her nuns . . ."

"But *that* takes saints," Padre Bracciano cautioned him.

"But at least openness and frankness where there are not saints."

"I would want my boys to be open and be frank with me. This has come as somewhat of a shock. . . . But you are right, Padre Riccardo. I have not been trusting you. I suppose I have been—at fault."

Someone walked by in the hall outside.

"I haven't always made it easy for you," Richard said. "I'm sorry."

"*Basta!*" said the superior quietly. "It's done." He shrugged. "We will talk more. I called you in . . . to reach some basic issues, and . . . it seems we have achieved them," he smiled. "Not as we thought, but, *beh*! Here we are." He shrugged again and looked up at Richard. "We will talk more." He looked at his watch. "It's time for rosary."

He slapped his hands down on his knees and sat there silently a while. "*Allora?*" He shrugged. Richard hesitated about asking him for permission to enter the Borghese exhibition. His sense of competition, his vanity, his zeal urged him to ask. But he was afraid that one more permission would be one too many. He overrode his desires and decided not to ask. The priest was waiting.

"Nothing, padre. No, nothing. . . . May I have your blessing?"

"*Certo,*" said the priest, rising.

Richard knelt at Padre Bracciano's feet.

"*Benedictio Dei omnipotentis, Patris, et Filii, et Spiritus Sancti, descendat super te et maneat semper.* Amen."

"Thank you, padre, for calling me in."

"*Niente. Beh! Buona sera.* I have confessions, so I'll be out tonight. Keep up the good work."

"*Buona sera.*" As he closed the door, the universe fell from Richard's shoulders. He hurried down the cool corridor filled with an immensity of promise. He regretted that he hadn't asked to enter the exhibition. But mostly he was glad. He knew now that he could talk freely with his superior.

18

THE NEXT DAY was a bright, brisk day. Light streamed into the refectory at lunchtime from the small square windows high up in the wall. Conny, who was a waiter, came over to Richard's table.

"Eat light, Ricky. We want to beat those fellows this afternoon."

"You really want to get them, don't you, Conny?"

"Dang right! I don't just like to *play* ball, I like to *win*." Conny was holding a platter in each hand and gesturing with his head. "Frankie and me got it figured out. If we keep Umberto underneath, never move him out, and you keep cutting back from forward to help with the shooting, well, we can keep poppin' from outside. If we're hot, well murder them!"

"Yeah, but if we're cold?"

"Why do you always have to see the bright side of things?"

"Go fill your platters. Just teasing you. I'd like to beat them, too. Really beat them. I haven't felt so much energy in years."

"You better feel it this afternoon. We need at least twenty points from you. Me and Frankie—"

"I know, you have it figured out. I'll get ten for *you*, too!" Richard pointed laughingly with his fork.

"Get 'em for Frankie," Conny tossed his head proudly. "I was out shooting this morning. Hotter than a firecracker! We're gonna win; I feel it!"

His tablemates were calling him to hurry with the platters. He looked over to see if the superior's table was watching him. Then he turned up his nose to his own table and said: "Aw-right, aw-right!

Hold your pants on!" He turned to Richard and said, since his table-mates were all Italians, "They prob'ly think I said *certamente, signori!*" He winked to Richard, bowed unctuously, and swept away.

"I doubt it," Richard said. "G'wan. Beat it."

"Thanks! Remember: *Be hot! We're gonna win!*" Conny was shouting over his shoulder. He nearly ran into Cesare, coming the other way. *"Mi scusi . . ."*

"Sure, sure. We'll win," Richard repeated after him, smiling. He turned back to the conversation of his table. He broke for himself a thick piece of Italian bread and asked for the olive oil and the salt for his salad. He helped himself to some more *pastasciutta*, too.

Lunch was over. Richard put his gym shoes and jersey in a canvas bag; met Johann, Umberto, Frankie, and Conny; and soon they were out on the asphalt court of the North American College, shooting, running, conferring, waiting nervously for the game to start.

After the first quarter, it didn't seem that Conny had been right —at all. The North Americans, in red pull-overs, had a solid sixteen-to-eight lead. The game had started very slowly and sloppily.

Conny was fired up. "We're nervous!" he gestured in the huddle. He pounded his fist into his hand. "That's the whole dang trouble. Trying too hard! Now *relax*. I mean, geez . . . we want some fight. But not too much. I mean, *relax!* Give 'em lots of room. Go easy. Johann, don't run after them so much. *Get the rebounds.* There's the whole secret right there. The *rebounds*. . . . Who you watching, Ricky?"

Richard was breathing heavily. He had a dirty smear across his face—the lawn near the court was muddy and slippery from yesterday, and once the ball had gotten wet. He rubbed his hand across his cheek. "Twenty-three. Fellow with the glasses."

"Switch to that forty-nine. He's hit three jump shots in a row. That's murder."

"O'Halloran?"

"I don't know what his name is. Forty-nine. Johann—"

"That's O'Halloran. The blond fellow."

"Johann, you take Ricky's man. You got it? He's fast. Watch him. Got it?"

Frankie butted in. "Look, Conny. Come outside a little more. Meet them right at half court. They're good. They can shoot from there."

"But it's not the defense, though, Frankie! They've only got sixteen points! It's the bloody offense."

Richard stood listening with his hands on his hips. His breath had nearly returned. The Annunziazione squad was wearing blue, without numerals. He watched Conny's excited face, his clear reddish-brown eyes, his freckles. *He really wants to win! It's a big thing to him.*

Conny looked right at him, challenge and laughter in his eyes. "Where're those thirty points, kid? Seems I've only seen four!"

"Coming. Coming!" laughed Richard. "Just hold your pants on." He bowed ceremoniously. He had never scored thirty points in his life. He had a good jump shot, that was all.

The whistle blew. The red jerseys were already on the court. Conny started a "Hail Mary" in the blue huddle. Richard reached into the pile of hands.

"Now remember. Fight! Relax! Take it easy!"

Contradictions? Richard thought, walking out to his forward spot. *Naw, just Conny.*

"I've got the redhead," a North American said, and switched with the man who had been near Richard. "Hi." He and Richard shook hands.

"Good game, Peter. Nice shot you have there."

"Thanks. Thought all you did was study theology. You're doing all right yourself."

"I'm full of secrets."

The whistle blew. They jockeyed for footing around the white ring. Umberto jumped very clumsily, so of course the Americans took the jump. They passed it downcourt speedily and scored.

"For cripe's sake!" Conny said. "*Cripes!* Johann, get your man! *Jee*-pers!"

Conny and Frankie brought the ball downcourt. Over to Johann. Richard broke across the middle. A bounce pass. Richard jumped, turned: two points! It felt very good to see the ball swish cleanly through the net.

"Six, Conny," he said. "Start relaxin'."

"You've got a long way to go!" Conny said without a smile. He never looked up but pointed towards his man coming down the court.

Richard picked up his own man. Conny stole a pass. He dribbled all the way down the court, alone until the very end. He lay the ball up. He turned, watching it. It rolled off. An American grabbed the rebound. Conny smashed his fist into his hand and stamped his foot in frustration. He ran, steaming, up the court to get his man.

Richard scored five more points that quarter. Frankie had ten, four baskets in a row at one stretch. He had a lovely one-hander from the circle.

"Nice shooting, Frankie boy!"

"Bee-*u*tiful!" Conny told him. "We're only five down. Keep it up! Keep it up. Nice covering, Johann. Nice rebounding, Bertie. We're going to get them! Watch!"

Johann was very serious. He never once smiled as they played. He frowned at Conny's praise, though it meant a lot to him. His blond wavy hair was bedraggled; he wore it very long—he was almost vain about it—and now he had to keep pushing it back into place with a sweep of his hand. He was a little fellow, short, thin, and wiry. He had on a pair of black pants. His skin was very white and reddened easily when he blushed or overexerted. He blew on his hands and shifted his feet in nervousness.

"Don't get tired *now*!" Conny warned. "And *you*—get those nineteen points, Ricky, or your name is mud."

"Ten for you!" Richard nodded. "After that lay-up you booted."

Conny colored. Richard slapped him on the back.

The whistle blew.

Richard had ten points in the third quarter. Rarely had he felt so good. He played easily, lightly; he didn't once overreach himself. He seemed to sense where the ball was going, who was going to pass to whom. He intercepted three passes. He found his own dribble working smoothly. Once he had changed hands and at the same time changed his pace and had floated in easily, alone, for an easy lay-up. His other points were on his jump shot. Conny was feeding him and, what was better, setting him up by feinting a drive through the middle. Richard waited in the corner, feinted towards the basket, and rolled out swiftly to the circle, took the pass, and jumped. He missed some, and Umberto wasn't getting too many rebounds, but the score was now fifty-one to fifty.

"*One* point," Conny was saying. "One measly point! Now come on! Pound them in the ground. Keep it up, Ricky! This time, instead of breaking for the circle, start out from there. When I give you the pass, fake your jump, then drive. Got it? Drive opposite of me. Got it, Ricky? Let's go!"

"Conny, you're going to win this for us yet."

"I *know* we're going to win. I *told* you so. C'mon. *C'mon!*"

Richard knelt to tie his shoe. The others waited impatiently. The referee bounced the ball with his two hands and caught it several times. He let the whistle fall from his mouth. Richard pulled the cords with his stiff fingers. He felt nervousness rising now within him. Ten minutes would tell the tale! Every play would count. A sizable crowd of spectators now lined the court. The *pock* of handballs hitting on the nearby walls sounded in the afternoon. Fellows in red and white jerseys kicked a soccer ball on the adjoining field, running cautiously to keep their balance in the mud. The sky was pale blue and misted. The sun was warm. The whole day seemed like a dream. He rose. He should talk to Padre Bracciano more often. The referee put his whistle to his lips. Ten players tensed. The whistle sounded, the ball went in the air. Umberto tapped.

Richard stole the rebound just before an American clutched it. A fast dribble, a change—he was alone with one defender racing to catch up with him. Two steps, the white line. Richard went in the air, turned slowly and easily. Underhand. Two points! The whistle screeched: take a free throw! Richard dropped it in. Fifty-three, fifty-one.

A moment later Conny passed to him. Richard threw it off to Johann. Johann feinted, passed to Frankie, Frank in to Richard,

Richard dribbled, spun, underhand. The ball spun round the inside of the hoop. In! Two points.

As the Americans brought the ball downcourt, Conny stole it. The teams formed, the Americans in their zone. The ball passed from side to side. Conny got it. He motioned Richard to come out. Richard came to the head of the circle, Johann raced in. Conny feinted, gave to Richard. Richard feinted behind Conny, broke the other way, dribbled, leapt, turned with a smooth underhand. Fifty-seven, fifty-one.

The Americans called time out.

Conny was delirious. "Ricky! Ricky! How I love you!"

"Really, now." Richard, too, was happy. The five of them grew strong, agile, quiet.

The time-out did no good. The Americans scored twice, but Umberto put in a rebound and Frankie scored again. A moment later Richard tried a one-hand set from the side. A perfect swish.

"Two more!" Conny said.

"Keep counting!" Richard hollered, but afraid now he wouldn't get the thirty. He had twenty-eight, with ninety seconds left. His hands were moist. The ball bounded towards him. He reached. He fumbled it. Pile-up. Jump!

He wiped his hands on his trousers. He jumped. He lost it. The game shifted rapidly. Then he was alone under the basket Conny shot. The ball fell from the rim. Richard put it in.

"You did it! You did it!" Conny shouted, jumping in the air.

Then Richard had another basket and Frankie had one. The Americans scored three, but it was too late. The whistle blew from the bench. They streamed for the shower room.

"Good game!"

"Good game!"

"Nice shooting, Ricky."

"Nice playing, fellows."

"Good hustle!"

"Yeah, thanks. Conny, you got my towel?"

"Frankie has it."

In the showers they sang and frolicked.

"I *knew* we would! I *knew* we would!" Conny shouted.

The noise rose above the sound of the water and the steam. Richard was overelated. Everything was so good! The smell of soap, running water, wet towel, sweaty clothes, clouded mirror—everything spoke of victory and joy. His mind seemed faraway, removed.

The North Americans invited them for tea and cookies. They sat around and talked. Richard's feet were very sore, and he rested them on their sides. Conny explained the strategy and his prediction. Well-wishers slapped the winners on the back. Especially those who said: "I didn't see the game, but I heard you won. Heard you had—was it twenty-five points, Ricky?"

It was an enormous temptation to correct them with a loud *thirty-two*! "Yeah," he said, "a good day." Cheating—but a man's entitled to some pride.

Then, afterwards, going home, down on the corner below the tunnels, Conny was talking excitedly, simulating a hook shot from the street. Brakes screeched; a truck racing to beat a bus to the piazza hit Conny with a dead sound and pulled him underneath. Frankie dropped his bag and the basketball and screamed to stop traffic. Conny lay there alone. His legs were soon swimming in blood. His cassock was torn, his gym shoes and towel were sprawled out in the street.

"Conny! Conny!" Richard shouted. He ran out and knelt beside him, screaming in his ears. Johann ran for help. Conny didn't move.

Richard, sick, arose and tried to keep the crowd away. A policeman came—no help at all. A priest came, looked at Conny, and anointed him. The sound of the truck went round and round in Richard's ears. At last the ambulance came.

19

HE PROBABLY will never walk again."

Padre Benedetto took off his steel-rimmed glasses, looked at them in the light. He spat lightly upon them, took out his handkerchief, and rubbed them stiffly. "How far along was he? First year, you said?"

"He only came in October. He was so happy yesterday and so excited. He won the game for us. I—didn't think he'd live. I thought he was dead in the street. The truck crushed him like—a fly. Padre Bracciano stayed with him all through the night. He's very broken up. Big circles under his eyes. He's down there again today. He'll have to tell Conny's parents."

Padre Benedetto had his glasses back on. "They'll probably be flying him home eventually, won't they?" He squinted. He was very serious, yet so concerned about his glasses.

"When he's strong enough. That truck was really huge . . ."

"He'll never be ordained now."

"Impossible."

"And yet, if the Lord would want him . . ."

"Padre, Conny was talking about leaving anyway. He hadn't told anybody yet—just Frank and me. He—wasn't very happy."

"His decision will be doubly difficult. What can a man do without any legs?" The old man looked at Richard with concern. "The Lord breaks us like bits of straw. Can the boy take it?"

"It will work out. He'll be O.K."

"It will. The Lord labors under only one necessity—to love. He can't do any other thing. The boy will find that, if he looks."

"He's a good fellow. A little boyish. Immature."

Padre Benedetto smiled. He relaxed. He closed his hands together on his chest, sat back, and asked Richard about himself.

They talked for a while of trivialities, Richard's painting, the vacation, school's beginning soon, the examinations in four weeks. The atmosphere of the room was easy and agreeable. The talk flowed. Only the quiet sound of their voices passed within the walls. The old priest was even more than usually kind, a little reticent and subdued. His face was towards the boy.

"I had a good talk with Padre Bracciano."

"Did you?" nodded the priest with lively interest flashing in his eyes.

"I feel very happy about it."

"I told him—just how I felt. I said I didn't think a house could work on suspicion and fear . . ."

"You told Padre Bracciano this? What did he say?" asked the old priest with a smile. "I can't imagine him relishing it."

"He was very good, padre. He wants to be a father to the fellows; he really wants to—I saw that. He is basically very humble, and he heard me out. He could have told me off, you know."

"Yes," smiled Padre Benedetto. "The wonder is he didn't."

"No! He was really very nice."

Padre Benedetto shrugged. "I don't mean to deny it, Riccardo. We shall see. But I'm very glad you spoke to him. It's a very good thing. Especially for you."

"I thought you'd think it rash."

"You're not rash, Riccardo! You're too timid."

"Timid!"

"You're twenty-five. You should be master of any situation, talk back to anybody. Instead you're too timid. You know you shouldn't be, and so sometimes you do rash things. If you were bolder on the instant, speaking out the truth, you'd be less rash at other times."

"I don't believe it. Too timid!"

"They fill you too full of docility and meekness. I'd like to see some men, some argument and boldness among you."

"You want me to get kicked out? Didn't we agree I should be quiet this year?"

Padre Benedetto smiled. "You are like a seesaw, aren't you? Too meek and then too bold."

"I positively don't understand myself."

"Who does? You'll learn, Riccardo. If you're honest."

Richard shifted his weight. "I have to tell you about something else." The sun was shining brightly through the window of the white cell. "I did a crazy thing the other night. I got up at two a.m. and went for a walk over to St. Peter's. Outside. Without my cassock."

He looked up at Padre Benedetto, who sat impassive, looking at his hands in his lap.

"Did anybody see you?"

"No. But I told Padre Bracciano about it."

There was a long silence. Richard wondered what he could be thinking and began to be afraid.

"And what did you—do on this walk?"

Richard flushed. "I just—thought."

"You got back with no one seeing you?"

"I think so."

His chair squeaked as Padre Benedetto relaxed again. "Good. We shall forgive it. But, Riccardo!"

"I won't. Don't worry. I feel so much better now. Now that I can talk to Padre Bracciano. I really think I can. I didn't realize how much it could get me down, being under suspicion so much."

Padre Benedetto shook his head, agreeing. "Be honest with yourself."

"That's so hard when you don't understand what you are."

"Men are like mountains of many levels, Riccardo. You never know where you are until you find your powers and one by one distinguish them. You come at last to the center."

"How do you do it? How do you get there?"

"In six easy lessons? You think it can be told in words?" Padre Benedetto laughed. He began to cough and brought out his white handkerchief from his sleeve. Wiping his lips, he said: "You want everything clear and bright and shining, don't you, Riccardo?"

Richard flushed. "How can you aim unless you know the goal?"

"But in this quest you don't know the goal. Because the goal is you. Each man has to find himself. Each man has to go alone."

"Your voyage, isn't it?"

"What's that?"

"Nothing. Just something Paolo said."

"Paolo Veronese?" When Richard nodded, Padre Benedetto went on: "He's a really good friend, isn't he?"

"There could hardly be a better. Honest. Kind."

"No, Riccardo, you can't know what maturity is until you find it. You can't find it with words. You can only do it in activity, in the actual taking of possession. Here. Here is an example." The old man thought a moment.

"Take a young man and a young woman who are in love. Is their love strong enough for them to marry? So. Is their love physical attraction? Is it passion and desire? Is it because of qualities of intellect or culture? Is it because of health or money or position? Is it in the Lord?" The priest looked at the wall for a moment. He could think of nothing more. "All these things are important, Riccardo. A man would not marry a woman without considering all of them, in his way. Yet how do a man and woman know? Really, how do they know?

"When they are young and in love, everything goes splendidly. We know that even in the novitiate. Everything is harmony. But do you know how they find out what their love really is? When one by one every element crumbles in their hands. When age takes away youth or sickness takes away health. When habit wears down the delicacy of desire. When money fails. As each level collapses, if the love remains, then the two know that it always existed on a deeper level. They can fall back upon it." Padre Benedetto illustrated with his five fingers, tips placed against the tips of his other hand. "Originality seems to disappear; intelligence that seemed quick now seems ordinary. In a year's time, husband and wife know every idea the other ever had. It happens even in a monastery, doesn't it?" His eyes twinkled.

Richard smiled wanly. "Conversation can get pretty difficult."

"Love must be deeper then. Contradictions measure its depth." Richard rubbed his chin, listening.

Padre Benedetto drummed his aged fingers on his knee for a moment. "God made the universe, I think, on one theme. Everything points to it. Love—free, superfluous—made to suffer." The priest thought as he spoke. "God is love. The Trinity is like a fire. The universe is something extra, something superfluous, which leaps from their love. Love has to do creative things, unnecessary things." Padre Benedetto thought of something else, began to say it, and stopped. Richard shifted his weight.

"Then, Riccardo . . . there is something else. The universe is competitive. The Lord wanted beauty. That meant variety and friction. The world isn't reasonable. Life is harsh . . . so creatures are called upon to love in suffering, too: to do the more than reasonable, to give, to bear the pain. You needn't, Riccardo. You can spend your days fighting the universe if you like. You can hate it. But if you are willing to love, you can own everything. Everything is yours and you are God's. It depends on your response, Riccardo."

"The other night I was so confused. I felt nothing, I knew nothing—only the most terrible dryness and desolation. I knew I could accept. But there was no comfort, only coldness."

"What else would you desire? Have you ever been so humble as you've been the past few weeks? Have you ever been more watchful for the movements of the Lord, more distrustful of your own emotions and desires? Have you ever been more distant from counterfeits? More cold and dark and pure?"

"Padre, you talk so backwards!"

"I?"

"To tell me to be happy when I am unhappy, content when I am desolate . . ."

"What else? Do you wish to live by faith? Or do you wish to live by emotions, or by complacency, or by intelligence? How do you wish to live?"

"Always questions for me, padre—never answers?"

"Ah! You are a slippery one! Won't you face the answers?"

"You want me to say 'faith' and then agree with you. That is hard!"

"I want you to say nothing, Riccardo *mio*. I want you only to consider how you wish to live."

"If I say 'by faith' . . ."

There was a silence.

"The Lord will come take everything. Love will come take everything."

"Absolutely everything," Richard said slowly.

"Everything."

They sat in silence for a moment. "How do you know?"

The priest nodded to his desk. "There is my master. It's all there. If you know how to look."

"So love is everything."

"Suffering love."

"Why do you stress the negative?"

"I'm only being truthful. You have to die to live."

Richard looked out the window thoughtfully.

"Love is everything," said the old priest slowly. "Love purifies, love liberates. It frees men and makes them expand. It is tender because it springs from pain. It enlarges the beloved and the lover. It makes both realize how beautiful they are. It makes them throw their heads back with pride, look into the sky, forget their fears and loneliness and insecurity. Love somebody and see the difference it makes to him. And to you. See the suffering it brings." The old man's voice spoke the words distinctly, slowly, almost laboriously. "You can love when you cannot feel. When you cannot think. When you cannot find God, you can always find your fellows. Even in your sleep you can love. Riccardo, you can take love as a star on the darkest nights. It is a borrowed light, not intellectual and clear, but sure and full of harmony. Love, and your life is worth its pain. Do not love, and you run counter to the universe."

"How can you be so strong?"

"Read the Scriptures, Riccardo. Listen. Think. What else of value is there? Measure up the world and weigh it. There is only one secret. Behind everything there is suffering love."

Richard pulled on the fingers of his left hand for a moment. He shifted his weight. He wanted to tell him about Mary Coleman but was embarrassed. Yet he knew he couldn't leave the room without telling him. "Padre," he began. "I have something difficult to try to say." He knew he was blushing, and his tongue wanted to stammer. "I met—a girl, Mary Coleman, in a store here. She's a painter, an American; she likes art. Well, we talked." The words tumbled out. "I know it's silly, but—as a matter of fact—well—I—in a way fell in love with her. I only saw her once, I mean—there was nothing to it. I mean, I just liked her, and it's been troubling me."

"I understand, Riccardo."

"I was just very tried, and upset, and cold. I've been so confused about my painting and this battle with Padre Bracciano—and—and everything! That night outside was the high point. I was afraid I was about to give up. I couldn't take it any more."

"I know."

A question leapt to Richard's eyes.

"You are very young, Riccardo." He almost said "immature"; Richard had said it of Conny; Richard thought he would and blushed. "You don't seem to grasp what is going on within you. A crisis was inevitable. The Lord is sure to try everybody to the break-ing point."

"It was very dark. I was very much confused."

"Of course."

"Do you think it will be over now?"

The good priest laughed. He lifted his hands to his face, pulled a white handkerchief from his sleeve, and laughed. "Over? Over? My lad, it's just begun! You've tasted nothing yet. Wait until the pain begins!"

Richard blushed crimson.

"These things take time. How well do you possess yourself? How much do you know of the Lord? You are an infant at the breast. He's only just begun to wean you, with a little bitters to make you turn away, to stand alone."

"That's why the loneliness?"

"God is not a body, not a prompter of emotions. How could you come to Him by sensibilities? How could you possibly know Him by emotions? You have got to move past all that, as He directs. Of course you're lonely. Do not rush the process. Be simple. Be faithful. His movements within you and without will teach you what to do."

"There are so many movements! In theory it is easy . . ."

"Ah, you will learn. In the beginning all is difficult. You do not even know yourself. The life of faith is not an easy road. Illusion is a million times more common. Superstition, Riccardo, selfishness, delusion—there is much of it! Much! In all of us."

"But if it is so hard . . . if there are so few . . . then—what does God . . ."

Padre Benedetto shrugged. *"Chi lo sa? Chi lo sa?* How God will judge? Perhaps God asks the barest minimum of faith, of love. He knows what we are made of, what our preoccupations and desires are. But some few must respond to Him totally. Some few must, must they not?"

"I desire to," said Richard seriously.

"Ah, do you really? You will suffer much," nodded the aged man.

20

RICHARD ALWAYS WONDERED when he came to the North American College what non-Americans thought of the immense, spacious building. From the outside, the buff brick building was huge and overwhelming, built in sprawling wings from a central box. The grounds were large enough for a green soccer field, handball and basketball courts, and a little gardening. The inner courtyard had a pool, walks, trees, and shrubs. Around the courtyard, upstairs, was a plate-glass corridor. Inscriptions of United States dioceses were graven on the walls; busts of bishops and cardinals were there for emulation. Plate glass, shiny metal railings, soft dark-red curtains, spaciousness, marble, a touch everywhere of the lavish and the big—what did they think of the taste and image presented by North America? What did they think of the witness to Christian poverty?

Beside Richard in the new auditorium sat an African, thin, small, very black in color, his head small and round. Johann, on his other side, sat talking rapidly to him in kitchen-Italian. Richard rearranged the coat on his lap and turned to look at the Irishman on his right.

"Excuse me . . . you're from the Irish College? What part of Ireland are you from?"

"You know Ireland, do you now?" smiled the fair, blue-eyed Irishman.

Richard smiled. "American Catholics are obliged to."

"They are now. . . . By whom?"

"It's written up in the Councils of Baltimore," Richard said. "No child shall be confirmed or receive Holy Communion until he be able to name the counties of Ireland in order."

The Irishman looked at him oddly. "Now that does sound like a wise ruling. It's second best to being in Ireland, isn't it?"

Richard laughed. "But aren't most good things the Irish do done away from Ireland?"

"Such as now . . ."

"Oh, Irish literature. O'Connor, O'Casey . . . Joyce."

"I thought you meant good things."

"Oh . . . what do you think of Joyce then?"

"Well now, we probably don't think he's as great as he's made out to be. He was a very mixed-up man."

"Have you read much in . . . Joyce? Or much in literature in general?" Richard asked.

"Some. I like to read a lot. Perhaps most of the lads . . ."

"You have a big library at the college?"

"Standard, I would think."

"In literature?"

"You mean novels—and poetry?" The Irishman flushed.

Richard nodded.

"I guess we have a few. Scott, Chesterton. . . . See here. We don't have much time to read. Theology, you know. There isn't a great deal of time to be reading. Later on, maybe." The Irishman shifted his weight.

"That's as most colleges in Rome," Richard said. "The reason I ask is that it strikes me how poor most seminary libraries are. In literature, I mean. In modern studies. They have lots of old stuff." He broke into a grin. "They're complete up to 1904."

The Irishman looked at him.

The lights dimmed. The audience stirred and grew silent. The curtain began to part. Richard knew the Irishman hadn't enjoyed the conversation. He guessed that he himself was being what Conny would call pretentious and superior. He sat back. His mood was very meditative.

The curtain parted on a lovely scene: a winter scene of snowdrift and pine tree and, far away, the moon. The audience applauded. The designer had shown restraint and taste, had been severe and suggested the coldness and crispness of winter on the snows.

The program was like a television Christmas show, a variety hour. A chorus, wearing now ski clothes, now suits and ties, now sports shirts and dungarees, sang favorite Christmas songs: religious, folk, nonsense. A master of ceremonies in black suit and white tie moved the show along with a flourish, reading from a witty, amusing script and introducing the performers. A tall seminarist in dungarees came forward at one point to lead a Negro spiritual; he sang with a moving bass voice and with intensity; the chorus responded with a quiver or with force, as the lines directed. A quartette sang several humorous songs and had to do them over and over for the encores. Another soloist, short and nervous, sang of Santa Claus; still another, in suit and tie, of the manger. Sleigh bells jangled, winter wonderlands spread their enchantment. Snow fell in the background of the stage quietly, effectively. Trains chugged and whistled as the chorus executed fantasy numbers and got Santa's sleigh sailing through the air. It was a pleasant hour and a half. Every touch to the show was professional. The talent was adequate, often excellent. A lot of talent on the stage, a lot of youth, Richard thought as he sat there watching—a lot of talent and energy in the darkened audience, too. A thousand young men willing to be chaste, to be poor, to obey—shock troops to go to every corner of the world. Moments of youth and joy sparkled in young eyes as singers or dancers entered into the magic of the stage. In their worldly costumes, they recovered a moment of imagination and initiative; they had conceived, written, and were acting out something of their own—a break from their ordinary, prosaic life, because now they were young and alive, now they were free and creative . . . and what would become of them?

As the last song of the first act drew to an end, he suddenly thought how Mary Coleman would enjoy a show like this. He wondered what her Christmas had been like. He wondered if there was some sort of an American Christmas party, on the Via Veneto or somewhere, where she might be going. He wondered if she was dating. He had been thinking of a thousand excuses to pass her shop and visit her again. Each time he went out in the city, his thoughts pictured how far she was away and how he could get there. He thought he better check his feelings. I'm lonely, he thought, and I desire comfort; that's not good for her or me. His fingers gripped the armrest of his seat. I don't think I'd better ask permission to see her. Not only for permission's sake—for *my* sake. I like her too much—it's foolishness! But I can't help it. The best thing is distance and time. Forget about her. Or try to. And keep away.

The lights went on and the theater began to stir. He had been thinking about her on his way down the hill from the North American College when Conny had been hit. He tried again to forget her. He tried to wonder how Conny was. Maybe he could go to visit him tomorrow. He was surprised how much he had come to admire him. Before, he used to think that he was cheap and substanceless. Now? He had seen the will power and energy he possessed. Richard felt humiliated by the pride that had kept him from understanding Conny. Conny was right: He was full of pretentiousness and superior feelings. Conny saw and felt things. Conny was a very living human person, but it had taken the crushing of his legs to make Richard care.

"Richard!"

Richard didn't know where the voice was coming from.

"Richard!"

He turned and saw George three rows behind him. The African flashed a white smile.

"Yes, it's you! I thought so, by the back of your head."

"How are you, George? Where have you been? I haven't seen you."

"Come out in the aisle where we can talk."

Richard excused himself past the African sitting on his left and climbed out into the crowded aisle.

"How have you been?"

"O.K.," replied George with the American expression, showing the light side of his hands in a shrugging gesture. "I was sick for a week. Then I didn't see you at the University."

"It's pretty hard, with my classes upstairs."

"And mine downstairs."

"How are you now? How do you feel? What was wrong?"

"Something I ate." George dismissed it with his hand. "I'm fine now."

"You really must have eaten something."

"Couldn't stop the dysentery," George grinned. "Stomach flu or something. . . . I wish we could get together."

"So do I. It's almost hopeless between classes. It takes the ten minutes to fight the stairways."

"During the holidays perhaps? I mean after the semester examinations."

"You haven't any free hours during the week, have you?"

"Not in first year," George said. "Only if a professor doesn't come."

"Yes, I recall!" Richard added wryly. "That first semester is a crusher. How are you finding it?"

George shrugged. "I don't understand all the lectures. When the professor finishes, I'm not sure if he's saying 'this is it' or 'this isn't it.'"

Richard laughed. "How do you like apologetics?"

George looked askance at him. "Not very much." He broke into a grin. "Is that why you asked?"

"I just wondered! How do you like the show?"

"Oh! Very much. The songs—" he stumbled and blushed; then he smiled. "They surprised me. And the costumes and staging. They are quite professional."

"And a little secular?"

"Well—yes."

"The songs are old favorites of ours; they make everybody feel at home. Were you—surprised by the street clothes?"

"A little. In Rome all I've seen is the cassock."

"In America we take off the cassock for things like this, for sports, and so on."

"I liked that song—about—*Santa*—do you say? *Who-A! Who-A!* The way they sang that, and the whistling. I liked that."

"The chorus is really good," Richard said with enthusiasm. "They learned those arrangements from television."

"Ah, yes. I have seen television once, in Rome. It is exciting, isn't it?"

"*Permesso!*" Somebody tugged at them to get into the row.

"Richard, they're beginning to sit down. Sit with me. There's an extra place beside me."

Richard looked for Johann. "All right. I'll find him afterwards. We're going over to the German College after this, so we'll have to hurry."

"That's all right. We'll at least enjoy this together."

They climbed in their row and sat down.

"Over the holidays?"

"Maybe we can organize a hike then. At any rate, we'll do something."

George shook his hand with polite exuberance. "Good!"

The auditorium was already darkened; the curtain opened. The chorus sang "Silent Night" around a Christmas tree in a darkened, silent living room.

"I'm going to leave right after the last number, to beat the crowd," Richard whispered in the dark. "I'll see you again at the Greg or call on you."

George waited in the dark a moment for the whispered words to register. Then he nodded, smiling.

Richard settled back, thinking of Mary and Conny and Herbert. He wished he could see what it was all leading to. He wondered where Herbert was for Christmas.

When the lights went on, he rose, said a quick good-bye to George, looked for Johann, and started out quickly for the Via Nicolo Tolentino. He looked back and waved to George as he got caught in the press near the door. George was waiting on the edge of the row for the crowd to move up the aisle. He smiled back.

"I wish we had more time," Richard said as they rushed through the throng in the outer corridor.

Johann looked at his watch. "We'll make it. They always have it late in the afternoon, and the ambassador is always late. We'll make it."

They crossed the city in the cold and the wind, most of the way by bus. They were met at the door of the tall building by seminarists in red and shown into the old, dark auditorium. There were not many people there, though the program was about to begin.

The atmosphere and the numbers were strikingly different. The German ambassador was there, in formal dress, with his family. In red cassock, the seminarist who was master of ceremonies walked quietly to the stage, bowed, and welcomed those present. Two violinists performed the first number. They entered the stage from the wings, bowed, and sat solemnly and played a Bach duet. The audience clapped softly as the violinists concluded, bowed, and retired. A seminarist in red bowed and read an old poem. Another delivered briefly a famous German dissertation on Christianity and freedom. A bass violinist played a long and sad solo, becoming then lively and passionate, then soft again. The audience applauded. Then five seminarists with rucksacks over their backs acted out a humorous skit, perhaps also from German folk literature. The five laughed, argued, slapped one another on the back, pretended to quarrel. They rested. One arose, trying to lift another to his feet as well; the latter always fell back down again, his long darkish-blond hair rising and falling with his violent movements. The hikers finally marched, singing, over the hills . . .

On the way home, Richard and Johann talked of autos and cycling, German industry, Russian progress. Johann was bitter toward the United States for allowing the Russians to be first with Sputnik. His brother had barely escaped death in Budapest; his family lived in East Germany. They reached home just as the bell was ringing for rosary and supper. They left their coats in the hall and went hurriedly, breathing quickly, into the chapel.

21

EAST OF ROME, the Apennines rose violet and white; in the cold, bright air one could look from rim to rim across the whole *campagna*. Then about eleven the sky began to cloud: High cirrus first streaked the sky, then gray cumulus massed on the horizon and blew slowly across the rim. The *campagna* darkened. The wind began to pull more sharply at the light-brown deadened grass about the ruined aqueducts of the countryside and to lift papers in the city. Chestnut vendors kept their hands near their tin-can fires and pulled their stoves nearer to walls or stairways. Frank Perrone and Richard pulled their collars up closer.

"It's a rat race, isn't it?" asked Richard as they hurried down the hill from the Via Nazionale. They turned their faces from the breeze. "I haven't even made my holy hour yet."

"Something every day," nodded Frank. "But that's what a vacation's for. Break the schedule."

They turned in at the Scots College on the side of the steep hill. Heavy-stoned buildings lined the street like strong canyon walls.

"Greetings!" wished a tall, spare lad, in the violet cassock of the Scots College, who met them at the door. "Place for your coats over here. They'll show you the amphitheater as you enter." He smiled broadly, eyes shining.

"Hello!" said the fellow who took their coats. "You chaps from Annunziazione? That was one of your lads, then, in the accident? I say, will he walk again? We were dreadfully sorry to hear about it."

"Yes, he was from our house," Frank replied. "He'll walk if it kills him—if I know Conny."

They went down the gray hallway to an open door. Inside was an incredibly small auditorium jammed with chairs and people. The air was already hot. The rows of chairs were wavy and irregular; every kind available had been pressed into use. The English ambassador sat down front with his family, one or two friends, and the white-haired rector of the college. Richard and Frank edged towards two empty seats, their knees barely squeezing into place behind the row in front of them.

"Libero?" Richard asked of a dark-skinned Latin American near the seats.

"S'accomodi" he smiled and nodded. They introduced themselves; he was Gabriele Mendez from Colombia, and he was in Richard's class at the Greg.

Gabriele was a handsome boy; he had black wavy hair, shining black eyes, straight, clear white teeth. He smiled easily and well, and his bearing was serious and gracious. His parents must be wealthy, Richard thought; he is surely of the upper classes. Before they could talk much, the lights went out. The show began.

The Scots knew Gilbert and Sullivan surpassingly. They had blocked every antic to perfection. A policeman—Guardsman of the Realm—fainted heavily with no one near, was caught before he hit the ground. "When the foemen bared their steel," the Guardsmen's knees trembled till the audience could take no more; they laughed and roared; the ovation was terrific in the little room. The entrance of seminarists in yellow and pink dresses, their faces heavily painted, made the room rock again. Singing voices were sure and firm: Singers could talk their lines or sing them, twist them or mock them, sweeten them or shout them. A deep-voiced Guardsman took all the lowest notes alone, with all on stage pointing towards him and rooting for him as down and down he went—until, once, on the very lowest, impossibly lowest, note, as he took a breath and opened his jaws, the tiniest, lightest voice on stage peeped out its highest squeak. The incongruity was perfect, the unexpected had been planned with thoroughness, and the audience roared.

"Delightful!" clapped Richard at the intermission.

"Very good!" nodded Gabriele. "It is my first—Gilbert and Sullivan. Very funny, no?"

"Delightful!" Richard repeated. "Would you like to walk out and take some air?"

"Yes, yes. It's very warm, no?" Gabriele lifted his cassock away from his chest.

They pushed through the hot crowd. It was impossible to talk. Even the vestibule to the street was filling up with smokers.

"Come outside?"

"Va bene," agreed the Colombian. "Coats? No?"

Richard looked around. He took two coats at random from near the door. "Take these. They won't mind."

Gabriele laughed and threw on his coat. "Thieves!"

Outside, they walked silently along the sidewalk. Gabriele sent a sidelong glance at Richard. He smiled. *"Amigo,* why do you overflow our country with Protestants?"

Richard wasn't sure what Gabriele's attitude would be. "Me? I'm not sending anybody. No one is. They go of their own."

"We are poor. They bring radios and medicines and printing presses. They are converting people who are religious already. They have money, techniques that are far advanced, organization."

"But you have had lots of time. Maybe it's a good thing, the competition. Maybe every country should have four or five religions." Richard shrugged casually but watched for Gabriele's reaction.

"There is no right to preach heresy. There is no preference between heresy and truth. Riccardo!"

"Is—an ignorant Catholic better than a faithful Protestant?"

"Catholicism has the Word of God. That is more important than ignorance and faithfulness. More important than what men do with it."

They turned back down the street. "Is Catholicism some set of abstract principles? A 'truth' which merely has to be handed on, unchanged, word for word? Is it words? Is it a code of laws? Is it an organization?"

Gabriele didn't answer him. He inhaled the cold air.

"It's a conscious life. It's a union that takes place in minds and wills. I think there are psychological laws—real, concrete laws— concerning individuals, which are never argued in our classes. These laws escape logic, organization, and, of course, canon law. They are laws about the inner mystery of persons, and this is where Catholicism lives. The rest is easier to see, but shallow, even ugly."

They walked past the door of the College.

"I'm frightened every time I think of Dostoievsky's Grand Inquisitor. Each man has his own soul to save, and no one can save it for him. No one. No one. Not even the pope himself. If a man makes an act of faith, if he chooses to obey, even if he takes a vow of obedience for life as we do, well, it is because he chooses to do so. Freedom is the most precious heritage of the Gospels. Men don't want responsibility, so they hide behind movements and simple laws; they hope for a simple, automatic heaven."

"But still there is the hierarchy; still there is revelation," Gabriele argued.

"Of course. But do you think medieval Christians were holier because there was only one church to go to? Do you think they were holier because the thing to do was to go to mass? Do you like what they did to the Jews and the heretics? You can't save people by the country. You can't save them *at all*. They have to save themselves. You can preach the truth *in season, out of season,* as St. Paul says, but you have to allow for good soil, and rocky soil, and bad. You can lead the horse to water, the proverb says. Well, why be afraid of competition?"

"You can speak that way because your people are educated. In my country they are ignorant."

"Competition will educate them. Your countries have the resources to be great. Your people do not have the energy."

"Ah!" said Gabriele.

"I don't think the Gospels would support this business of a 'Catholic country.' Power corrupts: I believe that. I think the cardinals believe it when they resent a pope who lives too long. Where there is no competition, the Church loses its ferment, its desire to grow and burst all the bounds, like the mustard seed outgrowing all its pots until it is planted in the whole wide earth. Pluralism is a good ground in which the human conscience can grow. What do they teach us that makes the conscience free? It is undetermined by others, it has alternatives, God hasn't forced it in a single fixed direction,"

They turned back up the hill.

"It's true. In Colombia the Communists have come, the Protestants have come. Many who once accepted faith as a part of being born are beginning to ask questions. All Latin America is stirring. There is great—psychologic life."

They talked rapidly for fear of returning late for the performance. Richard looked up ahead and quickened his pace.

Gabriele slowed Richard with his hand. "There is one thing you must understand. The mother's boys become priests. The men—"

"I've been told this before."

Oh?"

"By a friend from Mexico."

"Well, among us it is very marked. A—peculiar closeness springs up between the women and the priests." Gabriele grinned. "The *mulierization* of the priests. Neither one belongs to the world of men. Religion becomes impractical, devotional, otherworldly— irrelevant. It forms heroic saints. It is a good religion. But it is not a man's religion. It does not have intellect and force. Perhaps it is more contemplative, and that is good. But it is a very odd thing. Just the same, it is 'the faith.' You are a heretic if you dare to question it, a dupe of the anti-clericals. You are fighting stone walls if you attack it. Miracles are needed to change whole patterns of ideas."

"You are going to lose Latin America to the Communists; you know that, don't you?" Richard replied as they reached the door.

Gabriele nodded painfully.

Richard opened the door and they went in.

22

THE chapel was extremely quiet. A bench creaked though no one was in it. Richard knelt alone, before the tabernacle, on a *prie-dieu* pressed tightly against the altar stairs. The morning sun filtered silently through the amber windows on his right. Specks of dust moved slowly in the light like stars in a firmament. Richard's eyes were firmly closed, his head was bowed. He wore a white surplice.

He was late for his holy hour this week; every day had been occupied. His spirit had been taxed by the distractions and the excitement. His prayer now was not really prayer; it was spent in the preliminaries. He was barely able to withdraw himself from memories, feelings, loose velleities that had escaped him during the week and now in these moments of silence and inner freedom were flowing back on him with urgency.

He tried to realize who and where he was. He knew the Lord lay in the quiet, golden tabernacle: bread to appearances. "This is my body." Lord of stars, of space, of earth. Lord of history and men—each man with his sorrow and his secret . . . Lord so vast, belonging to all, immense enough for all, the Holy One before Whom he knelt. Richard tried, in the silence, to stir up old familiar thoughts, the old powerful images that usually gave his sensibilities wing and allowed his mind the freedom then to pray. His favorite idea was to lift himself out of Time: to think of what it meant to be in contact with the transcendent Lord, the Lord who knew the hearts of Barbarossa and of Teresa and of John and of Caesar and of Napoleon and of Newman and of all the men who had ever been and suffered or who would ever be. The Lord was outside Time. He knew them all, read the sorrows and the pride of their hearts. The thought always awoke Richard to some sort of objectivity, to realize how small, how petty, how selfish were his concerns in the stream of history. He wished to adore, to love his Lord in quietness. He wished by intelligence and will to throw his heart open before the Lord that he might kneel there patent and limpid. He wished the Lord to have access to his heart. The Lord, of course, saw through him; nothing was really hidden. But Richard wanted it hidden not even from himself. Gradually, inner darkness and calm peace stole over him. He knew that God cannot be found with the emotions or even with quiet sensibilities; he strove, with his naked will, to pray in faith, to believe, to affirm, to rest in darkness. Men don't see God, he knew, even in their prayer.

Richard knew that somewhere in his heart was the spirit's tip, so to speak, the fine point of flame, where resided his real identity in the depths beneath the contradictions of his hopes, fears, desires, joys. Somewhere, beneath conscious and unconscious, somewhere compounded of all he was and yet transcending all components, somewhere was the key to what he was. He couldn't find the key. But he wanted it, and wanted it as God's. He left it in God's care, giving Him what he himself found consciously to hand. Guilt he had, too, companionship with all the guilty, guilt so banal and so common. Pride, touchiness, selfishness, deception.

Padre Benedetto had not said much about Mary Coleman; he was free to resolve the problem in his own way. It puzzled him by its complexity. At times he thought it was merely his loneliness and his craving for the attentions and amenities of love. To be loved by somebody! And then again—to embrace somebody, to fondle, to kiss upon the lips. He wondered if it were really possible to love apart from bodily expression; surely he knew that the instant he loved, the body longed for presence and for demonstration. He longed, too, at times, when the sap rose high within his body, for the ecstasy of the flesh and its sweet surrender and its gift. He enjoyed at highest pitch the sensitivity of a woman's mind and heart and the delicate companionship and inspiration that a woman could afford his love for beauty. As by a whirlpool, the image of Mary Coleman was being sucked into the center of all these desires, standing for the satisfaction of first one and then another. His prayers seemed so dry and his inner life so dead that he wondered, too, if God did not call him by these desires to the married state and not the priesthood. How could one side be so full of life and beauty and the other be so drab?

Sometimes, at night, in a tensile silence, he would feel his longing greatest, and she seemed very sweet to him; he was usually very tired, though, and dropped heavily off to sleep. He might dream of her, and the little that he actually knew of her seemed but the better spur to his imagination. Occasionally, even in the daytime, the vigor and tenacity of sexual fantasies were very great and all the more alluring when he tried to resist them directly. He was learning what it means to be an animal, and he tried by reflection to learn to step back and laugh at the oddities and eccentricities of his desire. Could he live a celibate all his life? Perfectly? Better not to promise than not to keep the promise. He felt sure he could. He would need friendships. He would need frankness. He would need dedicated, determined work. Above all, he would need a tender love for the Lord. He wanted to foster that love, but the difficulty always was that he expected "tender" to mean emotional in spite of himself. It is hard to love with the will. It is hard to love by determination. But he knew that that was the kernel of the problem. Could he sell all for the pearl of great price—where all meant Mary Coleman and all her sisters, all their sensibilities, all their love, all their companionship? It was worth it. The pearl was the eternal Lord in wholehearted and endless intimacy.

He felt nothing in his heart. No emotion. With his mind and will he adhered to the Lord. There was no response. There was no voice or return, only emptiness. He adhered.

He followed a thought that flashed through his mind concerning Herbert and peacefully included him within his prayer. He had never had a letter yet. No address. He wondered if Herbert were sorry now or happy. He wondered if he'd found a job and begun his ambitious climb. He wished Herbert very much success.

His prayer began to steal away from him. Fragments of conversations came back to him with the dryness and pain of the last few days. One thing he hadn't thought about was lurking in his heart and nagging him: an immense despondency. It would be impossible for Catholicism to win men's minds and imaginations now—impossible. His hands grew moist. Who would accept her leadership in Africa? In America? His spirit groaned. It seemed senseless to beat blindly and in vain. The past was past. Lord! he broke, in an exasperated hope, how could You make the Church so high a dunghill? Have put Thy Truth in such a rigid, obstinate, unmoving wall? How *could* You?

He lay his head upon his hands, and he was sweating.

Richard tried to rest in quietness. He realized prayer was no place for thinking out his thoughts. Afterwards, perhaps. Better now to stay beside the Lord. Yet the terror of the walls loomed up before him. *Obey! Obey! Do not criticize. Be docile. Authority knows best. Authority knows best. Superiors know all the angles. Who are you to judge? That's authority's responsibility.* A terrible thought struck him and left him cold. He fought it from his heart. He wrestled with it, keeping it away. And then he let it rise up, full, before him, let it speak, and listened, struck numb, in the silence.

Master, what if to serve You I must break from the Church!

His life was based on the belief that the Church possessed the Word of God. He turned the belief over and over in his mind peacefully. Every ugly deed of the Church and every scar of history twisted like metal into his flesh. Every narrowness and smallness hurt.

But, besides, he would have to conquer the nub of obedience. He would have to sacrifice his art. He would have to submit to what he felt was an overemphasis on discipline and legality and a loss of Christian freedom and creativeness. In the process, he would lose the things he cherished. And he had better count on losing them—giving them—entirely. Or one day he would rue his ordination.

Pearl of price.

He knelt in silence for a long time. At length, when he arose, it was ten minutes past the hour he had intended. His knees were stiff, his feet almost asleep. He genuflected stiffly, moving his *prie-dieu* to the side. He walked slowly in the silence to the sacristy to hang his surplice. He removed it, hung it up, closed the closet door, and walked towards his room. The snap of the latch rang in his mind in the quiet, sun-filled corridor. His heart was full of emotion, deeply at peace beneath the storm, because he desired only truth.

He started up the stairs for his room, remembered the time, and started back down the stairs toward the recreation room. He went down to the basement. No one was in the room. Smoke hung lightly near the ceiling, magazines were in disarray. He found some letters on the nearest table. One was for him.

Mr. Richard McKay, P.A.
Collegio dell' Annunziazione
Lungotevere
Rome, ITALY

It was from his mother. He started to open it, then sauntered back up the stairway to his room. It has been almost two weeks since she'd written. Christmas and all. He wondered what was new. Dad all right? Kevin?

In his room he threw himself upon his bed, cassock and all, and read the letter. He laughed once, beamed towards the end. He thought over it a moment, then sat up and slapped the letter down on his knee.

"Well, I'll be! Kev's getting married. I'll be! And to Alice McKinley."

He picked up the letter and read it again.

". . . AND HE AND ALICE have decided on the 21st of June. Are you surprised? Had I told you he was going with her again? Well, he has, especially since September. And, of course, we've known the McKinleys all our life. Why, you used to date Jean, didn't you? (By the way, Jean just had a second baby girl, on the 19th. She always

says to send her best to you when I write. She and Jack are doing
nicely, moved into their new house. Small but nice, and he's got a
good job.) Well, I thought Alice might be a little young for Kevin;
she's younger than Jean, and Kevin's a year and a half older than you
and Jean. But then she's a serious girl, and it's all right if one's a little older, I suppose . . ."

"SO KEVIN finally up and surrendered! Well, the Irish won't be
vanishing any more, and I'll be an uncle!"

He lay back down. And Jean said to say hello. How hard it is to
picture Jean with two babies. And Bobbie has a boy now. Rebecca
married. Everybody settled. It's hard to believe. You go away for
three or four years, and they refuse to let the memories alone.

He got up again, straightened his cassock, put the letter in a
dresser drawer. "Well, good for Kevin! And for Alice. They'll make a
good pair." He rubbed his hand through his hair and stood there
absently a minute.

THAT AFTERNOON, Richard and Paolo started off to see Conny
at the hospital.

"I've got a sorry tale to tell," Paolo began.

"Oh, good! I'm in the mood for it," mocked Richard.

The bright sunlight on the Tiber, the blue sky, the buff and red
buildings on the Trastevere bank, and the shining billboards on their
walls completely belied the turmoil in his heart. He felt elated and
depressed all in the same moment. He felt as if the beauty of this day
outside would never be repeated—these buildings, the trees, the
gleaming yellow Tiber, the sun, the sky. In ten years perhaps all
would be changed, in a hundred years surely, and never again would
there be just today's sunlight, today's shadow, today's emotion to
greet them with. He got a sense of eternity he had never had before:
Beauty was out there—he saw it—there they met—and though all
else would change, outside and within, nevertheless the identity had
fused, beauty was captured, the moment was snared. Save it, O Lord,
for eternity, he thought; keep it outside of Time, with all things

good. That's it! he thought. Eternity is all the good things of Time, rescued, in the sight of God. How lovely . . . lovely . . . lovely . . .

"Tell me," he said. "I believe I could take anything."

"Do you remember Luigi Tasconi from *Il Capronico*? The one who was ordained before Christmas?"

"The tall fellow with glasses. From Milano. The one you went to school with . . ."

"He went to say mass yesterday at one of his favorite churches. Here in Rome. I won't say the name."

"Good!" interrupted Richard facetiously. "I love mysteries."

"When he finished mass—you know how serious a fellow he is. Well, the sacristan comes up to him, hobbling because he is a cripple. 'Padre,' he says, 'my daughter pretty. Clean, padre. Eighteen. Beautiful. She is fat, padre, very nice. She like to play.' Luigi told me he was sick. *'Leave me!'* he shouted. But the man dared to tell him: 'Padre, have no fears. There is a confessor here who gives absolution to the padres. It's quite all right. She is—' Luigi picked the man up by the arms, opened the back door, and heaved him out into the pavement, crippled leg and all. Luigi came back inside and sobbed. He told me of it yesterday and his face was still white about it."

"I wouldn't doubt it in the villages, from what I've heard. But in Rome! Surely someone would report it."

"Luigi won't. He's too sick about it. He only told me to get it off his chest."

"He *must* tell. If men like him won't, who will?"

"He hopes the sacristan will think just that and be afraid to try again."

They walked along in the sunlight up the Gianiculo. Paolo reached for a handkerchief to wipe his brow, though the air was cool.

"You know, Paolo, loneliness is really something you have to learn to live with, isn't it? I can imagine a man who thinks he is a failure, who is tired and never learned to pray or love, easily turning to a woman. It is not so strange."

"Ah, it is easy. No one denies it. But isn't that the choice!"

"How many know what they are doing?"

"*Beh!* Who knows the priesthood until he has lived it? But how many husbands would take their vows again?"

"How many husbands have as long as we do to decide?"

"There you are. We have a better chance of deciding well than anyone."

"But how many take advantage of it? How many talk of the difficulties? What do we learn of women and of love?"

"One thing: Stay away from them. It is not something you can have both ways, Riccardo. You cannot mate and still stay free. Somewhere there must come the choice, one way or the other."

"I know, Paolo, I know. But—"

"I hate the little seminaries, you know that. But there is room for a few of them. Some of those who come from them have—I don't know—a marvelous perfume, a splendid spirit. They make completely dedicated priests if they are mature. What can they know of women and of love? Yet they are often excellent, compassionate confessors. Ah no, Riccardo, it is not necessary or even possible to run experiments in love."

Richard felt uncomfortable for a reason he couldn't put his finger on.

"I will tell you why I am so strong on this. Riccardo *mio*, in our own house I see disaster happening."

Richard stopped short.

"No, come on." They walked along together. "I have never seen it or heard of it before. But I tell you one of our own men is building his ruin."

"Paolo!"

"He will not be ordained if I can prevent it, but I'll say nothing till the end."

"Paolo, I can't believe it. I thought I knew our forty very well."

"I speak the truth, Riccardo."

"You have—you have spoken then to your director?"

"Without telling him the name. He wants me to act on it, or let him act, but I will not. I made him promise to wait until our friend came to a decision by himself."

"Have you spoken of this to *him?*"

"Riccardo, I went out to the bathroom late one night. He was just coming in. He walked into my arms at the doorway of the washroom. He was in his street clothes and so surprised that he started then to cry. He told me of the family, friends of his own family. He had been trying to straighten out a family quarrel. The girl's brother-in-law was threatening the girl. He became her confidant. That night he was coming from her. Riccardo, you should have heard him cry. I held him in my arms. 'I did not mean to . . . I had not intended . . .' But now she is not pregnant, and he no longer wants to leave."

"Paolo, from our own house!" Just then Richard recalled his own walk outside the house. He thought of Mary Coleman. His heart turned to ice and his fingers went cold. The blood drained from his face. He thought of Padre Bracciano's imaginings when he told him of his own night outside the house.

"Oh, Paolo!" he cried.

"Che cosa?"

"Oh, nothing. Nothing at all. I just thought of something dreadful."

"It is dreadful. That I know," said Paolo grimly.

"More than I had thought."

"You—knew of it before?"

"Oh no, something else. Oh, Paolo, how dreadful and complicated life becomes."

"You sound so innocent. Dreadful and complicated? Nine-tenths evil and a small part good. . . . But do not look so downcast. You can build an optimism on that!"

"Oh no, Paolo. Innocent? I'm a fool!" He looked out over the Gianiculo, over the slate roofs of the ancient, tired city.

THEY SAW CONNY at the hospital. He was unable yet to speak. The nurse explained that they kept him under drugs. He smiled wanly, his face pale against the pillow. His light hair stood stiffly against the pillow slip. His legs were wrapped, temporarily splinted, lifted up by weights. He looked very weak and thin. It was difficult to judge whether he would live to leave the room. He didn't know yet about his legs.

The smell of anesthesia nauseated Richard. It was very heavy. And Conny's paleness and weakness entered his heart. Conny had been so strong until the truck—in a tiny moment, a fraction of a second, snap! He wanted now to take Conny's hand or stroke his head. He wanted to do something for him, something Conny's family could do if they were here. He only smiled, standing there erect, *romano* in hand. Paolo stood beside him impassively. All they could do was look. Padre Bracciano had sent flowers up yesterday and today. Both pots were on the dresser. He had probably brought the magazine or two, and Richard recognized the radio Padre always brought the sick. Padre Bracciano's brown rosary, too, the one he had bought in Jerusalem on his silver jubilee vacation, lay collapsed, unused, upon the table beside Conny's bed.

"You'll be fine, Conny. You'll be all right. We'll—pray for you."

"*Arrivederla, Conny. Auguri. Tante preghieri!* Chicago sends *auguri!*" Paolo leaned over and touched Conny's sleeve.

Conny tried, too, to smile, but they were sure he had not understood. They bowed, looked at the nurse, waved to Conny and left. Conny's eyes followed them helplessly, almost in tears. They waved again. He tried to nod *grazie*, it seemed.

Out in the hall they stopped. They looked at one another; Richard shrugged. As they walked on down the corridor; neither said a word. Each fingered his *romano*. At the door they put them on. They stepped out into the bright day.

"I hope. I hope," said Richard carefully.

"*Beh! Iddio provvedrà,*" shrugged Paolo. "It's up to Him."

They walked up the sunny street, in silence.

PART IV
Late Winter

23

"Y ES, ROSETTA, exams are over!"

"*Bravo,* padre! I'll bet you ranked the highest, didn't you?"

"Passed, Rosetta, I hope. But it's so good to be through with them! I could heave my books into the Tiber and shout loud enough to reach America!"

Rosetta clapped her hands to her ears in happy astonishment. Her eyes flashed appreciation for the zest of youth in the young *Americano.* He always stopped to talk to her if he could. She enjoyed telling him of Italy and a life that he had never known. "*Ai,* padre!" she would say. "Life is difficult. You have to laugh in order to forget. Yet one always manages." She would look out over Richard's head and see visions of hills and moving streams, of stucco houses, and goats slipping over rocks, and girls hauling water from a well, and *pastasciutta* in the hot sleepy summertime, and her husband far away. "They say in the South: nothing to eat, nothing to drink, one goes on living just the same."

"Did you . . . suffer much in the war?" Richard once had asked her.

She had laughed and smiled affectionately on him. "Suffer! When has Italy not suffered? Italy is poor. No factories. No work. But in the war? Hunger—you cannot imagine the hunger and the sicknesses of the winter. For six weeks my *bambino* lay in fever; he did not eat a thing. We forced goat's milk into his mouth; he spat it out. A boy of four, he would not eat! He was thin, thin like a thorn. He was wasted almost to nothing. All day I had to work in the fields. I came home at night expecting to find him dead. My heart was blackness. I do not know how I worked those days or how I lived. I did not sleep at night. I sat over him and cried. What could I do? No family, no husband, only the friendship of the women of the village, and they with problems of their own. Suffer, *bambino*? War teaches one how to suffer. When we came to Rome . . . the rubble, the destruction, armored cars . . . streams of people. No food! No homes! *Now* you cannot believe it. All this—built up again. Prosperous. Three times the people. But then! The homeless, the refugees, the hunger! We slept in caves made in the wreckage or in the hills. Children died, too weakened by the war. Families were reunited. The joy killed some of them. The news of deaths killed others. The war! Do not speak of war to me. It has destroyed my life. One child only, and he grew up without a father!"

But today Rosetta told him with joy. "*Bisogna una vacanza, padre!* Take a vacation. No more study! Rest yourself; you are looking pale."

"Me?" said Richard. "Well, we're taking one. Day after tomorrow, we're going for a hike. Paolo, myself, and one or two other friends."

"*Bravo,* padre! *Una gita in paese!*"

"*Si,* out into the open country. Not far. West into the hills. Just to walk a little, eat out, talk. Out on Via Aurelia."

"*Bravo! Auguri,* padre. You have to do this when you're young!"

Richard eyed the inner doorway of the vestibule as he talked with her. He ought not to stand long. "*Aliara, ciao,* Rosetta. I have to go in. . . . I notice today you have green pockets," he added in jest, pointing to her green dress. The expression in Italian meant that she was broke.

Rosetta looked down at her green print dress and plunged her hand in the pocket. She laughed. "Today and every day . . . green pockets! *Ragazzaccio!*"

He closed the door as she waved him away with her hand, repeating "green pockets" and laughing to herself. One part of his heart was light as he walked down the corridor. The other was pensive. He had great hopes for this hike; he hadn't asked permission yet. He stepped into the chapel for a brief visit. Then he hurried up to Paolo's room.

"Paolo, want to go on that hike day after tomorrow? I saw Gabriele."

Paolo lay down his pencil, slid his chair back from the light over his desk, and looked at him. He stretched. "*Si* . . . I'm tired."

"Almost finished?"

"Another chapter to go."

"When's your exam?"

"The same time as yours, but tomorrow. How was it?"

"He asked essay questions—take one out of three. I took liberalism in the nineteenth century. Italy, France, the Syllabus. I hope he doesn't mind the approach I took."

"Essay questions, *bene* . . ."

"A snap, Paolo. Don't worry about it."

"I'm not. I'm just tired." Paolo stretched again. "This time of year, Riccardo!"

"The hike will do us all good. But I hate to go in for permission. I think he hates to see me coming in."

"Imagination!"

"No, it's one thing after another. Visit this college or that, play, books . . ."

"Well, he shouldn't refuse a hike. A lot of fellows will be taking them."

"Maybe. Nobody did last year—just us. He wasn't too happy."

AFTER LUNCH, Richard descended the stairs to the recreation room. Cesare saw Richard enter the door and lifted a letter from the table. "I think it's for you."

Richard smiled thanks. It was an airmail letter, an envelope of light green: *Deutschespost*. His fingers hurriedly tore at the top edge. He walked quietly over to a corner of the room. "Caro Riccardo," the letter began. He lifted his eyes to see the date: "Hamburg, 22 Jan." His eyes turned speedily to the text:

Caro Riccardo:

Did you think I would never write? Well, I promised you, and now *eccomi*! How is everything with you? "The boss" still holding you in place? How are the good old classes at the Greg? I miss all of you, in a way. I'm glad to be doing what I am. But the companionship was something I didn't appreciate then as I do now. We surely had some good times! Do you remember the popcorn party we had one night at Villa Madonna with the corn your mother sent? And the beer Padre Milton bought us? He is a fine priest. I miss him. Say hello to him for me.

Well, about me. I couldn't get into the army. A bitter disappointment when I learned of it. It seemed everything was going wrong at first. Two years of service would have been an advantage for me—a time to think and reorganize my life, a time for gaining military experience for later on. Also, I have had difficulty finding work. I tried the consulates and embassies. I don't want the civil service. I went to the CDU party headquarters, but nothing doing there. Everything is tied down. Finally I took a job with an exporter. We export cars—to the U.S.! Would you believe it! My employer took a liking to me; he thinks my English is excellent—thanks for the lessons!

I have met a nice girl. Her name is Gretta. She is a good Catholic, very intelligent, very pretty. I do not see her much now. I am too busy. But someday!

The road to influence seems much harder now than it did. But my motto is, do all things well. In time I shall be promoted, step by step, until I can launch out on my own. Fifteen years, *caro* Riccardo. Look for Herbert Klein then. Meanwhile, pray for him in your quiet chapel as he does for you in a busy office.

In Christo,
Herbert

P.S. Write, write, write!

Richard raised his eyes to the top of the letter and began reading it again. Then he folded it. He started toward his room; he wanted to be alone. The letter stirred, as Herbert always used to do, his longings for activity, for expression, for achievement. He regretted now that he hadn't entered the Borghese exhibition; he would have had something to show for the year! But he had not wanted to offer an opening to another painful refusal. Self-pity rose in his heart. He seemed always to be running into stone walls and never to have the courage to unify his desires and inclinations. He'd never make a good religious.

In his room he sat on the bed and untied his shoes. A little nap will do me good, he thought. And then I'll begin another canvas. Tomorrow I may even finish it. He lay back and closed his eyes.

AFTER SUPPER, Richard went to Padre Bracciano's office. A little night light at the end of the hall cast a dim, dreary glow. A line formed behind him, restless but silent. Richard began going over in his mind what he would say. He hated to have to call Gabriele and George and tell them no. The door started to open. Light lanced out. Carlo passed him. Richard knocked.

"*Avanti!*"

Padre Bracciano sat fiddling with a silver letter opener. A stack of letters sat before him, waiting to be signed and folded. Richard closed the door and advanced.

"*Buona sera,* padre."

"*Buona sera,* Riccardo."

There was a silence.

"Uh, Paolo Veronese and I would like permission to go on a hike Thursday with friends of ours. One from Propaganda, one from Pio Latino. We want to go—all day. Out Via Aurelia into the country."

He waited. Padre Bracciano did not look up but thought for a moment.

"You'll miss particular examen, dinner, visit. They're religious exercises, you know."

"May we—make them up in private?"

"That's not the point. They should be made in common."

"We've—finished our exams. Paolo has his last one tomorrow."

"You won't turn this into a fraternity?"

"Oh no! These are just fellows we happened to meet. We don't see them often."

Padre Bracciano swiveled in his chair. He tapped on his letters. He looked up with a smile. "All right. You can go. I suppose you'll want money?"

"For wine, if we may."

"See me tomorrow night for it. See Fratello about the lunches. Whatever you need. . . . Don't forget your exercises—especially dinner."

Richard looked at his smile. "*Grazie,* padre. Your blessing, please?" As he rose to leave, he teased over his shoulder. "Want to come along?"

Padre Bracciano smiled wryly and nodded to his desk. "As you get older you have to *work*."

"*Buona sera,* padre."

"*Buona sera.*"

He stepped out into the dark hall and hurried jubilantly to tell Paolo, "It's all fixed."

24

On Thursday Paolo, George, Gabriele, and Richard set out across the ups and downs of Via Aurelia in the *campagna* west of Rome. Wayside trees made a corridor across the hills. Going up, the youths looked into the blue Italian sky, rich and swimming; down, into the narrow valleys. Stucco houses sat silently in the bright sun, pale maroon or gray. Milestones gleamed brightly along the road, marking the distance away from Rome, center of civilization. The youths pulled roadside grass to set between their teeth. They leaned over for rocks to throw at telegraph poles. They turned their faces away when roaring trucks kicked up dust and paper as they sped by, honking, along the narrow highway.

They spoke in Italian for Gabriele, English for George; Paolo tried a little of his Spanish; they used Latin in emergencies. Paolo and Richard carried knapsacks. One by one, the four took off their jackets as the sun grew warmer; the breeze, however, was very cool. Their steps rose and fell on the asphalt road. They had talked of the future of their countries, of school, of the religious life.

"You know," said Paolo, "I wonder where we shall all be in a dozen years."

"George here will be a bishop."

"Not I, never . . . you're teasing me. *You* will be—bishop of all Colombia."

"Paolo will be the most famous preacher in Italy, confessor to the Pope, and next in line for cardinal."

Paolo laughed. "I will be in exile in the missions."

"You, Riccardo?" asked the Colombian.

"I will be a plump American monsignor with a car, cigars, all kinds of curates, prestige, power, influence . . ."

"Will you speak to us?"

"Oh, I'll have secretaries. You can always keep in touch with me. If you need help or anything."

"Will you have a Cadillac?

"I was thinking of a Rolls-Royce. But then to import a car is a bit pretentious. Yes, I'll just take a Cadillac. A priest's tastes should be simple."

"Will you come to Rome every year?"

"Well now, that depends. There'll be a convention in Florida every winter, so the winter's out. Summers? Rome's damn unpleasant in the summers. Well, if I can get away in the spring or fall."

"Maybe we could get together every year for a reunion."

"Yes, yes, do look me up. Leave a note for me with the Secretariat of State. Yes, that should do it. I'm sure to find it when I come. If you let me know early, I'll even put it in my schedule. If I can at all, I mean."

They laughed and talked. Before long, their feet grew tired. They stopped on a hilltop, under a gnarled olive tree. The green field beside them swerved up to the sky. Lying in the grass, they threw pebbles, picked up blades of grass, lay back on the cool, solid ground. Across the way, a white villa sat back on a distant hill behind rows of vines and fruit trees. Sheep grazed on the knoll beyond it. Hills still farther in the distance rolled away in violet and blue.

The ground smelled moist with spring, cold with water somewhere near. They lay underneath the breeze. Richard could see the grass waving above him in the sky.

"One hates to move after a little while," Gabriele said.

"To think this is out here all the time while we are in the city," George remarked.

"Parts of Colombia are like this," Gabriele nodded. "Only we have forests and jungles, not these empty fields."

"Kenya, too, is like this in the hills. But they are rounder and larger. In the plains we see no hills at all. Just flat—with the long, high grass. I used to love the sun upon it when it waves. Like the ocean. The light runs towards you, right into your eyes!"

"Ah, you should see Chicago!"

All three laughed.

"We've seen it in the movies."

Richard sat up indignantly. The sun caught his brown hair and brought out the red in it. It brightened his green woolen sweater, his khaki slacks. It warmed his black hiking shoes.

"Chicago," he said, "is a wonderful place. It's not like in the movies."

"Are the hills in Chicago bigger than this?" George asked.

"In America, everything is bigger!" Gabriele said. The sun gleamed on his black hair and tanned Latin face. He flashed his bright, straight smile.

"There are no hills in Chicago," Richard announced. "But if there were, they would be bigger."

George sat up from the grass. "America is hard to understand. So much generosity and so much selfishness."

"No selfishness!" Gabriele mocked. "No selfishness! You have to understand the Yankee generosity. Look at the highway they built for us—all through Latin and South America. Pure generosity."

"All right, all right," Richard warned.

"No, Riccardo! It was for business, *vero*? What's wrong with business? Who's to blame the Yankees for being generous because of business?" Gabriele's eyes were full of mischief. "You must understand, George, that for the Yankees generosity is a business. There is no selfishness. It is a business."

Paolo laughed. "The funniest thing about Americans is chewing gum. All over Europe there is chewing gum, under the tables, under the benches, in the streets. It has all come from America. Never in the history of the world has the human mouth had so much exercise."

"Everything the Americans do is mild," Gabriele said. "They don't drink wine—they drink milk. They don't chew tobacco—they

chew sugared gum. They boil their own water when they travel anywhere. They brush their teeth three times a day." Gabriele threw a
little pebble with every thrust.

"And the mildest accent!" Paolo laughed. He imitated the
American twang on A's and O's. Gabriele roared with laughter, and
even George smiled.

"O.K., O.K.!" Richard threatened. "But remember, we don't
have to go to war with you, only stop feeding you."

"That is Latin America's mistake; she never declared a full-scale
war on you. Then you would have grown to love us and feel sorry
for us. This way, we have been friends and we hate each other."

"One thing I don't understand," said George slowly, as he crin-
kled his black face to squint in the sun: "It's how you treat the Negro."

Richard faced George slowly. "It's hard for us to understand, too."

"And the contempt you have for—the Latin peoples," Gabriele
added. He swung his legs up under him to sit with attention. Paolo
played with a blade of grass.

Richard ran his fingers through some tiny gravel on a bare spot
in the grass. "We're Nordics, I guess."

"You do not really like us," smiled Gabriele almost absently,
"We feel that. You think that we are lazy, careless, incapable. Yet you
tell us outwardly you want to be our friends."

"There is a lot we don't understand about Latin America,
Gabriele."

"Of course! But do you care to learn?" The question hung as
a dare.

Richard shrugged uncomfortably.

"People in Africa wait to see everything that happens to the
Negro in America."

"We know."

"But why are you so slow?"

"Things are very complicated."

"I thought—Americans could do whatever they chose to do."

"They can. They like to think so."

"Well?"

"They haven't decided to choose yet."

"Yes, but why?"

Richard shrugged. He threw some grass in the air and watched it drift. "The Negroes are our greatest sin. There's no way we can justify what we've done to them. So we have to push them down in our subconscious—we have to keep them an emotional problem, a problem of tradition. Otherwise we'd have to face our sin. Murders and whippings, calumnies, humiliation—we've done a lot to the Negro. But if we admit it, we have to admit to original sin."

"So?" Gabriele asked.

Richard smiled. "That's one thing America wants least of all to do. She is the new world. She has no part in the poisonings and feudings of medieval history. She is the land of Enlightenment. Sin belongs to the past."

"That's very convenient," Paolo smiled.

"It's nice not to have any history," Richard nodded.

"You're making one!" Gabriele said. "And Latin America is going to help you write one volume of it."

"That's beginning to worry me," Richard smiled.

"Sputnik is chapter one of another volume," Paolo added.

"We have another satellite up now, too!" Richard countered. "Put that in chapter two."

"But yours are both very small."

"Yes."

"At last there is something of which the Americans have not the first and the biggest!" Gabriele exclaimed.

"Do you like us better now?"

"Hm—_si_!" Gabriele conceded. He punched Richard on the arm. Richard punched his arm in return. Gabriele grasped his wrist and twisted him over on the ground. Richard pulled Gabriele on top of him. They wrestled awhile in the grass, staying away from the sloping bank. Gabriele soon pinned him. Richard drew his right leg up under himself for leverage. He lunged upward, but Gabriele put him down again. He rolled the other way quickly and caught Gabriele off balance. He rolled out and pinned Gabriele for a moment; Gabriele threw him again. They began to laugh and rolled, fighting, down the slope. At the bottom they rolled apart. They rose, brushing off their clothes. Gabriele had a grass stain on his light-blue slacks. Paolo and George stood smiling on the top of the slope.

"You carry the bags!" Gabriele called. "We're tired."

"That was very clever," George smiled.

"Americans are always clever," Gabriele answered. "It's their business. Isn't that right, *Americano*?" he asked, putting his arm around Richard's neck.

"Where are we going to eat?" Paolo asked, slinging his pack on his shoulder and starting down the slope.

"Wherever we can buy some wine," Richard said, trying to free himself from Gabriele's arm.

"There's a *trattoria* down the road a half mile, when we come to the railroad tracks."

"You hungry?" Richard asked Gabriele.

"Starved."

"Then get your arm off me and let's move."

Gabriele took his arm from Richard's shoulder and slapped him on the buttocks. George and Paolo reached the bottom of the slope, and the four of them set off on the highway again.

Gabriele began to strum the notes of "The Star-Spangled Banner," leading Richard along.

25

On the following Monday, hurrying into the house from school, Richard saw Father Milton entering the chapel. The sight surprised and gladdened him. He turned to look at Umberto, who was behind him. Umberto winked and broke into a grin. Richard stepped aside and let the rush of students pass him. The rule obliged them to keep silence once they entered the house, so the sound of voices died away just as they came in the door. Finally, Frank Perrone entered. Richard put his hand on his shoulder.

"Father Milton's back."

"Is he?" Frank's face lighted up.

"He's in chapel now."

Frank nodded. "Thanks!"

They walked down the hall together with their books. Frank leaned over and whispered: "Maybe to take Conny home."

Richard nodded. The explanation fitted into place. He hurried to his room and washed. Filing into the dining hall, he saw Father Milton standing tall and thin at his place at table. Just before Padre Bracciano began the grace, Father Milton raised his hand briefly to rub his lips. Richard smiled and looked for Umberto. Umberto, too, was smiling.

At the *Deo Grattas*, the traveler shook hands with Padre Bracciano and Padre Eugenio and the others at the table. The eyes of the household were on him. Speculation began about his return.

"I thought he was going to be in England until April," Cesare said as he lifted his water glass.

"So did I," nodded Umberto, shaking out his napkin.

"He's probably going to fly home with Conny," Richard explained.

"When's Conny supposed to leave?"

"Nobody's said."

"*Where* are they taking him?"

"Mayo Clinic."

"Do you think he'll ever walk again?" Umberto asked.

"He won't quit trying."

After the meal, Father Milton came down to the recreation room. He entered quietly, his hand on his lip, his head tilted to one side.

"Hi, father!" Frank Perrone shouted.

Father Milton shook his hand warmly.

"Buon giorno!" others called.

"Ben' venuto!" came other greetings.

"Ben' trovato!" smiled Father Milton.

"How was England?" Cesare asked him.

"Not so beautiful as Naples and Sorrento," Father Milton teased, because of Cesare's home in Naples.

"Are you back now for good?"

"Wish I was! Have to be off again, though. Moment's notice, you know. Never take an assistant procurator's job if they ask you!" Father Milton grinned.

The group led him to the chairs in the center of the room.

"How's England?"

"Foggy."

They laughed.

"What's the latest on the new foundation?"

"Not much definite yet. Oh, we'll be starting next year. Let's see now; can I tell you this?" Father Milton looked laughingly at the ceiling. "Don't want to be giving way any secrets!"

Everybody laughed. Father Milton threw one leg on top of the other and arranged his cassock over them. It was easy to see he enjoyed talking with "the troops" as he would say.

"We'll be buying an old place outside of London. An old summer house. It will make a lovely novitiate or postulate some day. We can build on the property too."

"Any vocations lined up?"

"Two. Not many, but it's a start. The bishop insists there'll be no trouble."

"What will we do there?"

"Send all promising Italians and Germans there to learn English." He looked threateningly around the circle of faces.

"Send Umberto," someone said.

"His English is perfect!" Umberto replied with dignity.

Everybody laughed.

"Say 'Coca-Cola,'" Father Milton said.

"Coca-Cola," replied Umberto.

"Perfect!" Father Milton said. "We'll send you other fellows."

"Are you flying to the States, padre?" Richard asked.

"Hello, Riccardo, how are you?" Father Milton shook his hand. "Yes, with Conny, Ricky. We're taking him to Mayo. . . . How did it happen? It sounded pretty awful to me in London."

"We were coming down from the American College, near where the bus stop is. Conny backed into the street just as this truck tried to pass another one. Boom! It happened just like that. Crushed his leg."

"It looked pretty gruesome," Frank said. "Blood all over the place."

Father Milton grimaced. "Padre Bracciano tells me the operation was successful."

"We go down to see him, two every day. He seems pretty good now," Umberto said. "At first he was unconscious for several days."

"Well, he'll be at the clinic in a couple days. They'll bring his leg back if anybody can. . . . Any of you like to go along this afternoon? I'm going over to see him."

"I would," Frank said.

"Room for two?" asked Richard.

"Posso io?" asked Umberto.

"We'll speak English," Father Milton threatened.

"Anch' io!" Umberto grinned. He looked for the words in English. "I—also!"

Father Milton laughed and looked at his watch. "Is three o'clock all right with you?"

"O.K.!" Umberto said in harsh English.

The group laughed as it disbanded.

"Father Milton! When did you get in?" A smile broke across Conny's face.

Richard, Frank, and Umberto followed the tall priest into the white room.

"Flew down special to see Cornelius McInerny! Think you can stand some English toffee?"

"Sure can. Thanks, father."

"How've you been, boy?"

"Not bad. Lots of rest!"

"You're looking good."

"I feel pretty good, father. Hi, Frank, Ricky, Bertie. How's school?"

"How're *you*?"

"Oh, I'm doing fine. Gee, it's good to see you, father. Sister said a priest was coming; I thought it would be Padre Bracciano."

"We told her not to tell you."

"Well, you surprised me. Not finding England hard, are you?"

"For a man of my abilities? Nothing's hard!" Father Milton laughed and looked at the others.

"How're the limeys treating you? Meet any good Scotsmen?"

"There aren't any good Scotsmen—living."

"Now wait a minute! I'll get out of bed and fight."

"We'll have you out soon enough! I'm just glad to see you strapped down a little."

"Don't say that, father! It's just beginning to get tiring."

"Well, it'll only be a little while now. You'll be walking soon. I'm flying back to Mayo with you, you know."

"You are? Oh, I'm sorry to cause you all that trouble."

"No trouble at all. I have to fly back to see the provincial, and you need company. We're killing two birds with one stone."

"I feel like a fool causing all this trouble, though."

"No trouble at all, Conny."

Conny blushed and looked at Richard and Frank. "All I remember is stepping off the curb to try a foolish hook shot. Showing off again! Honest, I never saw a thing. It took me three weeks to remember that I was a blank for all that time. It's a strange thing to have no memory. Except that I was too worn out to care! I really didn't care who I was."

"You're looking a lot better than three weeks ago," Frank said. He was running his *romano* through his fingers.

"The sisters take good care of me. A seminarian, you know." Conny grinned.

"You've got your color back," Richard said.

"Next I want this back," Conny said, nodding to his leg in traction. He fingered the leather binding with his hand. "It's an awful contraption overnight. I sure can't wait to be up and walking."

"In another month or two."

"The doctor says it will take more than that. You know, father, I wouldn't mind laying—lying; I'm forgetting my English—in bed if it was baseball season. But there's nothing on the radio. I'll probably get out of bed just on opening day. It would be my luck."

"You'll hear the basketball tournaments."

"Yeah, I'll get the tail end of basketball. Wouldn't you know I'd be hospitalized mostly in the off-season?"

"Conny, that's a fate worse than death!" Father Milton said.

"You know it," Conny agreed mournfully. "And another thing. I was just getting interested in soccer."

"But you used to hate that game when you first came," Richard said.

"I know it. I was just getting interested."

"Conny, you lead a tragic life."

"No kidding, father."

"When are you leaving for the States?" Richard asked in a lull.

Father Milton looked at Conny. "When will you be ready, boy?"

"This minute!" Conny laughed. "Padre Bracciano told me tomorrow."

Father Milton laughed. "Tomorrow it is."

"Tomorrow?" Frank asked.

"They didn't know I'd be in until last night. I have to be in Chicago Friday. So we thought we'd better get that plane tomorrow and get Conny all squared away at Mayo. Typical Annunciation planning, isn't it?"

"They told me last night," Conny said.

"That's a full thirty-six hours!" Father Milton exclaimed with a laugh.

"Oh, I'm not complaining. I'll be glad to go back to the good old U.S.A.—ask Ricky."

"I'll pack for you," Richard smiled.

"I was going to ask you. Don't forget my books in chapel, O.K.? And my baseball glove—it's in the locker room, unused. My gym shoes, too. You can leave those old pants and sweater there. If they haven't walked away."

"I have your gym shoes in my room. I took them home after— the accident."

"Oh yes—thanks. I think that's all there is. The rest is in my room."

"We'll take care of it."

"Thanks, Ricky. Tomorrow, father? Really? It's hard to believe now that it's here."

"I'll help you get those things," Frank nodded to Richard.

"Thanks."

"We've wired your parents. They'll probably meet us, won't they?"

"They said they wanted to. I had a letter yesterday. Dad was just waiting to get the arrival time."

"Have they been worried?"

"No, they seem pretty calm. I've been glad."

"Padre Bracciano's been keeping them informed. And the worst is over now. . . . Well, look, you boys better say good-bye, because it will be kind of hectic tomorrow and I doubt if you'll get down."

"Couldn't we see him at the airport? A few of us?"

Father Milton frowned. "It's during school, Ricky. He'll be going out in an ambulance. No, I kind of doubt it"

"I guess not."

"So long, Conny," Frank said, shaking hands. "Be good. Say hello to the States for us."

"You'll be coming home soon, Frankie. When's the ordination? Date set yet?"

"On Ember Saturday in Lent. I go on retreat this weekend."

"Is Lent that close? I've been losing track."

Frank nodded.

"Congratulations, old boy. When I see you next time, you'll be a priest. I'll serve your first mass at the college. Sorry I won't be here to see the ordination. Your father coming?"

"Yes, he couldn't have made it in December."

"Congratulations, Frankie. Send me your blessing."

"I will."

"Thanks for coming out, Ricky. Thanks for all the visits." Conny averted his eyes. He looked back again. "I'm sorry about the arguments."

"Forget it. I am, too. Just get better."

"See you in two years. You'll be a subdeacon in June, won't you?"

The reality surprised Richard. It was the first time anyone had talked of it like that. He nodded.

"Umberto, *ciao!*"

"Allora, ciao, amico! Give my regards to America."

"I will. I'll be seeing you. *Ciao!*" He waved to all of them.

Father Milton stayed behind for a few words with Conny. The others waited in the hall.

"He looks much better this week," Richard said as Father Milton rejoined them.

"He'll be all right," Father Milton said.

AT THE COLLEGE Richard stopped at Father Milton's door soon after the priest had entered.

"Come in, come in. How's everything?"

"Fine. I thought I better see you a few moments since you're leaving again so soon."

"Sure, come right in! How's everything been?"

"Just fine."

"And ordination coming up—in June, isn't it?"

"Yes, petitions should be very soon." Richard played nervously with the fingers of his left hand.

"Yes, usually in February–March. I guess you're right—in a week or two. So everything is all set, then?"

"Yes. I've given a lot of thought to what you told me in October."

"Yes?"

"About Padre Colletto—and Padre Bracciano."

"Oh yes." Father Milton colored and rubbed his lip. He wasn't sure what Richard was suggesting.

"I've had some good talks with Padre Bracciano."

"Yes? I'm glad."

"And I think I'm going to ask for ordination." Richard was surprised that he had said it. He hadn't intended to. But there it was—an announced decision. It had been building up in him; there was no avoiding it. He felt restless in making the commitment.

"Congratulations! I knew you would. I knew everything would work out."

It wasn't quite as Richard had hoped it would be. But he pushed on. "It's been a hard year, father. But I think that's what I want most."

"I'm sure it is." Father Milton leaned forward with his arms on his knees; he looked very tall and stringy doing it. "I gather that Padre Bracciano's been very pleased with the change that's come over you."

"The change?"

Father Milton smiled. "Well, I don't think I'm revealing any secrets if I mention that he's gone out of his way to speak of it in a letter."

Richard reflected upon his conduct. He wasn't aware of any change. "When was that, father?"

"About—January first, I think. Christmas time."

Richard nodded. Perhaps the one talk was all there was. "Well, anyway, I'm grateful for your advice in October. . . . Oh! Herbert Klein said to say hello."

"He did? How is Herbert? I was sorry to hear that he had left."

"He seems content. He's working for an import–export firm."

"He's a fine young man. The community will miss him. The Lord's will is the Lord's will, I guess." Father Milton rubbed his lip and grinned. He seemed anxious to get on with his tasks.

"That's really all I wanted to see you about, father. Thanks for your help in October. I hope you have a good trip with Conny."

"I hate to shoo you out, Ricky. I'd like to talk a while. But I have a lot to do before tonight. All kinds of paperwork to do. What would we do without all this red tape?" he asked, gesturing to the papers on his desk. "Buy fewer cabinets, I guess. . . . Say, you'll pack up Conny's small grip for him, won't you? Pajamas, slippers, a few things. Anything you think of? He might as well have some things of his own."

"Sure, father. I'll put it at your door. Thanks again. You'll be down in the recreation room with us tonight, won't you?"

"I hope so, Ricky. For a while at least. I should see the fathers, too."

"We'll be looking for you. Too bad you can't make the trip to Rieti with us!"

"I'd like to, Ricky. You'll like Rieti. It's lovely country. See you, now."

"See you, father. Thanks." He closed the door. He stopped to puzzle it out for a moment. He had changed? Well, as long as Padre Bracciano thought so.

26

TWO DAYS LATER Richard sat in the green ninety-eight bus as it
groaned up the hill of Gregorio Settimo for the monastery. The new
friendship with Gabriele and George had buoyed up his heart. He
saw Gabriele nearly every day in class. Sometimes they sat together,
other times they met in the halls.

"*Ciao, Americano!*" Gabriele would always say.

"*Hé, Colombiano!*" Richard would return. He found Gabriele a
fascinating mixture of the humorous and the serious, of the quiet
and the noisy. It was as if Gabriele had too much energy to contain
and periodically needed opportunities of demonstration. Richard
sometimes looked at his handsome face, his clear dark eyes, his
straight flashing laugh, and rejoiced to find companionship with
him. It seemed a miracle that men as talented as Gabriele and as
George would give themselves in all parts of the world to the work
of Christ. Their share in a love similar to his and in poverty and
chastity bound him to them by a bond that he really grew to cherish. He looked out the tinted window of the bus and squinted
against the bright afternoon sun. His own reflection hovered in the
glass; outside were the billboards and fields along the *corso*. Where
would it all end? he wondered. It was not impossible that he and
Gabriele and George and Paolo would end up their days in concentration camps. It was not impossible that the world situation would
worsen and career uncontrollably into a new dark age. He licked
his lips as he gazed at the countryside and the seminary on the hill.
He knew that great ideas were stirring in the tranquil world. He and

Herbert, George and Gabriele, shared them—Paolo, too, and Conny. No one quite escaped them. If you got to know their secret thoughts, there wasn't anybody who wasn't visited by fear.

The bus stopped at the curb. A Vespa raced by up the hill. The gears of the bus ground and roared, and the bus started up again. What would happen in fifty years to Rome? Would it evaporate in white-hot heat and need discovering in some other distant age? It was a strange sensation to be able to think of the future but unable to control it; to feel the ardor of resistance and protest arise but not to know against what enemy to exercise it. The age moved irrevocably onwards, compelled by forces it could not control. Men could only wait and be afraid. The time for acting seemed to have disappeared.

Richard lifted his *romano* from his head and ran his hand through his brown hair. Impossible to sit here passively! His ardor burned more angrily as obstacles grew more threatening. His hands were moist on the chrome bar. It was maddening to feel helpless against the times. The bus neared his stop. He pulled the buzzer and descended from the rear door. He was glad to leave the ugly fumes behind. The cool air invigorated him.

He was glad he had made his decision concerning ordination. It had stored up within him, and he felt confident in it. He watched traffic passing in both directions. He started out to cross the wide street. There was no one moment when he made the decision. It had built itself up gradually. Perhaps the interview with Padre Bracciano had marked the climax. Gabriele and George had helped. He stopped to let a gray Fiat speed in front of him. No use analyzing it: It was the kind of decision to be renewed every day, not something finished once and for all. He felt relieved to be so confident and only a little ill at ease. He squinted up at the sky. It was light blue, with many little clouds in it. He turned from the dusty road at the monastery gate. He wondered what Padre Benedetto would have to say. He pulled the bell.

After a time, shuffling footsteps came towards the door. An old brother Richard didn't recognize asked him what he wanted. The brother had a hooked nose and was small and bent. His skin was old and wrinkled like a pickle. "Padre Benedetto," Richard said.

"Always Benedetto!" rasped the brother. "Does he think this is an office building? Come in."

The brother was sharp and brusque and merely pointed the direction down the hall; he shuffled away without another sign.

Richard shrugged and was puzzled. He had never seen such an attitude at San Girolamo.

He walked slowly to Padre Benedetto's door. The corridor was very still.

"Avanti!" came the familiar cry as he knocked.

"Buon giorno, padre."

"Ah! Riccardo! Come in, come in!" The old man lay aside his pen and his book. He straightened his heavy glasses. "Sit down. Is it cold outside?"

"Like spring, padre. Warm and mild. A little nippy."

"Pneumonia weather, Riccardo, pneumonia weather! A trap for men like me." The old man's eyes flashed and he rubbed his nose.

"You look very good, padre. Better than several months ago."

"Si . . . si," said the old priest, touching his cheeks. "Yes, I feel very good. I feel almost young again." He laughed. "How were your examinations?"

Richard sat up a little. "Easy."

"Good."

"We took a trip out Via Aurelia—Paolo, George—he's an African—Gabriele—from Colombia—and myself. We had an awfully good hike."

"Yes."

"I heard from Herbert, too. He's doing very well. . . . It's so good to have friends!"

Padre Benedetto nodded.

"Father Milton's back now from England; he's taking Conny home. Conny's legs are pretty much better. They're going to try to make him walk at Mayo."

Padre Benedetto nodded.

Richard changed his tone a little. "I talked to Father Milton. I told him I was going to petition for ordination. I thought I better talk to you about it."

Padre Benedetto shifted his weight in his chair. "You want to make the petition?"

"—yes."

"Then by all means do. As long as your choice is conscious and willful, nothing can shake it."

"I hope not."

Padre Benedetto was silent but watched him closely.

"I mean, I'm so enthusiastic now about George and Gabriele—they're these new friends—I feel better than I have all year. There's real communication with them. I think I need that in order to survive."

Padre Benedetto waited.

"They're a lot like Herbert. Good ideas, enthusiastic—it's contagious. You sort of need friends to buck the *status quo* and hold on to your ideals."

"Is it the *status quo* that is troubling you?"

"What do you mean, padre?"

"I think you're your own trouble, Riccardo."

"I?"

"Not the conformity or the conservatism or anything else. Not even your desire to paint, which you haven't mentioned. You're still hiding from yourself, Riccardo. When you get close to the answer, you run away. What earthly difference would it make to you what sins and negligences other men committed if you yourself were full of charity and lived in God? What difference would it make?"

"It still would be wrong on their part, padre. It still would need opposition."

"Catholicism is very *hard*, Riccardo. It doesn't ask reforms in other places, but in oneself. Reforms come and go, sounding brass and tinkling cymbal. It is a very human, often very ugly Church. I know that. The question is, how much charity have you?"

"But I'm not afraid of *my* charity, padre. That's *my* problem. *I'm* afraid of being hit from left and right, not allowed to paint, not allowed to speak, looked on as a nuisance—or a danger."

The priest shrugged.

Richard pushed on stubbornly. "There isn't much freedom for those who speak of freedom. A lot of ideas are very hard to voice."

"When I was young, Riccardo, I met Charles Péguy. I met him in Paris. I know the difficulties of being free."

Richard hardly listened. "Besides, I want to paint. I really want to paint. If I can't give my life to art, at least I want to try to make it possible for other men to do it in the future."

"Riccardo . . . what is your motivation for all this?"

"They're wrong, that's what it is! The Church has become a machine. The priests are mere administrators. There's no love and freedom ruling things."

"And you believe that that's sufficient motivation?"

Richard didn't answer.

"Your motive is not the love of God or you would not be so upset. You would be calm and strong and sure. Not so fitful and erratic. You're full of emotion. Your pride is being wounded. You don't want to subordinate yourself. You want everything your own way and at once."

The white curtain in the window was suffused with sunlight.

"You don't have to be so pained, Riccardo," laughed the old man softly. "I've told worse to people. You didn't think I thought you were perfect, did you? You didn't think you were perfect, did you? You're a common piece of clay. It's good for you to know that."

Richard felt his speech would be unsteady if he spoke. Yet he didn't want to sit there passively. He gathered all the energy he had. "I'm sorry I'm so foolish." His inner tension was relieved. He felt the strength of manhood beginning to gather in his heart.

The priest sat back. "You are an artist, Riccardo. Your whole way of thought reveals it. The way your eyes regard things, the comments you make on things, the moodiness and introspection you carry about within you. You are even too delicate; you take everything to heart; you are not as strong and aggressive as you should be. I get the impression sometimes that you don't want to bruise things, that you hold back and let things injure you. An artist likes the world in some perspective, in symmetry, in form. Disjointed things annoy you. You are torn between contemplation and righteousness. You want to act, you want to be at peace. An artist sees visions, his own visions, and he blames the world when it does not conform. But the mature artist comes more and more to love reality. Recall that, Riccardo. He lets his tears fall on the real earth, the imperfect, stony earth, and not on any other, on God's world as it is. Don't waste your tears, Riccardo."

"I know I want to be a priest," said Richard with a new firmness. "I know I want to be a priest. After that, I become confused. I'm pulled apart by a thousand inclinations. One half of me does not want to work by charity! One half wants to labor with the world's weapons in the world's way. I want to paint. I want to speak. I want to act!"

The priest looked at the resolution marking Richard's face. "Reality will never please the artists. The Lord was not an artist, Riccardo. He was small, pragmatic, realistic. Would you have done things His way, Riccardo? Would you have left men to themselves, human causes to have human effects, human machinery to need human sweat and suffer human scars? Or would you have worked it all out—like that!—and made it all 'without spot or wrinkle' from the first?" The old priest smiled wryly.

"We're not supposed to *accept* evil and mediocrity."

"No."

"Well, then?"

A smile threatened to break across the priest's face. "Where will you begin?"

Richard flushed.

The priest hid the smile behind his hand. "You feel an immense weight of ugliness, Riccardo, and it is there. Sometimes, at night, one can hear it pressing on the earth and feel men stifling under it. But hidden, some places, is the fire of charity. Many people are living by the love of the Gospels—many thousands, perhaps many millions. You will see one day and be amazed. The world is charged every day with many kindnesses, much integrity, much truth at the cost of pain. The amount of goodness is immense. And every bit of it is a miracle; remember that. The world belongs to vanity and to decay; it belongs to nothingness and Satan. Everything rescued is a fresh new miracle, something extra, something gratis. Remember that.

"You will find it anywhere, among the very poor, among the wealthy—surprises of it, hidden veins of it, perhaps only a moment or a gleam of it—but surely you will see it often. Men need not be good. Every smile, every helping hand is a new creation, something unnecessary, something made from the heart of man."

"I know that's true, padre. I know it is! But it doesn't answer something—here. It doesn't ease everything that is pulling at my heart."

"Do you know what you are really concerned about, Riccardo? You are worried because you do not love enough. You sometimes believe that you hear a voice calling from the mountains, where the air is new and cold. But then you are afraid, for you know somehow that God will take everything from you. And so you listen for noises in the world, and there are many of them. There is a great deal of sickness and corruption and rottenness. And so you begin to believe that you know why you are anxious: You are in an evil world. But you are anxious because you are not faithful to yourself. God is calling you as the target calls an arrow. You are eternal, but you postpone remembering. Your heart cries out for life, but you stifle it for fear. Why are the men in our age so afraid to be? Why does it spread even to the monasteries? Why such hesitance? Why such timidity?" The priest's almond-black eyes were flashing. He spoke with long-accumulated earnestness. "It is everywhere! In everyone who comes to talk with me."

"I am not afraid, padre, but I don't see what I should do," Richard said after a little silence.

"I can't tell you, Riccardo. You must see for yourself."

"I know that I should be a priest. But what does that mean? A time of rush and worry, routine and overwork. I'll never get to touch my art. I'll never see much fruit in my work among the people. No one does. Things go on very much the same."

"That is the image of reality I want you to maintain."

"But I don't want to maintain it! I want so much to break through it! I want a force to be generated—an inner force that will change the face of everything."

"Then don't think of 'natural' and 'supernatural' as two different worlds. There is only one God, one real world, one Love behind existence. Cherish every form of love. Realize that love twists its way into every heart, that it is the core of every ideology, that it is in the hearts of families and friends and strangers who are kind. That is how the Lord gets His way. No matter how men try to escape, they end up driving one another back to unity and love. War does it, bitterness does it: there are many means! But the universe has only one source. Every reform, every evil parody, every act gets its force from love."

"And where do I start?"

"Where do you start?" nodded the old man. "Humble charity is the only force that moves the world." The priest set his steel-framed glasses on the desk. The sun shone on the dull leather books.

"I still don't understand," mused Richard in the silence. His hand was on his chin. His heart was moved; he struggled to straighten out his ideas. "Herbert and I used to talk of things. We never understood where things were moving to. We saw great forces, we saw ideas, we saw the bloodshed and the wars. I wish I understood!"

"Of course. A new consciousness—I think that is the word," said the old man after he had thought a moment. "That is what I hope it is. You and your African and Colombian, you are speaking the same language now, you know the same ideas. You are conscious that life on earth is flux. Men are better educated. They are more disciplined than in the past—their schedules are harder, their lives move faster, efficiency digs into them. Men are more sophisticated—every day they have more alternatives to choose among than they can possibly exhaust. Through psychiatry they know their strengths and weaknesses. They know the risks of every choice. This is what I mean by consciousness. Men know so much about everything they do. It was much simpler when they didn't know, when they simply acted out of instinct, believed from instinct, loved from instinct, brought up children by their instincts. Perhaps people were even happier. But now we are more conscious. We have got to live with our greater knowledge. We have got to live with our greater freedom."

Richard shook his head. "Freedom is a burden. Thought is a burden."

Padre Benedetto nodded. "You will see it in people's eyes. And love must fill that consciousness—conscious love, chosen love, bold love, new love—with more and more intelligence. Were more of it to fill human consciousness . . . were evolution to speed in *that* direction . . . Riccardo!"

Richard saw a vision too intense in Padre Benedetto's eyes; he looked away.

"But never, of course, on earth. . . . Were happiness to come, were symmetry and form to come, we would lose the cross. We would lose suffering. And, with suffering, we would lose the ardors of perfect love. So, many men do not love, mediocrity is given reign, transitoriness crushes us . . ."

They sat in silence for a while.

"Riccardo, you will make a fine priest, if once you learn to suffer, if once your will becomes adamant. You must be determined. . . . You go now. Make your petition for ordination. Stand on your own. When I see you the next time, tell me how you've changed."

"You're optimistic."

The old priest shrugged with a tired smile. "If no change, why should we continue talking?"

"You're absolutely right," said Richard slowly.

He was lost in thought until he reached the college.

27

THE SEMINARISTS were scattered on the hilltop above the valley of Rieti. The sky was glassy bright. A purplish mist hung on the horizon. A long white mountain rose across the valley, and other violet hills marched off in the distance. A bird cawed on the hillside. It was Mardi Gras, and warm, and quiet.

Richard had wandered over the brow of the hilltop, behind the monastery, to the cave where Francis had lived while he wrote his religious rule. He stood within the shadow of the cave and listened to the wind. A pine bough hung in shadow before the cave. Sprigs of green had begun to appear where the ground was soft. Trees rustled in the wind. The bird cawed again. The birds St. Francis talked to? Richard mused. He reached forward and moved the stiff pine bough with his hand. Below, the valley of Rieti gleamed in the sun. Patched fields of different colors, tiny flashes of stucco, red roofs, a gleaming creek bed. The air felt fresh and clean. The mountains in the distance almost shouted aloud. It was strange to feel so in possession of the valley and yet so powerless, unable to respond or lose oneself or halt the flow of Time. . . .

He looked about at the damp stones of the tiny cave. Could a man have lived in here? He wondered if it were only legend about the writing of the rule from here. But he knew St. Francis saw the valley. No wonder he wrote such a fresh and open rule. Modern congregations had been conceived in ugly provincial cities of the North.

His heart cried out for God, genuinely and deeply.

"Riccardo! Riccardo!"

Richard listened to hear where the voice was coming from.

"Riccardo!"

"*Sono qui . . . giù!*"

It was Paolo up above. He heard him coming down by the path.

"*Che fai?*"

"I was thinking."

"*Il Pensieroso.*"

Richard grinned defensively.

"Very beautiful, no?" Paolo said, stepping in.

"Lovely. This is the place to write a rule."

"Like Subiaco."

"Or Montserrat. Where there is beauty—and spaciousness."

"*Romantico!*"

"*È vero!* I can't deny it"

"Come, they're almost ready to start eating lunch."

"I'm hungry enough. Let's go."

"Look, Riccardo. Have you seen?" Paolo pointed through the grille of what seemed to be a cellar window.

Richard put his face against the bars and peered into the dark. He drew back quickly. "Oh no! Bones and skulls."

Paolo laughed. "The old monks. It's the burial room. From six centuries."

Richard grimaced. "They could close them off from view."

"The monks aren't afraid to see them."

"I think it's hideous!"

"*Beh!* You aren't a medieval."

"There are few things I'm happier about."

"*Allora!* I hope you haven't spoiled your lunch."

"Paolo, appetite is one thing, aesthetics is another. I could eat a horse."

A gleam came to Paolo's eye. "You may. I swear I don't know where the sisters buy their meat."

Richard slapped him on the shoulder.

Padre Bracciano was beginning grace before meals as they appeared. Conversation in the courtyard ceased, except for two groups that hadn't noticed prayer beginning. Somebody hissed to them, and somebody else cleared his throat. Hats came off and faces reddened. In the wind, Richard didn't hear the prayer. The regulator rang a tiny bell for the Angelus, but the tones sounded light and tinny out of doors. Padre Bracciano blessed the boxes of food laid at the base of the high wooden cross in the courtyard. Then he said *Deo Gratias*! and all picked up the phrase. Hats went back on tonsured heads. Lines began to form. Shouting, pushing, and conversation resumed as if never interrupted.

Paolo and Richard came away with two cheese-and-ham buns, a hard-boiled egg, and a cup of wine: Paolo had red, Richard white. They bit into their rolls and sipped the cold, bitter wine. The buns were hard and salty to the tongue. The wine warmed their stomachs.

"*Qui,* Riccardo. I have the salt."

"Thanks, Paolo. These eggs are good. Where are you putting the shells?"

"Here, I have a paper."

"Thanks. Eat up! Tomorrow begins the fast."

Paolo smiled. They were sitting on the edge of the courtyard, overlooking as best they could the sun-filled valley. They balanced their cups on the ground. Paolo took off his beret so they could rest their extra sandwich upon it. They sat on a log; the drop below, through the underbrush, wasn't sheer, but it was very steep.

"Petitions in a week or two," Paolo mused. "Vicariate exams in April, the Greg in June, and then—ordination."

Richard smiled. "Take your last fling. Think it over. It's not too late."

Paolo laughed. "Well, I'll feel better when all these exams are done."

"Relax. It's not even Easter yet."

"Only ten weeks until the first exam. At most. Probably nine."

Richard picked up a pebble and threw it into the underbrush, trying to send it down the hill. "I never thought I'd see the day! Veronese nervous!"

"You don't know Veronese very well. He can't let his steam out on canvas."

Richard looked sharply at him and laughed.

They both stood erect and walked back for a piece of cake and more wine. Richard selected two ripe peaches. Paolo picked up some sugar biscuits.

"The sisters really make a feast."

"I bet they're glad to see us go for a day."

"I wish they had a chance for some of this themselves."

"Nuns are the greatest women in the world."

They sat back astride their log. They were silent for a while as they ate the soft chocolate cake. The cool wine tasted good even with the cake.

"I can't keep my eyes off that mountain."

"The white one?"

"It's so serene and silent."

"Molto betta," Paolo nodded.

"We go over there next? Richard looked towards another mountain. He bit into his cake.

Paolo nodded. "There's a little cave where they say St. Francis and his companions slept. It's only—this big. They must have been midgets." Richard laughed. "There's a red cross on the wall, which they say St. Francis made."

"When were you here before?"

"Once with Luigi."

"Luigi?"

"Tasconi."

Richard nodded.

"We liked Assisi best; everything was quiet and calm."

"I'll try to go there this coming summer."

"Where else?"

Richard smiled. "Florence, Venice . . ."

"You've been back there every year."

"Where else?" Richard smiled.

Paolo bit into a peach. He changed the subject. "Have you designed your chalice yet?"

"Yes. And yours?"

"I don't think I'll get one, Riccardo. My father wants to buy it, but—there'll be one anywhere I go. For the sake of poverty, I'd rather not."

"I would like to say mass with a chalice that is beautiful, clean, significant. I couldn't stand a factory model. I want mine to be in silver—for earthiness, for time, for use. Gold is for show. I want a heavy cup, large and deep. I want a node of amethyst or anything red or purple."

"No inscription?"

"No. But I may have Rouault's 'Christ Mocked by Soldiers' engraved on the cup. It's my favorite image of Christianity."

Paolo smiled. "It's impossible to believe we're almost there, isn't it?"

"In nine months we'll be saying mass."

"In another six months hearing confessions, preaching, counseling."

"It will come soon enough; there's a lot to do between now and then."

Richard looked at the tangled gray underbrush on the cliff. New shoots pushed through the bed of leaves. New white-green slips of briars began to grow alongside their hardened forebears. The stiff branches of the trees and shrubs were beginning to unbend and course with life. His own heart felt the same kind of change. He had begun to spend the entire evening, every day, in prayer. At recreation after supper he redoubled his efforts to admit mistakes when necessary, listen to what others were trying to say, be scrupulously honest and generous with his own speech. At night prayer, when the entire community droned the prescribed prayers for the ending of the day, he tried to stir and revitalize his attention, if not to the words, at least to God. As the others left the chapel, he would take out his own breviary, which felt so comfortable in his hand, and say compline, the evening prayer of the Church. He would read a little from St. John of the Cross or from St. Teresa. Then he would sit in silent prayer. The benches creaked; others left or entered; lights went off and on. He kept his eyes closed and kept as near to God's presence as possible. His heart was usually dry and without inspiration. It didn't matter. He didn't want to feel or think. He wanted to believe. Sometimes he said the word over and over as his defense against distractions. Often he said: "I love." He didn't want to use words but did so because it was necessary. He knew that God understood him thoroughly, even if he did not see God; that sufficed. He rejoiced in the dry silence. When emotions came, he accepted them. He preferred their absence, because they were distracting and misleading; they were not prayer, though faith was.

Previously, he had never had the time to give this last hour of the evening to God. There was always a thesis to outline, a chapter to digest, a letter to write. Besides, he had always felt he would be restless, his mind would wander, there would be only distractions anyway. But now he had made up his mind that he wanted to pray more than anything else, whatever the result. That decision changed everything. His body still shrank from the hour's effort; studies, letters, duties called him away from it. Some days he cheated by putting off some of the breviary he was obliged to say each day until the evening. He caught himself cheating and resolved to keep the final hour free of obligatory things.

Already his life had taken a sort of new root. He was like a ship that had taken on ballast and evened out its stability. He knew now what he wanted to do. The cold, searing light of confrontation with the Lord was beginning to expose many of his hidden faults. He began to dislike precipitation and impatience; minor matters no longer set his nerves on edge; his judgments concerning other people were calmer and deeper. He began to sense how truly lonely all creatures are and how each seeks completeness—but usually by sham and pretense. And, seeing his own pretenses, he began to feel compassion for the strugglings of other men. He felt as if a light in the dry silence was burning into him; or, rather, he felt nothing, but noted the change in his judgments. He was no longer troubled when his faults came to the attention of others, and he couldn't quite bring himself to defend himself: A part of him still longed to, but another part insisted that the truth could not hurt him or hurt others. He felt that these changes in his life were themselves misleading, however, because they came too swiftly and too easily. He didn't find in himself the struggles and long turmoil that St. John spoke of, or even Teresa. He felt that the Lord was leading him like a child, the easy way, for a while. There would be long days of drought and relapse into fault and struggling with his pretenses before he would achieve real progress.

He knew, with his mind and cold will, that he was face to Face with God, whether his emotions sensed anything or not. As his mind searched this conviction, the implications became more and more extensive; horizons widened rapidly. He came to feel a certain closeness to creation. Creation surrendered itself to him; it wasn't hostile, it was friendly; it was enigmatic and brief, like a lover's letter; it stirred his heart with every gesture and event. It no longer appealed to him as a source of beauty and emotion; Wordsworthian romanticism made his new heart uneasy. He didn't want creation, or ecstasy, but creation's Maker: in a very quiet, ordinary way, without excitement, without joy, without tears. He was sure the Lord was touching the deep point of his soul in these silent, arid movements, beyond what the sensibilities could detect.

"Riccardo!" The voice shocked him. "What are you thinking of?"

Richard colored a little. "Something."

"Eh, for sure! Another painting?"

"No." Richard smiled and regarded Paolo's smooth, red face. The light fuzz of adolescence seemed to have been just shaved from it; Paolo had no signs of a beard heavy like his own. Paolo's merry eyes questioned him, but without intruding. His threadbare but neat cassock shone lightly in the sun on his plump, active body. One of the best things he liked about Paolo was the silence they could share; Paolo didn't feel any compulsion to be always chattering or hearing noise.

Paolo thought he had been enjoying the valley. "It's beautiful. It's worth looking at."

Richard nodded.

"Don't let me interfere in the processes of a great, creative painter. I am not jealous of your thoughts."

"I know," Richard laughed. "But I'm afraid the great, creative painter was hardly thinking of the view. It's a shame, too."

They felt the sun upon their faces as they looked. Richard picked up a twig and took the bark off it absently and pushed his nail into the soft wood until the twig split. He was looking at the white mountain, and he felt a great contentment.

28

THE *COLLEGIO* BUS was still new and shiny. The interior was in silver and in red. When he stepped aboard at Rieti, the fumes inside made Richard a trifle sick. But as the bus began to move, the odors either disappeared or were forgotten. Richard looked out the green-tinted windows and watched the bus gain the open country. Facing him, on the back of the seat in front of him, was a picture of the Rialto Bridge in Venice; facing Padre Bracciano was a view of Bressanone in the Tyrol. He was glad to be sitting with Padre Bracciano, though the arrangement had come about by accident. He felt that a genuine friendship had sprung up between him and the superior, even though it was unspoken.

"You enjoyed the trip, Padre Riccardo?" the superior asked. His voice had its usual raspiness.

"Our Lady of the Angels was beautiful, padre. The valley too. *Lei?*"

"Of course, I've seen it many times before. Every four years I bring a new group back. But it's one of my favorite trips."

"Did you see the children down at the cathedral?"

"No . . . I didn't. Were there children?"

"About four or five in Mardi Gras costumes. They were little girls dressed as gamblers and dancers. One even had a mustache painted on. Cute as could be."

"Rome is probably full of them today. The mothers parade them down the Via Nazionale."

"I saw them yesterday: George and Martha Washingtons, cowboys, Indians, Chinamen—it's a panic. And all of them throwing confetti."

"The carnival at Frascati is going full tilt, too."

"And, of course, the Piazza Navona."

"From time immemorial," smiled the superior. His large face was comfortable and relaxed. His dark eyes shone behind his rimless glasses. "But the big carnival now is in Frascati. Of course, you've never seen it?" he teased.

"We have a strict superior."

"No one ever came in to ask if he could go."

"Padre, what would you have said?"

" 'No.' But they should come in."

They both laughed.

"Have you heard if Conny and Padre Milton arrived all right?"

"*Padre Generale* got a note from Padre Milton yesterday. They arrived safely at the hospital, and Padre Milton went on to Chicago."

"I suppose Conny's parents met them."

Padre Bracciano was disturbed for a moment. "I suppose so—I don't know. . . . He is very lucky. The doctors here worked very hard to save his leg. He is very lucky."

"Yes, he is." Richard sensed Padre Bracciano's pride in his handling of the mishap.

"It took them fourteen hours to operate on him. They had to collect every piece of bone, tie the cartilage, and so forth." Padre Bracciano tried to imitate the operation with his hands: plunged with forceps, tied, and then scraped things together and pushed them in for the final sewing.

Richard smiled.

The bus roared on through the late afternoon countryside, down the narrow winding road. Signs in blue and white announced towns that three years ago Richard had never heard of. Billboards announced Italian products and sometimes American ones as well. The bus driver blew the horn on long curves, speeding relentlessly on the narrow asphalt. The passengers looked over sheer ridges as they rounded their way up hills, descended into valleys, climbed again. The hills were peculiar: small, rounded, bare, humped torturously in gullies and steep defiles. . . . Sometimes a castle stood dark upon a hilltop. It was hard not to picture medieval knights and armies winding through the valleys. The sun was a white ball above the grayish-blue horizon. There were not enough clouds for a brilliant sunset. Winter grass waved gray and restless, though in some fields new wheat or barley waved a fresh, tentative, young green. A stream lay white and silver in the dying light. The sun cast large shadows from the moving bus, the lines of poplars that sentineled the asphalt, the hills opposite the road. Inside the bus, the drone of movement dulled into the riders' consciousness.

Richard and Padre swayed with the motion of the bus. Padre Bracciano said *"mi scusi,"* and began to say some of his breviary. Richard said a small section of his to take advantage, like his superior, of the remaining light. In the back of the bus, six or seven voices were harmonizing softly, singing "Santa Lucia." Their voices barely filled the bus but were like a soft undertow just above the rushing of the tires. There were occasional shouts and bursts of laughter as those in the back seat quarreled over the last of the cake and wine. A lot of teasing and lightheadedness was going on.

After a time, Richard and Padre both finished saying their office. They sat in silence for a while. Outside, it was darker as dusk descended.

"Italia è molto bella," said Padre Bracciano in the silence.

"Yes, I like it very much . . . this view in the evening."

"Very tranquil."

"Very."

"America is too busy, too hurried," smiled Padre Bracciano, turning to watch Riccardo.

"Yes, it is."

"And Italy is copying America. The whole world is copying America."

Richard smiled, nodding to a billboard: "Coca-Cola."

"But also . . . its spirit. . . the American spirit is something I do not understand," sighed the older man. "It strikes me first as . . . wrong. I do not like it. But I think perhaps it is only me."

Richard listened, rocking in the bus.

"Americans are so . . . free. They are very brash. They do not have the respect that—say—well, Italian people have."

Richard felt very strong in his own convictions and at peace. He didn't fear to argue with his superior and tried earnestly to be faithful to what he really thought. "But the poor of Italy have been so oppressed, padre. They are too respectful."

"Ah! They are humble. They understand the laws of life. They keep their place and do not ask too much. Americans . . . seem to break those laws."

"You are right, padre. There *are* laws Americans don't consider 'laws.' Social stability, for one; keeping one's place. But there are other laws which Americans respect and Italians don't. Responsibility, perhaps, or social discipline. The way people get on or off a bus, for example—without all this pushing and confusion. Or the attitude toward red tape and the letter of the law. Subtle differences . . ."

"We are different peoples. We must learn to understand."

"Affection teaches best, padre. I know that even from my art. The more I love a subject, the more I come to see."

"It takes more than love!" The superior's face became very serious. "There is the future. That is what concerns us—in authority." He slipped his fingers up underneath the bridge of his glasses for a moment. "Will Americans throw out all laws with their love of mobility and freedom? What will be left? What will be left in Italy when the American ways are accepted? What will happen to her religion, her traditions, her patience and suffering?"

"You worry because of the movies, the comic books . . ."

"The spirit!"

Richard tried to force him to use the word: "Materialism?"

"*Beh!* Perhaps . . . I am not so sure that that is not too simple. Freedom is not a materialistic value. It is freedom that worries me."

"Padre, why would *freedom* worry you?"

"What does it mean for the people, the common people? You tell them they have freedom, that Americanization means freedom, and what happens to their lives? Do you know what happens? Values collapse, sins multiply, contrition vanishes . . . society dissolves . . . infidelities, divorce, loss of respect for authority, for law . . ."

"Padre, are there not many sins anyway?"

"Even *with* stability there are many sins. Without it . . ."

"Americans are among the most law-abiding people in the world."

"Yes, yes. But I do not mean *law*. I mean . . . I mean . . . authority. Every American is a law unto himself."

"Padre . . . isn't that . . . good? In a certain sense?"

"No! No. . . . It leads to . . . relativism. Who is right? What is truth? Where have authority and reason gone? What happens to order and stability?"

"But look at the stability of the American government."

"Pragmatism! Sheer pragmatism! America has no ideas to show the world—nothing but . . . pluralism and freedom! Yes—and mass production. What will they bring us?"

The bus droned on. The sun was a white-and-orange ball on the horizon, easy to look upon, like a fruit about to drop away. The sky behind it was dull pink and violet. It was a most unusual sun, brilliant yet not blinding. A stream in the valley far below the bus caught the silver sheen and flashed it towards the high road.

Richard began to sense how deep the argument was going to go. He saw that Padre Bracciano genuinely wished an exchange of ideas and was not merely judging him. Besides, he felt inside a deep peace and honesty. He began again to try to explain. "Padre, it is difficult to put in words. But I'd never . . . worry about freedom at all! It seems to me the very basis of the Gospel, the very root . . ."

"Ah, but as a *means*, not as an end . . . or, rather, as a *condition* . . ."

"But so important! Society can't offer anything more than a condition. Individual men must do the rest. Men must make the choices. Society can only offer an atmosphere. That is the American idea."

"But is unguided atmosphere a help to man? Is not pluralism a disease—a—swamp that breeds diseases? Men are not intelligent in the mass. They have puny minds: The movies aim at twelve-year-olds. Men's minds conform to current tastes—in droves, in flocks, in herds. An original mind is as rare in a society

as . . . snow in the desert! You will not live much longer, Padre
Riccardo, before you see that men, even men of intelligence and
education, love to conform, love conformity better than anything
else. They want to overcome their loneliness. They disagree on
little things just to salve their pride. But most of all they crave the
security of being up-to-date . . . or even avant-garde if it is con-
ventional to be . . ."

"Padre, you frighten me."

"Why? Why?" laughed the priest.

"You do not think that men are capable of choosing for themselves.
If they had to think for themselves, you fear that they would . . ."

". . . follow the fashions of the moment! Is that so frightening?
So . . . terrible?" The priest was smiling.

"Do you think the Church is set up on that principle?"

"Oh, I do not mean to say *that*," the superior shrugged. "Certain disciplinary laws, it is true. The Index, some of the examples
you read under 'Occasions of Sin,' the attitude on movie censorship
. . . *'Praesumptio est. . . .'* The presumption is that for the majority
of men this or that would constitute a danger . . ."

"The presumption is that the majority of men do not have a
moral sense . . ."

"Exactly!"

"How strange! Democracy operates on precisely the opposite
assumption."

"Of course! Liberalism is fundamentally an optimism, even an
utopianism. Liberals have forgotten all about original sin."

"Yet the Gospels . . . the Gospels are utterly rooted in freedom.
There is nowhere else where freedom is so important. No one
stands for free will as the Gospels do . . . heaven and hell—nothing
makes sense unless there is individual responsibility. The Gospel
appeals to the person . . . to one at a time . . . for love . . . for understanding. The state, the law, the doctors, all—all are brushed aside.
You! You! You are what counts. You and the Lord, alone. Freedom,
padre, freedom is the beginning of everything!"

"The beginning, yes!"

"And the end! 'The truth shall make you free.' Don't you think it is freedom to be a saint, to love only God?"

"Of course, of course, Padre Riccardo; but most men are not saints."

"Will you try to make them saints by law?"

"Oh no! Of course not," laughed the priest. "Of course not! Merely to guide them. Oh, there are few saints—the Lord knows, very few! To legislate for *them*!"

"What happens to the mass of men? To the mediocre?"

"They must avoid mortal sin, that is all."

"Then there are two kinds of Christianity: one, a Christianity of freedom for the saints, for the true Christians; the other, a Christianity of law, of mediocrity, of discipline and guidance, and avoidance of mortal sin . . ."

"What else? Of course, you disparage it in the way you speak. But we are only human. The Lord knows what we are made of. Talk all you want, men remain the same. Take up Nietzsche's superman: You think that will help? Nine men in ten will be too lazy to listen to you; of the others, one in a thousand will submit himself to Nietzsche's discipline. . . . Oh, you can get a whole nation aroused, as Hitler did. You can march and sing and hold games." The priest lifted the bridge of his glasses again and rubbed his eyes. "Look what Mussolini tried to do in Italy—his forum and his nude statues on the post offices in all these little towns! In the end, the common man is deadweight, *ignobile vulgus,* as has been said from time immemorial. Padre Riccardo, these are facts. The Church must work with facts. The Church is here to save men as they are."

"I don't see that . . . I don't know why. I don't see that, not the way you explain it. It just does not meet everything that I have seen and felt. In America . . . the people . . . democracy . . . well, it works! There are the sports enthusiasts, there is the vulgar taste, there are the movies and amusements and the smell of factories, but . . . it works! Somehow, there is kindness . . . and humanity; there is thought . . . and concern. Somehow, it works! Europeans—excuse me, padre— Europeans speak of 'the masses'; Americans do not. Who coined the *ignobile vulgus*—a European, wasn't it? And didn't Thomas Mann write of the beautiful and the fair against the ugly herd? It's built into everything here in Europe—in the Church and into ideology. The artists pick it up. The artists *started* it. The avant-garde falls into it. But they have never won in America. America is run by common, living, working, uninspired men, and they are free."

"America will last only until she uses up the capital of her Protestant inheritance. Then she will lose her respect for law, her institutions, her morality. And that has been happening, Padre Riccardo; that is already far along."

"But many more than Protestants have respect for law! The humanists, the unbelievers—they respect and defend the law as much as anyone."

"But on what grounds?"

"The needs of peace. The requirements of order. Law for Americans is the protector of the peace and of the right to pursue happiness. Law is a friend."

"What happens as the relativists in your universities teach that law is a convention, a taboo? What happens as artists depict and praise the defiance of the laws? As 'progress' comes to mean dissent?"

"Padre, you misunderstand!"

"I do not think so. I have been in America and have observed. I hear confessions! Man is not what your Americans think he is. . . . Here, I will tell you something. How can the liberals praise a man like Freud? Freud! Now there was a man who knew what the confessional was like. There was a man who knew what could be dredged along the bottom of the human soul! There was a man who knew original sin, much as he despised the name! What are all these dark longings, these impulses, these repressions that he spoke of, if not man's blindness and animality, which he inherits from his parents? *There* was a man who knew. Now, how can the liberals idolize him? Amazing! Utterly amazing!"

"You go from . . . to Freud . . . I cannot understand you!"

"Human life is very complicated. That is why I say, follow the Church. The Church is slow with things. Freud, for instance. Now, when I went through, we weren't allowed to read him. In certain clerical company, I still would not speak of him! But, Padre Riccardo, she comes back to pick up what was good after the excitement has passed."

"I don't admire the Church for that."

"What's that, padre?"

"I don't admire the Church for that."

"Why not? Isn't it the highest wisdom? 'Wisely and slow'—isn't that Shakespeare?"

"It is pretentious! I . . . frankly, I . . . hate this show of wisdom!"

"Padre Riccardo . . ."

"I do! I hate this pretense of always being right. If we were afraid of Freud thirty years ago, well, then we were right or we were cowardly, but it's not fair to come back later and pretend to perfect wisdom when the issues are all dead!"

"Ah, but it's that very conservatism that guarantees . . ."

"Nothing! Nothing at all. . . . Oh, I see the need . . . excuse me, padre . . . I see the need for slowness with dogmatic definitions. Yes, dogma should be formed very slowly and always worded negatively: 'it is *not* this . . . *this* is not it. . . .' There's a kind of wisdom and courage in taking a stand like that. But I can't see this caution with ideas. I have a passion for ideas. Ideas are gateways, doors, openings. I can't understand those who run around barring out the sky, closing people in! There ought to be room for experimentation, too. There must be room for newness and advance, as well as for dogmatic carefulness . . ."

"You are very optimistic. However, time will teach you . . ."

"I hate time, too! Why must we be always put off by the threat of later experience? Does experience mean forcing everybody into the same mold?"

"The same mold, Padre Riccardo?"

Richard flushed. "I didn't mean it that way exactly."

"I know what you meant. But, padre," the superior smiled gently, "you must be more temperate. You talk . . . like a very young man. . . ."

"No . . ." began Richard, then stopped. He shrugged to himself and relapsed into silence. He smiled and said: "I'm not really being carried away, padre. I mean what I say. I like to argue like this."

"I, too, Padre Riccardo." The priest lowered his chin and looked up through his glasses with a smile. "As you once said, it's good for an old man to argue with the young."

Richard blushed. He wanted to say "and vice versa," but feared that it would sound too much like flattery. "Anyway," he said, taking a deep breath, "it's been the close of a lovely day."

"Yes, it has," said the superior.

In the back of the bus, seven or eight fellows, Umberto leading, were singing light, frolicking Italian songs again. They sang softly and low; the songs grew more melancholy as one led to another, and the day's wine and excitement were lulled by the steady hum of the tires. Twilight was falling rapidly. The bus lights went on. In the middle of the bus, many of the students were dozing. Padre Bracciano looked around and pulled out his rosary. He held it up. The word spread throughout the bus.

"Rosary!"

"Time for the rosary!

"Shh!"

"Hey! Rosary!"

"Credo in unum Deum," began Padre Bracciano.

One side of the bus joined him in leading the rosary, the other side responded. They alternated the leadership at each decade. The words droned on.

"Ave Maria, gratia plena . . ."

"Sancta Maria, Mater Dei . . ."

"Paternoster . . ."

The bus rounded the hills in the twilight. The Western sky went from pink and violet to pale blue, then to the darkness of the early night. The buildings of Rome appeared on the horizon, then the lights of the suburbs, then the side streets. Richard thought of Padre Benedetto and said a prayer of gratitude for his advice and counsel. He tried to understand what Padre Bracciano had been arguing and how to answer it. He tried to think of God as he should be doing. Rome at night was like a fairyland. The sky was big. America was far away. The rosary was concluded, and all sat in hushed silence a moment before the stirring began, when each would gather his belongings and troop into the dark and empty college on Lungotevere.

29

LENT ALWAYS LOWERED Richard's spirits. It was a time of year when there were few free days, when professors counted on doing the heaviest amount of work, when, outside, the rain fell and, inside, just as relentlessly, attention was confined to studies and routine. At least there was no fasting: In honor of the Pope's residence among them, citizens of Rome were dispensed from the light Lenten fast that Catholics elsewhere in the world observe.

Richard tried to compensate for not fasting by sitting more erectly, eating of dishes he didn't like, and taking less of things he did like, without anyone's being able to notice it. He tried to keep his temper mild. He gave more attention to what others were saying when they talked; he tried to detect circumstances or inner trials from which they might be suffering. In a quiet and unaggressive way, he tried to make them feel liked and respected. He tried to root out from under cover his own desires for affection, agreement, sympathy, and praise, in order to make himself capable of needing God alone.

In a week or two, he revised his resolutions to include fighting against discouragement. He resolved that most of all peace would mean, for him at any rate, relinquishing the desire to be perfect and being content with his temperament and persistent faults. Paradoxically, if only he could be unconcerned about his faults, he neutralized them. He learned to ask the Lord constantly for mercy.

He didn't see Gabriele at school for a while and heard that he was down with the flu. He met George once in a walk through the piazza of San Pietro. But, like everything else, friendships seemed to have been driven into deeper recesses by the rains and by routine.

In the slow, dreary days, a more morbid form of sensuality than usual began to trouble him. At first merely sneaky and vague, fantasies became lurid and violent. The worst part about them was that they were attractive; it would have been folly for him to pretend that his flesh did not long for its completion. The legend of the little bird cloven in two by the Creator—each of whose two parts thereafter flew through the world ardently seeking the other—occurred to him forcefully and hauntingly; it slipped out from a pen sketch he was doing on the margin of his notes in Scripture class. At other times, in half sleep or in an unguarded, tired moment, the temptations took more ugly form: Nudes appeared to him, or his own body strained with desire.

He sometimes saw Mary Coleman in his fantasies, and awareness that it was her disgusted him; he wanted to keep her out of it. He had not seen her since that day in December, but somehow she had become part of him. Her blue eyes, her smile, her soft voice, her love of art and beauty were the concrete focus for which his heart was reaching. His heart was no longer without defense; he had gained the mastery. He admired her as a person. He felt a certain closeness to her, a certain sympathy, and if he was denying it for the sake of a higher love, still he cherished their friendship, fragile and momentary as it had been. Some day, in eternity, it would be reclaimed.

Sometimes in the street he saw the quick solid curve of girls' legs, the full movement of their breasts, the rich skin of their throats, the undulation of their buttocks as they walked. His heart would be alarmed, his mouth become dry. He tried to turn his mind to prayer. He fought with his imagination. He tried to think of basketball, studies, friends, anything to drive the demon from his thoughts. He was glad his flesh was young and alive; but it seemed cruel that the more he wanted to belong solely to God, the more rebellious his body became. He had thought that many of these battles had been passed, that in the past years he had laid much of this struggle to rest. He was almost tempted to give up his extra prayer in the evenings, for it was from about the time he began it that the new struggle started.

Once, walking with Umberto near the Fountain of Trevi, a typical incident occurred. It was, for a change, a bright clear day, but the breeze was nippy. A girl in a light-green dress stood near the rail of the fountain in front of them. The calves of her legs were gracefully formed, her thighs pressed against the tight dress, the breeze flashed a hint of her slip. She turned and pointed for her companion to a rooftop nearby. Her breasts were tight and high, her stomach firm. Richard saw all this in a glance and looked away, fighting his quick appreciation—and the desire that arose—trying to regain the thread of his conversation with Umberto.

Umberto shrugged and smiled as soon as they were past and leaned over to Richard. "Thanks to God for beautiful things!"

Richard grinned. "Almost too beautiful for me. She could launch nine hundred ships easily."

Umberto chuckled: "*Beh!* She is springtime." And he nodded towards an old woman walking in front of them, huge and twisting on her thick legs. "Think of winter." The old woman turned her head at a fruit stand. A great pimple lay beneath her nose. Her eyebrows were stiff and fierce. Her hair was straggly.

Umberto rubbed his large nose and chuckled again. "Think of their mothers when the daughters are so beautiful."

"Think of almost anything, but not of the daughters," Richard laughed.

He was glad Umberto had a sense of humor. He thought how oppressive it would be to be walking with Luigi Alessandro. Then he hoped it wasn't unkind to be so truthful. He took a mischievous delight in playing true speech against kind speech—because in the Lord's eyes such things were insignificant, so long as love was served. He felt happy and full of devilment and looked up at the gray clouds racing above the roof tops in the blue sky.

THE NIGHT for petitions came a few days later. Richard hesitated in the chapel for a moment, then hurried to the line outside Padre Bracciano's office. Paolo, Richard, Umberto, and four others were to ask for major orders: subdiaconate, diaconate, and priesthood, to be conferred in July, October, and December, successively. These were the major steps of the priesthood, each bringing new powers and each, beginning with subdiaconate, irrevocable. The subdeacon could take part as a major minister in the mass; he chanted the epistle. The deacon could distribute communion, could prepare the Body of the Lord for exposition, could preach the Word in public. The priest could offer mass, absolve sins in the name of the Lord, represent men before God, and for God minister to the poor, the contrite, the brokenhearted.

Richard waited for his turn to enter. He was sure he was making the right decision. But it was a little like proposing to a girl: the future consequences, the possibility of rejection, and the sudden concentration in one act of a decision long in making threatened to inhibit speech. The council might question him or raise objections. He might not have thought something out. As the line diminished in front of him and the door opened and closed rapidly—for the formula was brief—Richard found his hands were moist. Still, he knew the petition was routine. Difficulties would have been ironed out before this.

At last he was next. The door opened. The light blinded him. He entered, closed the door, and bowed clumsily to the crucifix behind the desk. He knelt and was vaguely aware of the black figures over him, sober and ominous. Padre Eugenio was carelessly twirling a light-green pen. Richard found his moist fingers leaving prints in the booklet from which he read the formula and his mind on everything but what he was saying.

"I, Richard Francis McKay, humbly beg of you, Most Reverend Fathers, for the glory of God and in the name of His most holy Mother, the favor of being admitted to ordination as a priest of Jesus Christ, according to the will of Mother Church, through the holy orders of subdiaconate, diaconate, and priesthood."

"Do you make this petition of your own free will?"

"I do."

Padre Eugenio's pen scratched.

Padre Bracciano looked around, although Richard didn't yet raise his eyes. "Are there any questions?"

Silence.

Richard lifted his head. Padre Bracciano nodded, expressionless.

Richard rose to his feet, tripping over his cassock, blushed, and bowed to the crucifix. The corridor outside seemed very cool and airy. The step was made! The rest was in the Lord's hands. He hurried down the dark corridor for his nightly hour of prayer. He was not unaware that the first- and second-year men envied him.

Three weeks later, well into March, a gray mist fell over the *campagna* and the Eternal City. All morning it rained. Once, early in the afternoon, the sun broke through, but the clouds edged it out again.

Richard, Paolo, and Father Frank Perrone walked quietly through Trastevere on one of their weekly walks.

"We take a left here, father."

"Sì."

The cobblestones were wet and shiny. Bits of cabbage, wet papers, and sticks of crating lay in the street. It seemed strange to talk to Frankie as "father" now. A month ago, just Frankie. Today, in the same cassock, with the same mannerisms, the same intelligence, Father Perrone.

"Eccola! Santa Maria" said Paolo. The old church loomed out of the foggy rain.

Inside the door, candles dripped heavily before a picture of the Virgin, casting eerie, flickering light. The tray beneath was full of old green wax with areas of yellow wax upon it. An old woman knelt before the picture with her hands upturned, articulating her prayer with cloying exaggeration. She turned her eyes to see if they were noticing. They disregarded her with annoyance and walked down the darkened aisles. The church smelled damp and cool. They knelt and prayed before the altar of the Blessed Sacrament a while. The red sanctuary lamp flickered dully. They arose and walked toward the main altar.

"Any sign of the sacristan?" Richard asked with a mischievous grin. He intended to turn on the church lights without permission. He had found the switch once by accident.

"I don't see him," Father Frank whispered.

Richard ran his hand along the carpet on the edge of the altar platform. When he found the bump, he thrust his fingers underneath and turned the switch. Brilliant light slowly flooded the huge mosaic of the apse. The Lord, in gold and blue Byzantine splendor, looked silently down upon them from the entire wall. They backed off a little, necks craned backwards, in the stillness.

"What beauty!" Paolo finally said.

"Too stiff, too artificial," Frank commented.

"But I like that, father!" Richard turned to him enthusiastically. Then he checked himself. "Of course, to each his own. But that formal restraint, those strong lines—I think it's so perfectly pure!"

Frank shrugged: "Too stiff for me."

"See the bishop who built it—over there on the left?"

"The running water, the deer, the reeds, the sheep . . . I love those symbols."

Richard walked up in the silence and turned out the lights. The switch clicked; the apse filled with darkness. The men walked slowly down the center of the church. They stepped out into Trastevere.

A WEEK LATER, Paolo and Richard took as their weekly trip the Vatican museum. They had wandered slowly through the colorful ancient library, to the Borgia rooms of Pinturicchio, which both of them deeply loved, to the Sistine Chapel for an hour once more of Michelangelo, to Fra Angelico's chapel—Richard's favorite—and now to the Raphael room. They had talked of art.

"I mean it—which one is your favorite, Byzantine, Renaissance, or modern?"

"Progress, everything is progress!" Paolo laughed.

"Seriously."

"I believe," said Paolo pompously, "the Italian Renaissance is the peak of human history." He waved his hand in an arc. "A miracle of beauty!"

"Seriously," said Richard. They walked along; Paolo didn't answer.

"How can I be serious in so huge a matter? Riccardo, such questions."

"But important ones! They are the ones nobody talks about but everyone implies. 'Change,' 'tradition'—what do they mean?"

"Riccardo, there is birth and death. There is a little love in between. It doesn't matter 'where we are in history.'"

"It does! Not for individuals in particular. But for the *atmosphere*. And that affects all individuals. Institutions change—what should we keep, what should we abandon? Questions like this affect individual lives."

"*Beh!* Something consumes all individual lives. Art is what is snatched away."

"Art!"

"*Si.* Art rescues things. It records a moment for as long as the record lasts. . . . Ah, *Raffaelo*. Have you seen such lovable, living figures?"

"The young man here . . ."

"It's himself."

"Is it?"

"So they say. . . . I love the reds."

"I love the movement."

"Richard!"

Richard turned. "Mary! How are you?" He stepped towards her. Paolo was silent. Richard looked at both of them.

"Mary Coleman . . . Paolo Veronese. Mary works over on the *corso*. She runs a religious-goods store, Paolo; I met her there once. . . . How are you, Mary?"

"Fine. Yourself?"

"Just fine."

She looked down at her white-gloved hands, then up at him. "You never did come in with those paintings."

Richard colored. "I thought of it often. I need permission, though . . ."

"But you will bring them in?"

"Yes, if you would like. At least I'll ask. . . . Mary is a painter, too, Paolo."

Paolo nodded and bowed.

Mary was wearing a light-blue spring coat. She carried a shiny black purse. She was alone. Her face was fresh as ever, her eyes dancing and lively. She wanted to talk with them a while; Richard would have loved to.

"Do you like *Raffaelo*?"

"We were just admiring him."

"I like him very much," she said. "I've been here almost an hour."

Richard noticed the hook-nosed museum guard eying them suspiciously; clerics in Rome didn't stop to talk to young girls. He resolved to speak a little louder, in English, to convey the fact that they were strangers operating by different standards.

"Did you hear our profound discussion?" Paolo asked.

"No. But you looked very serious." Mary looked from one to the other with her smiling and quick eyes. "Did I interrupt something of great importance?"

"Of worldwide importance. A preliminary summit conference on the destiny of the world," Richard said.

"To prepare for a ministers' meeting to prepare the preliminary conference," Paolo clarified.

Mary put her hands to her face and laughed. Her pocketbook lifted with them and dangled, shining, before her. "I'm terribly sorry; I didn't know!"

"How is your own painting coming?" Richard asked, forgetting the guard.

"Oh, so-so. I haven't got to it much this winter. The winter doesn't give me much time to paint."

"The whole year doesn't give me much time," smiled Richard. "Have you been in to see Michelangelo yet?"

"No, I won't bother today." She looked at her watch. "I'm due to meet Angela soon and have dinner . . . then a movie. I've spent nearly all my time here. Today is my day off. I like to spend a long time with one painter at a stretch." She looked at Richard tentatively.

"Paolo and I like to visit all of them slowly, but over and over."

"I like that, too, sometimes," she said.

People strive to find things in common, Richard thought . . . like cloven little birds. . . . "I'm awfully glad we bumped into you," he said.

"So am I. I waited every week . . ."

Richard laughed. "I'm sorry!"

"I even thought you might submit a painting in the Borghese exhibition," she said, lowering her head and looking up at him. "But I didn't see anything of yours there."

"No, I didn't enter that." He was sorry now he had missed her there.

"I'll write you my address," she said, opening her purse. She wrote in a little yellow notebook. Richard thought of the guard's interpretation. "It's near Trevi Fountain, not far from the *corso*. Very easy to get to. It's not much of an apartment . . . but both of you are welcome. The family that owns the place is very nice. They're very good to me—like a daughter." She smiled. "I couldn't . . . take you out to dinner, could I?"

"You may not even be able to entertain us! I'll ask."

"Do that, Richard. I hope I can . . . I . . . guess I better be running along . . . it was a pleasure meeting you, Paolo. Do bring the paintings, Richard. *Arrivederci!* And please try to come." Her blue eyes looked deeply into Richard's.

"Good-bye. I will if I can. It's a promise."

"Arrivederla!"

She waved.

"Nice girl, isn't she, Paolo?" Richard's heart still stirred at the sight of her; he felt lighter and happier. But he was rather proud, because he felt a new inner strength in talking to her, as if he had, at last, the mastery of his heart.

"Very nice," nodded Paolo. "Attractive . . . refined."

"Imagine Padre Bracciano giving me permission to visit her?"

"He can only say no."

"I'm afraid that's all he will say."

They looked at Raphael's Aristotle and Plato and glanced once more around the colorful, lively room. They walked out again, through the narrow passageway, then down the long wing past the bright library cases and the metalwork and lavish vases. Richard was happy amid so much art. His heart expanded and he felt talkative.

"Art is what is saved," he said, picking up Paolo's theme. In the Vatican hills, with the work of so many centuries and continents, the words had a special beauty. "I like that. I like that very much! It fits a theory of mine . . . but then, also, I think the chief thing about art is not memory but understanding."

"Capire?" Paolo asked. *"L'intelligenza?"* He seemed skeptical.

Richard nodded. "Not like . . . science—or even a prose sentence. But a kind of harmony. Or a kind of sorrow. Art gets those things—those things that won't go into words."

"Allora, what about poetry?"

"What's important there, too, is what won't go into words, the things gestured at, the ideas distantly evoked, the experience concretely called to mind. It's the same in the novel—it's the levels underneath, never talked about, that are the important ones."

"You sound like an existentialist . . ."

"Not at all! Just the contrary. It is just that there are many more forms of understanding than rationalists—or existentialists—know about. There is more than logic, more than concepts, more than concrete experience. Art is not concerned with concepts. The artistic idea is nothing like the logical idea. Paolo, I think understanding is an activity hardly at all exploited. Understanding runs through everything. Children understand—they begin to organize experience: they babble. It is fantasy—but it is already a first step in understanding. The ancients told myths: That is a form of understanding. Knowledge, I think, is like a little center of light in an enormous darkness. Men move outwards from this center in little forays. Some forays are successful, and more light is added to the circle. Some are misguided. But always the circle grows. I think art sends the forays farthest out—the myths, the fantasies. Scientific intellect is not as fast as art. It is a lot more sure. Everything, I think, springs from the center, and the center is wonder. If men were satisfied, they would stop. But men wonder because they yearn to understand. That, I think, is our salvation."

Paolo listened carefully. "That is how, if at all, men come to God."

"By wonder."

"*Sì*, by wonder. When they keep asking questions. Of every finite thing: Why? Why? Things cannot respond."

"I never thought of that. Wonder even is the path to God."

PART V
Spring

30

"RICHARD! How good to see you! Come in, come in! Paolo, how are you? I see you have the paintings. I'm so glad. Here, let me take your coats." Delight filled Mary Coleman's eyes. She stood at the door in white blouse and pleated blue skirt and waved her visitors in. Her short hair bounced as she reached for their coats. "Go in, go in! I'll just hang these up."

Richard and Paolo entered the sitting room. Paolo leaned the canvases against the wall. The room was light green with a white ceiling. Bright modern paintings were on the walls. On an end table was an old Gothic Madonna, a newspaper, a maroon glass ashtray. The floor was covered with a worn but clean gray rug.

"I'm so glad you could come!" Mary said, rejoining them. "Do sit down." She folded her dress under her and took the chair near the bookcase. "Did you have any trouble finding it?"

"No, none at all." Richard looked at Paolo. "No trouble getting permission either—that had us worried a lot more."

"You're right off the bus line. We got off on the *corso* at Via del Tritone."

"It's within minutes. Can I get you something?" she sprang up. "Would you like a little wine? A little Marsala? Really, I don't know how to entertain seminarians." She lifted her hands to her face as she smiled.

"No, thanks," laughed Richard. "Don't be disturbed about us. Really, it's entertainment just to visit in the city. Padre Bracciano was very good about allowing us to come." He looked into her lively eyes.

269

"Is he your superior?"

Richard nodded. "He's been awfully good of late, hasn't he, Paolo?"

Paolo laughed. "When he gives us what we want, he's a very good superior."

The three of them laughed. There was a slight silence.

"Are you going to show your paintings?"

"We want to see yours," Richard countered.

"You have!" she said, pointing to the walls. "But most of them are in the other room. Come on! I'll show you mine first. Save the best till last." She turned her head to look at him before pushing open the door.

"I'm afraid you'll be disappointed," Richard said. Her vivacity pleased and soothed him—and excited him.

"My pride and joy!" she exclaimed quietly as they entered the white studio. A light bulb dangled from the ceiling. Easels stood around the room. Sketches and canvases hung upon the walls; paint and turpentine were strong in the air. Sunlight streamed through the large window and the skylight overhead.

"What a large room!"

"And all this light!" Richard nodded.

"Watch your cassocks," Mary said. She walked to the window. Richard knew that she was pleased to show her room to him. She was proud of her paintings, sensitive and hesitant concerning criticism.

He walked slowly from one painting or sketch to another. Impressions of orange and yellow and leaflike daubs of green filled his eyes. He saw mauve sunsets and purpled shadows, gray valleys and pale-yellow shores—mostly in impressionist or cubist style. "Lovely colors!" he remarked. "What a bold eye you have for colors."

"The detail is excellent," Paolo said.

"Thank you. I'm sorry the room is such a mess. I really didn't know when to expect you, or if you could come, and I've worked late every night. I even slept in and went to the noon mass today. I just finished doing up the dinner dishes when you arrived! This is my latest love. . . ." She pulled them to the window to look at the easel in the center of the room.

"The roofs of Rome!" Richard said.

"From Santa Sabina," Paolo mused.

"We're fond of the views of the city. From Garibaldi's Park on the Gianiculo, from the Pincio, from the Palatine." He turned to look at her.

"Oh, I *love* Rome!" She stamped her foot and they all laughed. "I hate to leave."

"We all do. It gets into your dreams and thoughts . . ."

"Do you know what I do?" she asked ironically. Her hands came up over her mouth to hide her laugh, and her blue eyes looked at Paolo, then at Richard. "I throw a coin in the Fountain of Trevi *every day*! I not only want to return, I don't want to leave!"

Again they laughed. "You think I don't do it, don't you?" she said.

"Oh no! I believe it," Richard smiled.

"I really do," she said. "Well, that's all my paintings."

"They're lovely, Mary." Richard stood with his hands on his hips surveying them and nodding. A note of affection crept into his voice. "I wish I had your eye for color and your boldness. I haven't tried enough of these things yet. I'm always afraid of getting reckless. I don't have control."

"Oh, I'm pleased you like them! I love to toy with colors. My teacher told me once color was my strength. I'm not so good with composition. I overcrowd or undercrowd."

"The impressionist pieces are your best. I like them better than the drawings."

"I do, too, Paolo. I do the designs because that's where I'm weakest."

"But even the designs have such lovely colors," Richard said.

She lowered her chin and looked up at him with a smile. "Now is it time to bring the real masterpieces in? That's why you came, remember?"

"All right. But now I'm ashamed." He wasn't ashamed, but nervous.

"I'll bring them in," Paolo offered.

"Thanks, Paolo."

"So, Richard," Mary said, now that they were alone. "I'm glad you like these. It makes me feel very good. I enjoy the work so much." They turned to the window. "I've not much view, as you can see. Just the courtyard. Those orange walls and old green shutters. The tile roof. The sky." Her voice was delicate and affectionate,

"It's a pleasant view, though. It's Rome. It's quiet." He looked into her eyes, then away.

"You like quiet beauty, don't you?"

"You know, Mary, you should try to sell some of these," he replied as he nodded to her question. She was innocent and good—and less aware than he of the possibilities of mutual attraction; he forced himself to take the initiative in guiding their conversation.

"Angela told me the same thing. She wants me to bring them to the store. She even wants me to have an exhibition professionally." She looked into his eyes.

"You should."

"I will, before leaving Rome."

"When will that be, Mary?" He was, in spite of himself, disappointed to see Paolo at the door. He smiled inwardly at the contradictions of his own heart.

"In another year, I'm afraid. . . . Over here, Paolo, in the light. We can take this one off the easel. There! One at a time. Watch your cassock, Richard. . . . There . . ."

They looked at Richard's painting a long time. Richard felt his hands grow moist and his heart begin to beat swifter. The verdict seemed long in coming. The seconds passed slowly.

"Richard, that's powerful," she said quietly. She was silent a long time. "That's the only word I can say: Powerful!"

"Thank you. Thank you, Mary."

"What do you call it?"

"No name. Paolo said to call it 'Abandon Hope.' after Dante's Hell."

"Riccardo, I told you she would like them."

"I—was afraid. I've so rarely shown my work. Even to talk about it is an event. . . . Put up the others, Paolo."

The first had been the falling city Richard had painted at Christmas. The second was of the Adriatic at Villa Maria. The ocean was amazingly restless, expansive, longing, lonely. The sky was pale and empty, save for a solitary black gull, little and tiny, dipping to the water. The rocks and the beach were vague and impressionist. Pale yellows and grays and violets broke the shore to a kind of receptive haven for the yearning ocean.

"So different from the first, Richard! So quiet; yet the same strength is hidden there. How did you do it? A quiet ocean with such hidden power. Richard, you have talent!"

He felt her heart beating with his. "I'm glad you like them. Very glad." He felt a great release, a dam of longings for recognition breaking safely out, the corroboration of his faith in himself. The feeling was immensely peaceful.

Paolo put up the third painting—of Florence from the hilltop piazza of David. Quiet, serene, with a suggestion of the passion and history that had made the city. There was a feeling about the picture that the serenity was not serene but ready to explode, that beneath the quietness and sense of tranquil antiquity surged all the crimes and dreams and violences of long ago.

This time Mary was silent, and Paolo, too.

"Richard, I won't tell you any more. You know that I like them." She looked up at him. Her eyes were full of warmth and esteem. "Silence is best when real art is in question. This is art."

He nodded this time but did not speak.

"The *conception* of those three paintings! Why, there is so much *underneath*, churning to get out . . ."

"I've always thought," began Richard slowly, trying to check his joy, trying to still his intoxicated mind, "that art lies in restraint . . . in suggesting just a fraction of the strength available, in seeming a lamb, but with the fever of the lion flashing all around . . ."

"You've done it here. May I . . . keep these? I mean, to look at them and show to Angela? She'll love them." She looked into his eyes.

He turned to Paolo. "What do you think?"

"She could always send them to the house. Or bring them over herself."

"I think I'd rather call for them. At the store. I hate to ask another permission: I could just call and pick them up. Yes, that's what I'll do."

"I wouldn't want to cause you any trouble. . . ." She wrinkled her nose in concern.

"No, no! It will be all right. I just hate to abuse Padre Bracciano's goodness. He let us come over, and I don't want to keep asking him for more."

"If you think it's all right, then, I'd really like to keep them. I'll enjoy looking at them. And Angela will be delighted. She's due home about four-thirty. I hope she comes in time to meet you."

"We must leave about five. It's—four now?"

"A little after," Paolo said.

"Let's go in and sit down then. I'll take good care of these; you needn't worry."

"I won't."

"Well, then, tell me something about yourselves, won't you? We see the seminarians all day long and know nothing about their life. I'm so curious. . . . When will you be ordained?" She arranged her blue skirt neatly over her knees. It was good to be in female company again. It had been so long.

"In December."

"It hardly seems possible, does it, Riccardo?" Paolo asked.

"You wait for so long, and then—there it is!"

"One thing I'd . . . like to ask . . ." she stumbled. "Do you mind if I ask something?"

"Go right ahead," Richard said.

"One thing that's always puzzled me. How—how do you *know* you are meant to be a priest? I thought I wanted to be a nun once. My parents disapproved. But I don't think I really wanted to be. I didn't even argue."

Richard squirmed for a moment. "You have to really want to be. If you really want to be and have the ability. . . . There's nothing really mysterious to it. You make the choice or you don't. You can't stay on the fence forever. You have to choose. If you want something, if you're willing to die for it, God's helped you with that choice by everything that's ever happened to you. That's what I think. . . . That's a vocation. As long as you stay in the middle, it's —hell. The decision changes everything."

"The grace of vocation," Mary said, "is the history of your life."

Richard nodded. "I think it's a mistake to make too much mystery of it and throw the responsibility on God. He works through nature and events. There's no such thing as a supernatural world apart from the natural. There's only one world; it's all nature and it's all grace. . . . I think I always wanted to be a priest. More than anything else in the world. Maybe, at first, if it was only boyish idealism. Serving mass and all that. And a priest being a different sort of person— and an Irish hero. You know how the Irish are: 'no one like a priest!' Maybe there was a little sexuality in it, too." He blushed. "A priest is pure; he's above the flesh and all that. That's the most dangerous part of all, and I think I'm pretty clearly past that: I'm just me, and not so very angelic at all." He tried to smile, and he was blushing. "And then there used to seem so much for a priest to do. I can remember visiting Chicago: the tenements, the bad plaster, the faded clothes, the smell from the stockyards, the Negroes in the streets. I felt so bad for them because they didn't have the chance to move out if they wanted to— or the desire or the training. It's an awful sight to see a whole people living out their one lifetime without the chance. There seemed to be so much for a priest to do . . . I guess the idea—got stronger. Now I wouldn't—exchange it for anything!"

"But why not a—social worker? Or an editor? Or—something else? Couldn't you help people that way, too? What about a vocation in the world?"

Richard shifted his weight. "Yes, but I . . . the problem is too deep for anybody but a priest. Oh, not that a priest can handle it . . . or even that, in fact, he does . . . it's so difficult to say! But see . . . what good is all the social work in the world, or ideas, or movements, or reforms? Padre Benedetto is right—he's a friend of mine, my director. They're all for the *future*, for future generations. Then they're only partial. But, above all, they leave present men pretty much the same. They don't ask about eternity. They only make the present generation restless and anxious, with no home and no place to go, with no satisfaction and only flux. They haven't touched the basic issue—the issue of what men *are* and what can change those who are alive."

"But can you make men happy? Do you really think it is possible to be happy—here?"

"No, Mary, you are right," Richard said, sitting up. "That's another thing Padre Benedetto is always saying. 'Happiness is a mirage, a fiction. Suffering is our happiness.' He sounds backwards at first. He wants to turn all the wheels and gears backwards. You ask him about happiness; he tells you to learn how to suffer. But love along with it. It—it makes sense if you're not slow to catch on! As I was. It's so hard to learn to suffer! It doesn't bring . . . peace or comfort or anything like that. But it brings . . . order . . . and pain that seems sensible . . ."

"Couldn't—a social worker do as well? I mean, let me be cynical for a moment. Couldn't a social worker tell people to go on suffering—to accept reality?"

"But it's not a question of that. We should go on trying to eliminate suffering and poverty even more actively. But we're only *creatures*. It's a question of a total point of view . . . a whole vision of the world and human relations and existence . . . oh, everything! Padre Benedetto has a way of saying it . . ."

"He sounds like a marvelous man," Mary said, to break the silence.

"He is! I don't know how I'd get on without him. He's meant everything to me. You should get to meet him—Paolo, too. He likes young people. He meets with several from the University of Rome. He's at San Girolamo, out above the Vatican."

"Between Via Aurelia Antica and Gregorio Settimo," said Paolo.

"He's a saint. I owe him so much!"

Mary crossed her legs and sat back. Her chin was in her hand. She looked especially pretty. "What about . . . your painting? Is that too personal a question? I mean, if you are a priest, will you have a chance to paint? I'm awfully sorry if I'm trampling on something sensitive . . ."

"Oh no! That's all right." Richard smiled wryly. "It's just difficult to answer." He sat forward, with his hands dangling between his knees on the skirts of his cassock.

"Don't answer, then! Don't bother."

He looked into Mary's eyes briefly and felt again the bond of trust that would make talking easy. "No, I will. I'd like to—it would do me good. I've spent so long trying to clarify it." He sat a moment and he thought. He rubbed his hands from nervousness. "I love art. I love art a great deal. *Almost* more than anything. The priesthood more. And therefore I figure . . . therefore I figure . . . that I should do what I want most to do. And if the Lord wants to give me painting on top of that, then I shall be the happiest man in the world!"

"But . . . if he doesn't?"

"Well, then I won't like it so well! Because I truly love to paint. I truly want to make beauty. Somewhere, somehow."

"What a shame if you couldn't!"

"But not at all unlikely. I've thought of that. We've a small community. We need teachers and preachers and pastors. We don't need painters. So I've had to *choose*."

"What a stupid situation, Riccardo!" Paolo interrupted. "Talent cannot go—wasted! Talent is too rare. We must honor talent, love talent, cherish talent! We have all the poor teachers and pastors we need. Riccardo, this makes me so furious!"

They all laughed, for Paolo's good nature made indignation seem so unlike him.

"Still, my task is to follow orders. Superiors have to worry about the use of talents."

"But you must push, too! You are not worthy of your talents if you do not fight for them."

"Oh, I'll fight for them. They are part of me. My salvation depends partly upon them. I'm not one of those who believe that obedience means to become a sheep. I'll speak my mind. But then they can do as they wish."

"Good," said Paolo grudgingly. "I do not like to see you passive. That's not obedience! Every man has a self to be faithful to. That is as much a part of his sanctification as anything. You must be true to your conscience and vocation."

"Mary, this is turning into a debate for your benefit."

"I find it fascinating. I'm new to much of this. But I can appreciate the difficulty. And I admire your . . . decision."

"You're nice to have around. You're full of compliments."

Mary smiled and looked into his eyes. "They're true. I admire what you're doing. What else can I do?"

"I've probably exaggerated and made it seem more than it is. I'm doing what I think is right. Actually, in practice, day to day, it will take care of itself. The Lord will manage it."

"It makes my job seem so insignificant."

"Funny!" he laughed. "I've been wishing I had your freedom and your dedication in your painting and your store. The grass always looks greener, I guess."

She laughed and seemed very glad for what he said.

"There is another thing, though," Richard said seriously. "I really believe this. Maybe the possibility of losing one's art is very important for finding one's priesthood . . . and oneself. And maybe even for regaining one's art, much stronger in the end."

"You don't want to bargain, though," Paolo warned.

"No! It's not a bargain." Richard blushed. "But it is a thought."

They talked for the remainder of the hour. The time flew. Paolo laughed about his father's theories of government and world politics; Mary spoke of her younger sister in college, her own hopes concerning painting, and her need soon to return to the States. Richard sensed her concern about marriage and knew that this was one of the reasons leading her to return. Then it was time to leave. They waved good-bye at the door and descended the silent stairs.

Richard felt glad and free as he walked along with Paolo and inhaled the cool air. He knew he both loved Mary and was detached from her in realistic observation of his vows. And he knew it would be good to see her seldom, think of her little, and turn his thoughts gratefully and steadily to his work and the Lord.

"She is a lovely girl, Riccardo," Paolo said.

"That she is," Richard nodded happily.

They passed the Fountain of Trevi on their way to the *corso*.

31

THE BELLS of St. Peter's sang in the air over the piazza. They donged and counterdonged, trembled lightly and joyously, clanged, boomed, rang melodies in delicate patterns. It was an Easter Sunday sky, fresh, blue, and infinite. The white dome of San Pietro felt the joyous sun. Bernini's columns turned from winter brown and gray to white. A huge crowd thronged the piazza, made it come to swarming, slowly moving life.

Richard stood near the origin of the curve of one of Bernini's arms, well out in the throng. He craned his neck to see the altar far up on the vast steps of the basilica. Tiny figures in red and white moved about. A loudspeaker broadcast the mass. Richard lost his balance and looked down quickly at his feet to see that he stepped on no one. A little boy looked up at him and was then lifted swiftly to his father's shoulders. Richard smiled and looked up at the sky. The little boy turned around to look at him while his father was trying to describe for him what was going on at the altar. Richard winked. The boy slowly smiled. Richard looked out over the throng and wiped his brow. It was getting hot, very hot. A woman in front of him a few rows held a newspaper to her eyes. Her husband was in shirt sleeves and wore a cap made of paper. A German girl in front of him kept tucking the straps of her bra under her white dress; her neck and shoulders were a northern white. She talked a rapid German with her companion, who squinted through a compact camera which he occasionally held above his head and aimed at the far-off altar. Nuns, seminarists, priests, pilgrims, Romans, buses from afar . . . the world had come to Rome.

"Viva il Papa!" shouted the crowd when the Holy Father appeared to deliver his Easter address. Again and again the shout went up.

The high, shrill voices and low, throaty roar burnt themselves into his mind. He didn't shout but felt the words rising hot within him.

Kerchiefs waved, with newspapers and handkerchiefs: The piazza was a sea of rippling white. The breeze blew overhead.

Two thin arms reached out above the people, far above from the balcony—two thin, reaching arms, vibrant and aged.

Richard felt for a moment the history of the papacy and the ardor of the common man's faith, from the day of the barbarians and the plagues to this. But his emotions were ambiguous. He was ashamed of much in the papacy and felt guilty for it. He knew the contributions of the popes to civilization but could not bring himself to feel pride and glory. He was suspicious of mob hysteria; on the other hand, he was afraid of pseudo-sophistication and holding aloof. He settled for a warm act of faith and a long glance over the crowd, assembled from all Europe and the ends of the earth. The hope and sincerity and longings of mankind. The people! Those who endured and persisted and refused to die. Those who suffered, and were redeemed.

A loudspeaker grumbled and crackled; it picked up the thin voice of the pope. One word kept being repeated: *"Pace . . . pace . . ."* The pope said it as the Romans do: *pa-shay.* Richard noted that. It went through his mind again and again: *pa-shay, pa-shay. "La gioia . . . il mondo tenebroso . . . la miseria . . . la nostra epoca nella storia del mondo . . ."*

The pope gave his benediction, and a bevy of white doves was released from the square, winging upwards into the blue sky, over the arms of Bernini, and away.

". . . il Papa! Viva il Papa!"

The little figure turned away. The white disappeared from the balcony.

The buzz of many voices began. The crowd began to mill towards the basilica and outwards through the colonnades. Where was Father Frank? Richard looked for him but didn't see him. Richard's cassock felt like an oven, holding in the heat. His *romano* left a ring of sweat around his head. His heart sang. *"Pace! Pace! Viva il Papa Viva!"* He walked almost aimlessly in the crowd out to the bus line. It was good to be flowing in a crowd, good to see the white shirts and dresses, the new prints, the shiny black shoes, and the laughter and vitality and energy. The sky was beautiful. The glassy blue went on and on. And the white doves . . . winging . . .

He heaved a deep sigh. He was happy. Time soon to begin concentrated work for the exams. Another year all but over. A few more weeks of hard study, then exams, then over! Where did the time go?

He arrived home for dinner hot from the crowded streets, dusty, and sweaty. He looked at his watch. He had time to sneak up for a shower. It would have to be a cold one, for there was hot water only on Thursdays and Saturdays. But he felt lucky: Until Father Milton came, there had not even been showers. What had they done before then? He grimaced.

The cold water felt very good as it struck his shoulders and slid along his body. He flinched at the first contact and stepped back and forth under it. He couldn't bear the burst of it too long upon his chest. He shut the water off. He toweled himself, put on a fresh T-shirt and cooler trousers. The bell rang for dinner. He was hungry.

There was chatter in the recreation room, where they had an *aperitif.* They stood with their glasses, joking and laughing. Father Milton was the center of attention. Padre Bracciano walked from group to group, wishing a happy Easter and exchanging a few words. Richard stood aside for a while and watched the others. They were his "neighbors," his immediate circle, among whom Providence expected his destiny to be worked out. He felt close to them in Easter ebullience but wished that the good spirits weren't the result of just one day's joy—and perhaps the stimulation of a good martini.

"Eh, *buona festa,* Riccardo! *Auguri!*"

"*Buona festa,* padre," Richard replied, lifting his glass.

"A beautiful Easter, isn't it?"

"Very beautiful. The new Easter Vigil went very well last night."

"You liked that?" The superior's dark-brown eyes smiled at him. "I didn't think you would get your taper lit to light the paschal candle."

"I burnt my hand! Look, there are no hairs on it. Every time I put the taper in the new flame, the taper melted. I couldn't light it! They made the fire too big. It was a bonfire."

"Well, it was liturgical."

"It was like the *Inferno.*"

The priest threw back his head and laughed.

At dinner they had chianti with their meal and a sparkling rich champagne. They ended with a liqueur and demitasse. They ate *pasta-sciutta*, a soup, roast lamb and roast beef, beans, salad with oil, *finuchi*, peppers cooked in oil, small loaves of bread. Since dinner was later than the usual hour, Richard was especially hungry. He ate heartily and festively. The sisters had baked a cake for each table in the shape of a paschal lamb bearing a small banner of the cross—the lamb one sees in the missal, lamb of the Apocalypse. Apocalypse, he thought: *"Come, Lord Jesus!"* The champagne was delicious. Life is good!

Then after the banquet he intended to go to bed. Father Milton stopped him in the hall as he came out of chapel and told him he was wanted on the phone.

"Thanks, father," Richard said. "Happy Easter." He shook the tall priest's hand. Father Milton smiled and went out the door with the car keys.

Richard hurried down the hall and picked up the phone. *"Buon giorno."*

"Padre Riccardo?"

"Si."

"This is Padre Francesco from San Girolamo. Padre Benedetto is dying. He asked for you. Would you like to come out?"

What? It took Richard a moment to answer. *"Si . . . si . . .* right away! Right away!"

He hung up the phone and asked Cesare, who was just passing, if he had seen Padre Bracciano.

"He was talking with Padre Eugenio after dinner."

"Thanks." Richard ran up and down the halls looking for him. Was he taking his siesta yet? He looked in the refectory, chapel, priests' recreation room. Everything was silent. He went to Padre Bracciano's room. *What if he is sleeping?* He looked at his watch. He raised his hand to knock. He waited. He raised his hand again and knocked lightly. No answer. *Hurry! Hurry!* He knocked loudly. No response.

He ran to look for the brother-steward.

"Avanti!"

Brother was just lying down for a nap.

"May I please have forty lire to go up to San Girolamo? My director is dying and he asked for me. I'm awfully sorry to disturb you."

"Who?"

"Padre Benedetto, my director," waved Richard impatiently. "Please hurry!"

"Adagio! Adagio!" said the old brother, eyes twinkling. "Forty . . . lire." He lifted them from the desk and dropped them one by one, four coins, into Richard's hand.

"*Grazie, Fratello, grazie.* I'll tell Padre Bracciano later. He doesn't seem to be around."

Richard's throat tightened as he hurried down the hall, down the steps, out the front door. The heat met him in the street.

It seemed the bus would never leave from the corner, and it poked up the long, sunny hill. It stopped halfway up. The gears ground again, the bus slowed, it gathered momentum. The fumes seemed particularly rancid. But finally Richard spun off, out into the hot Easter air. He almost ran across the boulevard. The sweat gathered on his sides and back; his shoes became coated with dust. He clutched his *romano* and hurried.

The bells of the monastery began to toll and his heart felt sick. Tears burnt into his eyes.

The impossibility of directing his own life was like a thick mist that blotted out all else from his thoughts. Just as he had changed and begun a new and serious tack! *Dead! Dead!* Incredible . . . incredible . . . incredible . . .

He hurried over the pavement and pulled the bell. He pulled
again. The sun beat silently upon the yellow brick. A white butter-
fly darted and spiraled across the silent, dusty courtyard.

"*Buon giorno,*" said the brother at the door.

"Padre Benedetto . . ."

A look of consternation: "*Si, ma lui è già . . .*"

"Please, may I come to his room! Please, just to see him. He
sent for me . . ."

"*Va bene,* padre. *Van bene, Avanti. Di qà.*"

"I know the way."

He hurried past the little brother, whom he did not recognize,
and walked swiftly towards the familiar room. Don't hurry, he
thought. Be respectful. But his heart pounded loudly enough to
drown out his thoughts, and he took the steps two at a time. His
cassock ruffled with the noisy movements.

At the door of the cell and in the small room the monks were still
saying the prayers for the dying. Richard slowed his pace and felt a terrible depression. He walked sickeningly to the edge of the circle opposite the door. Two candles burnt on the familiar desk, beside the books
and manuscripts, on either side of a crucifix. A priest in surplice and
stole stood by the bed. He turned a papery-thin page; the candles flickered. Padre Benedetto lay in a white nightshirt, whiter against his yellow skin. The blanket over him was dark and still. Two of the monks
glanced up from their breviaries to identify the newcomer; one of
them suppressed a yawn. The others recited their prayers and turned
their pages. Padre Benedetto lay so skinny, yellow, and leathery. His
face was twisted to one side in a grotesque humiliation.

Richard dropped to his knees, overcome. He saw, clear as in sunlight, his own death. He would be like this. Exactly. Alone, among
brethren whose love was warm yet detached. The withered bones
and skulls of St. Mary of the Angels in Rieti came back to him. He
looked in terror at the faces of the monks. A tear did gather in one or
two eyes. One of the older monks was shaken. Richard recognized
Padre Francesco beside this monk inside the room. The others were
accustomed to death within the brotherhood.

Padre Francesco became aware of the young student. He arose and came to kneel beside him. He offered a controlled but warm smile. "Padre died only several minutes before you came. I knew you would like to come. I heard him breathe your name, and I knew he was close to you. I could not call you earlier. It came—suddenly." He nodded toward the bed, on which the body of the dead monk could scarcely be seen under the blankets, too thin and wasted to exert himself against them. "He was conscious to the end. It was . . . painful. You can see, he struggled . . . to the very end."

"Did he . . ."

The priest looked at him. Richard could not continue. Some of the other monks looked at him curiously as he knelt there whispering.

". . . say anything?" asked the priest. "He couldn't. He didn't seem to remember any of us. He seemed to have lost his clarity, except of pain. The Lord . . . took everything."

Richard's throat tightened and his eyes blurred. His heart became hot, heavy lead. "Oh, God . . . God . . . God!" He pressed his fingers into his eyes and saw blackness and reeling lights.

He felt cold, distant—in a spinning void. "Padre, padre!" But, of course, no response. Of course, no response. Coldness and silence— and the ugly twist in Padre Benedetto's face. He buried his eyes in his hands, but he couldn't cry.

That he himself would end like this, that he and Padre Benedetto would end up as one: The coldness overwhelmed him and frightened him. He could not stir his faith. He could not do it. There was not an ember, not a spark, to warm his heart. Only coldness and distance and repulsion.

Fiat, he said. *Fiat, fiat, fiat, fiat* . . . He could do nothing but say the words. His eyes grew tired of the dark. He looked up. The priest was finishing. He sprinkled with holy water. The candles leapt and danced. The crucifix stood metallic and still. The drops of water thumped coldly on the bed. Padre Benedetto lay motionless, his thin form hardly apparent, his face and hands thin and yellowish.

"*Un santo . . .*" murmured an old priest, getting up to leave. The others left silently.

The infirmarian went to the bed and waited for everyone to go.

Padre Francesco put his hand on Richard's shoulder. Richard wiped his eyes, but they were dry, only aching.

"He is with the Lord."

"*Si,* padre," said Richard. He whom he loved was dead.

"He burnt up everything," said the priest.

"Everything," said Richard.

"He would have liked this death. Nothing but human weakness in it."

Richard began to cry. The tears came slowly, warm, hot, then in great bursting sobs. He had never really cried before, and he couldn't control it. A passing brother looked in wonder, but Padre Francesco took the youth's head to his shoulder and stroked his neck softly. Richard pushed his head against the strong-smelling heavy habit, against the bony shoulder, to fight off the hot tears. A warm release of emotion surged through him, he shook, and then he was quiet. He gained control again.

"*Grazie,* padre," he said, still unsteadily. "*Grazie.*"

"Nothing at all. It's a hard thing, Riccardo. One needs faith."

He looked up at Padre Francesco. There were the pure, compassionate eyes, not dark and intense, but steel-gray. You are Padre Benedetto's spirit, thought Richard. He squeezed Padre Francesco's hand. "Say a prayer for me."

"I will . . . to him . . . to Padre Benedetto . . . he is closer now."

Closer? thought Richard as he left. Closer? he thought as he stepped out into the beautiful clear day. Closer? The sky swam and spun above him. Birds sang, the whole sky seemed to whistle and hum. Closer? How? How? How? Inside he felt the cold. He felt far away from everything, chill, alone.

32

"BUT, PADRE, I *have* to go. He was my director. *Please* let me go."

Padre Bracciano turned in his chair. "Padre Riccardo, I know you are full of grief. But tomorrow is the house trip. All of us should go together. All of us. I will say mass tomorrow for Padre Benedetto; you may serve, if you wish. But today, no. Is your presence at the funeral *that* important?" He looked at Richard's crestfallen face. "Riccardo, my answer has to be no. You will go on the house trip with the others."

Richard opened his mouth quickly but realized that protest was futile and even unfair. Disappointment made his throat tighten. "As you say, padre," he said. "But I had to ask—extra hard."

"I understand."

Richard left. Not to go to the funeral! Not to see him once more! Not to say a last prayer in his presence. Everything crushed under the weight of community this and community that: 'all of us together; all of us!' He hated the herding. The word stopped him: *Everything*. He stopped near the wall in the silent hallway and saw very distinctly in his imagination Padre Benedetto saying the word and heard his accent. He hurried to the chapel, laid his head against the seat in front of him, and, kneeling, came close to tears.

Easter Sunday night, the night of the death, he had knelt like this. He hadn't cried. But desolate images of his own vainglory and pride, desire and lust, smallness and selfishness had besieged and tormented him. He had almost cried out in pain. He had never seemed so empty and dry, so totally without support. He seemed so useless, so contemptible, so unfit for everything, so unhappy and dismal. His spirit had writhed in agony. Today the tears began to press on his eyelids. It was easier as the tears arose. Torrents of conflicting emotions tore through him. The tears gave him warm and finally soothing release, though he could not tell just what it was that was making him cry.

Fiat, he kept saying. *Everything.*

He went to bed and, tears threatening again, turned to his pillow. He was asleep before he could cry. He tossed somewhat, but awoke in the morning refreshed.

Entering the bus for Hadrian's Villa the next day, Richard made a determined effort not to sit with Paolo or even Father Frank. His heart was heavy with sorrow as he thought of the funeral he was missing and the farewell he could not give. But he didn't want to begin his new life with a surrender. If the Lord had cut him off from his great support, he would try to keep the cut clean for as long as he could. He would depend solely on the Lord, not on human consolation. Padre Benedetto's face, framed in the bright light of his window, kept assaulting his mind. He had to dismiss the image as earnestly as he could, for it cut his heart too deeply. He tried to wear a smile, but he felt nothing but coldness, distance, and the desire to be alone.

"*Occupato?*" he asked.

"No," said Attilio.

Richard sat with him. Attilio was short in stature and very quiet. He had straight black hair, cut short, and soft brown eyes. He was from Turin. He was good-natured, very mild, prayerful, generous. Once Richard had entered the rec room to find someone help him move the benches in chapel so that he could mop the floor; Attilio had come immediately. Another time he had been looking for a companion so that he could make an errand into the city; Attilio had quietly volunteered, with a smile, at the expense of the afternoon. Attilio had no great talents: He was bashful in giving a sermon, barely adequate in studies (he wouldn't qualify for a degree), not very at ease or polished in company; he was only good. He possessed a quiet, moderate, steady generosity that never failed. He was gullible and the butt of countless jokes; he was loyal, unthinking, docile. He was obedient and disciplined, and in this sense was a perfect seminarian, lost as he would be in confronting the world. His goodness redeemed his mistakes; other people soon respected his innocence and in spite of themselves made provision not to take advantage of him.

Richard was cheating. He had not planned it, but instinctively he had chosen the easiest companion. Attilio would talk little during the short trip. He would be mild, gracious, unimaginative. It would be restful to sit beside him.

"It's a beautiful day," Attilio began.

"A friend of mine is being buried today," Richard said.

"You—couldn't go to the funeral?" Attilio was concerned and sympathetic.

"I asked. Padre Bracciano thought it would be best to go with the house."

"Oh."

"He was a great man. A great man. I feel so sorry to lose him. I—didn't know how much I loved him." Richard was talking straight ahead, almost as if Attilio weren't listening.

"Did he—die suddenly?"

Richard nodded. "He had cancer. Only the infirmarian and he knew about it—and the abbot. I didn't know."

"An uncle of mine died of cancer. He had it in the stomach. He used to groan all during the night. But they didn't tell him how serious it was. They operated, but there was too much to remove, only they didn't tell him that, and he died in three weeks." Attilio spoke very seriously.

"They should have told him."

"I told them it was wrong not to. Men should know the truth."

"It is a hard truth, though."

The bus had started and was turning through the streets, along the wide *viales* on the way across the city.

"I *want* to die. I keep thinking everybody does. You get used to looking forward to death and forget that other people think so differently . . ."

Richard listened to the motion of the bus for a while. "You want to die, Attilio?"

"Yes, of course! It wouldn't make sense if I didn't. I mean all the sacrifices . . . and everything. You do, too, don't you?"

Richard was silent a while. "Yes, I do . . . I do."

"We're all humans. It's hard to . . . but . . ." Attilio shrugged. The things he believed so intimately entered a hostile environment when voiced, and he always had trouble articulating them. He preferred his own inner world.

Richard saw—as by a direct insight—into Attilio's soul. All of Richard's own romantic insights about Time and pain and eternity seemed like so much froth. He rode on in silence. Attilio squinted as the sun poured directly through the window. The bus raced through the undulating *campagna* across the flats toward Tivoli in the hills. The soothing motion and sunlight and quiet fields gradually lifted Richard's spirits. They talked briefly of the view, the silent aqueducts, the Easter ceremonies, the coming exams—but no continuous conversation took root. The trip was relaxing.

At Hadrian's Villa, at the base of the hills of Tivoli, Richard decided on the easy way: He walked alone as much as possible, to collect his thoughts. His mind filled up with the fresh sky. He studied the large, heavy cumulus that sped low and white over the *campagna*. He looked up at the olive trees of the green cliff that bore Tivoli on top and the Villa d'Este on its face. His spirit frolicked over the new green grass and the wet earth, over the white and pink blossoms bouncing in the breeze. The air was cold and he drew his jacket about him; then, when the breeze stopped, the sun was too warm and he opened it again. Sky, new leaves, waving grass—he loved the day. Padre Benedetto would be glad to be buried on a day like this. Spring! New life! New dreams! The wind slapped at his face and streamed over it. His thoughts followed the wind across the *campagna*, under the same sky, to Padre Benedetto's grave and the requiem mass. They were one in consciousness. Yes, now he could talk to Padre Benedetto without any of the opacity of before: Every thought and feeling was limpid instantly.

Did the blessed with God see and understand their old friends? Did they come closer than before? Yes, but how? Surely they didn't have to wait for death, for reunion after death.

What is it, Lord? he asked. What is consciousness? How do we live in one another? But there was no answer. He watched the wind-whipped sky, and the clouds, and the bouncing, blossomy trees. He walked over the soft turf, hands in his cassock pockets, and he felt the wind whip at the black cloth. He looked down over the artificial lagoon, shimmering dully like a mirror while the sun was behind a cloud, then bright and blue like a deep penetration of the sky into the earth.

He looked to right and left, at the ruins of great halls, of amphitheaters, of barracks, of aqueducts—crumbling gray-red walls of small ancient brick. He walked on, over soft turf and tile floors eighteen centuries old. He looked up through broken roofs at the rich blue sky and the white clouds. He felt the wind whistle in the ruins. What had the barbarians thought when they came upon this splendor out in the fields? What visions did they think they'd seen? And when they had plundered it, how long afterwards did the wind buffet it and the rains come, before it began to fall and was forgotten? In the Middle Ages, did knights and bishops and superstitious peasants visit it? What had the ages of people thought, united by a focal point that remained as they took their turn and departed?

He felt himself rising on a strange swell, part of a great movement, and immense history, in which all of civilization was a late moment . . . going where? Going where? Living together in consciousness? Or he alone living? His generation alone? Was it all dead . . . the past? Every bit of it dead? Nothing but sun on the ruins, and the wind, and the sky, and the fresh, living grass.

Well, you know, he thought . . . I take a resolution. I promise you, Padre Benedetto. I couldn't get to your funeral. But I promise you. I know what you meant about love. And I know what you meant about me. I'll stand alone now. I'm not afraid. I've got these two hands and a heart and a mind. And I'll do with them the best that a man can do. I want to live as a man, a perfect man. I want to fulfill every hope that a man is capable of. And if we can't know, well, I'll live in darkness. I'll believe. I'll stake my life on your love. I'll take my chances . . . that all this suffering . . . all this ruin . . . all this death . . . has been in a vision of love . . .

Tears were in his eyes and he wanted to run over the hillside, run as in a dream, in silliness and joy, run in the grass and the wind, run to the horizon and the sky up above, run in delight with creation. But he took hold of his heart. He looked around for his companions. He wiped his hand across his eyes, but the wind had already cleaned them. He felt new and fresh. Now came the struggle of living.

"Riccardo!"

"Look at the lonely explorer!"

Luigi Alessandro, Father Milton, and Umberto came around the corner of the road and waved to him.

"What are you doing—contemplating?" Umberto called.

"Just enjoying the day," he shouted, and started down the hillside to meet them. His cassock flapped in the wind, and his strides were long and carefree. Father Milton looked at him suspiciously for being alone, but Richard smiled to disarm him. "The view is lovely from there," he said, nodding back up the hill with his head. He saw a puddle in the road in which the sky was reflected, with its white and gray cumulus.

"We're walking over to the corner to see if we can see the city," Father Milton smiled, squinting in the sun. He passed a hand over his mouth. "Like to join us?"

"Sure! I'll bet you can see it beautifully from up there." He looked towards Tivoli.

"We'll be going up there after lunch."

"I've been out there before. Johann and I did it by bike once—and Herbert and Cesare."

He walked along with the group and they talked about nothings, but he thought how significant their companionship would be in eternity.

33

THE LAST EIGHT WEEKS of the school year rolled on at a dizzying pace. The vicariate exams came and went. Classes all morning, intensive reviewing of theses, outlining, memorizing, analyzing used up long afternoons and as late into the evening as was permitted. Nervous tensions mounted in the house. Headaches became common. As the afternoons grew hotter, papers stuck to the varnish on the desks; collars, and then whole cassocks, were removed; and the seminarists sat back on two legs of their chairs in T-shirts and Bermudas, looking out the windows and sighing, with folders of notes upon their laps.

The June exams were the only exams of the year in the major courses, and they were orals, fifteen minutes per course. On the scheduled day, the students waited outside the appointed room, the professors came, and the students' spirits rose or sank according to who they were. The students nervously ushered one another into the room, four of them at a time. They rotated from one professor to another in each of the four corners of the room. They came out in an hour; another four went in. The professors were often of worldwide reputation but, no matter, behind the dark-green tables they all looked formidable, even when they smiled. Waiting outside to face them was a torture.

Richard remembered the ordeal and his hands sweated. Questions could be on anything, broad questions or detailed questions, questions of principle or of application, of theory or of history. Study, study, study . . . and an aspirin before going to bed. Up at five, mass, trying to clear the mind of study, breakfast, talking Latin on the way to school, quizzing one another, classes, lunch, a nap, study . . .

On weekends, once the comparatively easy orders examinations at the vicariate were over, Richard began going out on hikes or bike trips to keep his mind clear and fresh. According to house rules, as long as at least three went along and they received permission, they could go out on any of their free days—Thursdays or Sundays or some holy day. Paolo and Father Frank and Umberto and Johann were usually willing, the other Italians less so, as they took their examinations with ruthless seriousness and devised all sorts of means for staying up late at night and studying all through their free time. Twelve hours a day was not too much for some of them, and it was a matter of maintaining face to score at least a 9.5 out of 10. Richard aimed for a 9 but wished anything over the passing grade of 6. The perfect memorizing of detail was not worth the extra points.

ONE THURSDAY, Richard and Father Frank and Johann stood over their bikes on the last hilltop before the plain to Fiumicino on the sea, about twenty kilometers from Rome. The breeze stirred in the wheat on the hillside. Silver water poured musically into a drinking trough off the side of the road. The once-famous marshes that Mussolini had drained lay before them, green in the sunlight. Flashing poplars lined the road across the plain to the sea. The wind pulled at their jerseys and caps and made the sweat on their backs seem cold. They stood for a long moment, catching their breath from the long climb up the other side. Then up on their pedals again, sitting down, speeding, and the wind beating on their ears, stinging their faces as they hummed down the steep asphalt road. The bikes rattled and jarred with the momentum. The cyclists clung to the inside edge of the asphalt, blinking the wind and the tears out of their eyes so that they could see well in advance the rough spots, cinders, or breaks in the asphalt. At the foot of the hill, they sped past an intersection, jarred over the railroad tracks, and began to slow up. Then along under the poplars to the sea. They passed the Communist Party signs of the fishermen's city, the movie house, the smelly wharves, the side road to the beach, hot and silent in the noonday sun. They pushed their bikes through the hot sand. To right and left, Mediterranean. An abandoned concrete pillbox sat on the dunes. A two-engined airliner throbbed in the sky overhead, silver, its propellers tiny circles in the sun.

They stripped off their shirts, shoes, trousers, and ran in their pre-donned trunks over the boiling sand and into the icy sea.

"Like Lake Michigan in May!" shouted Father Frank to Richard. Their flesh sparkled, wet, in the rolling, stinging water.

They dried in the sun, shivering, put on oil, ate their sandwiches and drank cool red chianti. They felt the wine burn inside. They lolled in the delicious sun. Lazily they watched the minute life in the sand, ran its crystals through their fingers, and enjoyed the sound and smell of the beach. Richard felt his inner force restored. He rolled over, shielding his eyes from the sun.

PAOLO AND HE went once, too, to a beatification at St. Peter's. The crowd inside was already restless at the barriers along the center aisle as they entered; cardinals and bishops arranged themselves in line. Richard and Paolo had two tickets each, one large and colorful, the other a small green one. Hurriedly they showed the nearest gendarme the large one. "Di là, padre!" he pointed, pulling Richard's arm. One bored officer after another sent them down the line. They searched with frustration a place along the barriers. Finally, meeting Sandy and others from the North American College, they tried to go down the center aisle to the front.

"Momento!" A gendarme lowered a rifle across their path. He looked at their tickets. "Vial" he said. "Vial Parasites!" The others, with their large tickets, turned aside. In a moment of desperation, Richard showed his little green ticket. "Va bene, padre." With a grip of steel, the gendarme pulled Richard out into the aisle. A moment later, Paolo was beside him. "Avanti!" ordered the guard. "Hurry!"

Richard and Paolo looked down the long center aisle, toward the main altar, and swallowed. They thought it was a joke. There was no escape but the long, open center aisle. They began walking down the aisle, afraid at every step of being sent back. Paolo kept his eyes straight ahead. Richard's stomach was queasy. Expectant crowds in a mass of blue and red and black leaned over the barriers and stared at them. A ripple of excitement passed along the aisle.

A gendarme one quarter of the way down the aisle stopped them; then a chamberlain in tuxedo and knee breeches and light-blue shoulder sash halted them; then four Swiss Guards, halberds erect, closed off the end of the aisle. Paolo and Richard walked steadily closer. They threw their heads back and tried to appear at ease. The chamberlain among the guards barked an order. Halberds crashed on the floor, the guards came to attention, heels clicked.

The chamberlain looked at their small tickets. "*Avanti,* padre," he said, and waved first Richard and then Paolo into the circle around the main altar. He found a bench for them in the first row, seating them between two bishops in red. The young men looked at one another with joy and mischievous delight; they scrutinized their tickets.

Trumpets crashed out, echoing in the great basilica. "*Viva il Papa!*" rent the air. Under the clusters of little lights and the long maroon drapes on the pilasters, Richard and Paolo looked up with full hearts to see the thin old pope carried above the waving kerchiefs and the shouts. His thin arms moved from side to side, blessing and touching proffered white beanies to his head, handing them back then to the crowd. When the Holy Father descended from his chair and walked the inner circle around the twisted-columned altar, he allowed the bishops next to the young men to kiss his ring. He looked into Richard's eyes very deeply. Shouts still filled the air. Then he was past.

The shouts still rang in the ears of Richard and Paolo as they pushed their way through the streaming, shoving crowd out into the brightness of the piazza.

"I'm going to frame this," Richard said, holding up the small ticket. "And as for this one . . ." he crumpled up the large colored one and threw it in the air.

Paolo laughed.

"Paolo, I'm so happy!"

"*Romantico,* it is the afternoon sun and the sky!"

"And the crowds and the air . . ." Richard smiled. "Everything."

They finished exams. Richard felt the jubilation and release of racing down the colored marble steps, out the great door, out into the sun.

"Finito! Finito! Finito!"

He whistled in the street, all alone, until he remembered that clerics in Rome did not whistle: Unbecoming. . . . A tightly dressed girl walked by on the other side of the street and a man in the doorway licked his lips and looked after her. Richard smiled and his heart flew: It's so good to be a man and alive and free! And he almost threw his *romano* in the air till he thought: really, now . . .

Then there was the eight-day retreat, and silence and seriousness, and his extra-long prayer in the evenings concerning his coming ordination. He lined up the factors in his mind as best he could. He had achieved a measure of independence. He was beginning to know which ideas and feelings were his and which were merely received. He wanted more than anything else in the world to be a priest, and to suffer, and to serve. He longed to paint. But that would depend on superiors. They could make him a janitor for all he cared! No, that is not true, he thought. That is too exuberant. But, Lord, you know what I mean. I'll do what you will.

At the end of retreat came the day of ordination. The ceremony was at St. John Lateran's. Hundreds of clerics took part, receiving minor orders or major: porters, lectors, acolytes, exorcists, subdeacons, deacons, priests. Gabriele was with him among the subdeacons; George received porter and lector. Richard and Paolo and Umberto marched in their part of the procession of youths from all nations, clad in the pure white of new albs that covered them from neck to foot. They marched slowly, hands folded, golden chasubles folded across their arms. Richard's heart pounded steadily. He would be God's forever.

Six months later, in December, Richard again walked in procession at St. John Lateran's, to be ordained a priest. He would join the line of young men stretching back to the first apostles and to Christ. He would stand before the altar and plead, "*Abba!* Father!" He would say "Father!" not for himself but for the world, for the forests, and skies, and animals in their lairs, and men. He would say "Father!" for our own age, and its wars, and ideologies, and fears. He would take into his heart, with Christ, all of creation, all of history—every tear, every joy. The real world, the concrete world, he kept telling himself. And this would be his politics and art and life. He listened to his own footsteps and those of the procession as they marched ever nearer to the altar. His parents were watching him; he was proud for their sake, but his heart was far beyond them.

> *I will go in to the altar of God,*
> *To God who gives joy to my youth.*
> *Why are you sad, O my soul,*
> *And why are you in turmoil within me?*

The ancient prayers and the ancient church filled his heart with joy. He lifted his eyes to the great mosaic of the apse, to the Lord majestic and stern and distant. He felt a reservoir of sadness and of joy opening within him; but his emotion was so intense he felt almost nothing, only a pervading calmness and dryness.

At length—for the ceremony was long and tiring—there came the time for the prostration. All in white, the subdeacons, the deacons, and the priests-to-be lay flat upon the stones of the basilica, ancient stones, while the choir chanted the litany of saints and the invocations for mankind.

> *From pestilence . . .*
> *From famine . . .*
> *From fire . . .*
> *From lightnings and storms . . .*
> *From wars . . .*
> *From our evil desires . . .*
> *Deliver us, O Lord!*

With his body pressing on the stones, and his face resting on his white linen sleeve, Richard thought of Padre Benedetto, of his parents and brother Kevin, of his own immaturity, his vainglory, his wilfullness, his lust. He thought of the dry, routine days ahead. Cold fingers of fear slipped around his heart; he felt a black abyss opening before him. He reached out, accepting everything. He gave his life to Love—the Love that dwells in all things and everywhere.

In an hour, he was a priest of Jesus Christ, forever.

—finis—

Afterword 2004

THERE ARE JUST two points I'd like to make, in expressing my gratitude to Sapientia Press of Ave Maria University for bringing my first novel back into print.

First, back in 1960, I had just left the seminary of the Holy Cross Fathers and was living in a one-room apartment on West 23rd St. on Manhattan's West Side. It was a room so small I had to put my feet up on the bed in order to open the big drawer of the one old dresser in the room. It stood just down the hall from a blind man whose dog's food tray must have been constantly overrunning, for tens of cockroaches wandered from under it down the hall. Exhilerated even in such circumstances, my aim in completing this book was to accomplish something artistically very difficult.

I had read many novels about seminarians or nuns "jumping over the wall." In fact, I had seen the movie by that name. It is easy, I thought, to portray a healthy, fully sexed young male or female wearying of the disciplines of religious life, yearning for ordinary freedoms, and deciding to throw over an arduous vocation. Indeed, when I myself left the seminary, I was the very last of the 39 youngsters who had started out with me in the seminary twelve years earlier. Almost everybody leaves. "Many are called, few are chosen," is an aphorism as true as it is succinct.

What is really hard, I thought, having studied Dostoevsky's troubles with Alyosha in *The Brothers Karamazov*, is to create a character who is struggling to be good, even saintly, and to place him in the circumstances of normal human temptation, and then so to arrange things that readers sympathize with his decision to go forward into the priesthood, even at great emotional cost.

Since I myself, in an analogous fashion (no two testings of vocation are alike; each is different in its own way), had come to see, after much turmoil, that I must leave the seminary—that was the calling clearly intended for me—I knew well enough how to write the story of walking out the door of the seminary. In describing credibly the opposite decision would lie the artistic triumph, if any.

Secondly, I must say it outright. My wife Karen is a painter by profession, and she did travel to Rome as a postgraduate student—but, no, we did not meet then, but rather at Harvard some years later, when she was on sabbatical from Carleton College as an assistant professor of Art, and I was studying the History and Philosophy of Religion. The novel, then, was oddly predictive. It reflected perhaps a desire that long preceded the fact.

And a kind destiny, too.

As my dear friend Ralph McInerny notes in his kind introduction to this edition, this novel even had in it a prominent character named "McInerny" many years before I ever met one—and whose nickname was "Connie," the name of Ralph's beloved wife. But let us not carry coincidence too far. As novelists have long said, "any resemblance to persons living or dead is purely ". . . uncanny.

Michael Novak
Lewes, Delaware